THE DAILY TEXAN

THE FIRST 100 YEARS

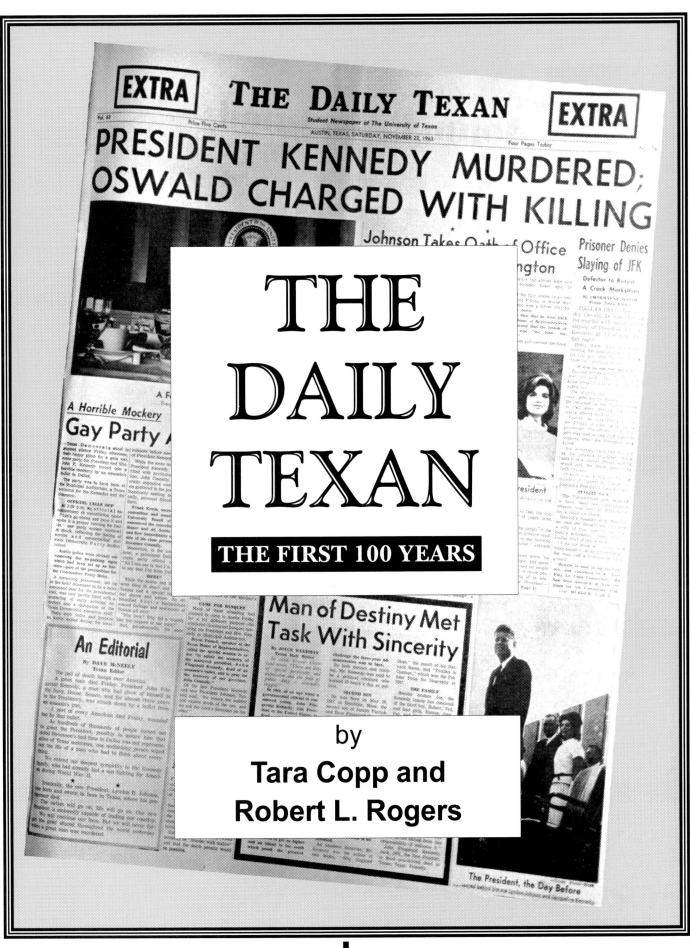

THE
DAILY
TEXAN

THE FIRST 100 YEARS

by
**Tara Copp and
Robert L. Rogers**

EAKIN PRESS ⚔ Austin, Texas

FIRST EDITION

Copyright © 1999
By Tara Copp and Robert L. Rogers

Published in the United States of America
By Eakin Press
A Division of Sunbelt Media, Inc.
P.O. Box 90159
Austin, TX 78709-0159
email: eakinpub@sig.net
www.eakinpress.com

2 3 4 5 6 7 8 9

1-57168-302-X

Library of Congress Cataloging-in-Publication Data

Copp, Tara.
The Daily Texan : the first 100 years / by Tara Copp and Robert L. Rogers.
  p.   cm.
Includes bibliographical references and index.
ISBN 1-57168-302-X
1. Daily Texan—History. 2. College student newspapers and periodicals—Texas—Austin—
History.   I. Rogers, Robert L. (Robert Lawrence), 1974–. II. Title.
LH1.U764D357   1999
378.1'9805'0976431—DC21   99-13404
                                                                       CIP

To *The Daily Texan* staff — past, present, and future.

CONTENTS

WILLIE MORRIS
Texan editor 1955-56

As this book went to press, former *Texan* editor Willie Morris, who contributed the Foreword, died on August 2, 1999.

Willie Morris was a hero to *The Texan* and to the press. He was a student, a prankster, a sportswriter, and a Longhorn football fanatic. In 1955 he led *The Daily Texan* in one of its most trying years. The 20-year-old editor began his term with these words: "Joseph Pulitzer once said a newspaper has no friends—to rephrase, *The Texan* has no obligations. . . . *The Daily Texan* is bigger than any one man. We will protect it and its tradition with our youth and our strength, and if necessary, with our personal reputation. You will be jostled, cajoled, embarrassed. Yet, through our telescope of ideas, you will see your life here in much nobler focus. We have been appalled by the tragic shroud which cloaks our undergraduate. This student apathy, this disregard of all save the most material, is a thing of the mid-twentieth century. If we do not kill it now, here on a thousand campuses, it will eventually kill us—an ugly cancer polluting the bloodstream of democracy."

In 1955 Morris stood tall against an administration hell-bent on shutting him up. He hollered for integration, for intellectualism, and for an end to corrupt "business as usual." In response, the Tower installed barrier after barrier to keep his content "to a college yell." He fought back by running blank spaces where revoked editorials should have been. He enlisted help from papers nationwide. In the end, his voice was heard. And *The Texan's* independence, though battered, survived.

Willie graduated, but kept close ties to *The Texan*. In the decades following, scared editors sought his counsel when the paper's independence became shaky. In the late 1990s, he came to the staff's aid when *The Texan's* elected editorship was threatened.

We researched the paper's first 100 years to collect and protect *Texan* folklore for journalists to come. There were so many staffers like Willie who carried treasures inside of them, and many of them had already, as Willie put it, "gone the way all of us will go."

We wish he could have celebrated *The Texan's* 100th birthday. Thank you, Willie Morris, and all staffers who passed before you, who in your words "have given to *The Texan* its substance and color."

Foreword

THE WORLD HAS taken a couple of turns since my University years, but I would take nothing for my experience on *The Daily Texan*. It has been invaluable to me as a writer and editor, and the friendships I formed with my *Texan* contemporaries forever remain a song in the heart. I remember as yesterday the fun and camaraderie in the old journalism building of that 1950s era, and also the bone-wearying work, the late-night deadlines, the arduous responsibility we all felt when we stood up to the Board of Regents on censorship.

In its finest moments, and they had been often, *The Daily Texan* had defended the spirit of a fine university even when the University of Texas itself was unable or unwilling to do so, and in these periods it had reached an eloquence and displayed a courage that would have challenged the mature profession. In that watershed year of 1956 my colleagues and I were aware of that background, and passionately felt that we must pass on to future generations of *Texan* editors and writers the lineage of editorial freedom. We made youthful mistakes, but I believe we fulfilled our duty.

Tara Copp and Robert Rogers have performed a splendid service in researching and writing this history of our beloved newspaper to honor its centennial year. Along the way they have not only mirrored the changing times and realities and nuances of the student generations, but have also discerned the common threads that unite those thousands of us who have labored in *The Texan's* vineyards since the year 1900. They have successfully captured something of the spirit and singularity of these young men and women, so many of them now gone the way all of us will go, who have given to *The Texan* its substance and color.

The University itself has changed tremendously since my days there, and so indeed has Austin. UT was a rather somnolent provincial institution then, easily dominated by entrenched political elements, and Austin a wonderful, drowsy state capital town. Now Austin is all bristling and high tech, and the University has become one of the grand, powerful American universities in physiognomy, population, and temperament, not unlike, say, Ann Arbor. Never mind. The good old *Daily Texan* in its verve and independence will always be a *sine qua non* of the life and ethos of its University. Every decade or so certain factors come along, out of whatever motives, which want to stifle its editorial autonomy. To the young student editors to come, I suggest you have a century of notable example behind you. This is the *students'* paper.

The Texan remains one of the signal student newspapers in the nation. My abiding hope is that its future editors and reporters will see this book as a vivid and reliable guide to what this venerable institution has traditionally embodied, and how unerringly its editorials and reportage have reflected, and indeed shaped, the ineluctable character and personality of its passing generations.

God bless you, *Daily Texan,* and happy birthday!

WILLIE MORRIS
Jackson, Mississippi
May 1999

INTRODUCTION

PUBLISHING A COLLEGE student newspaper is an audacious undertaking. Students in their teens and twenties add to their books and coursework a second full-time job as journalists. They often have little formal training. Their on-the-job mentors are fellow students. Turnover is high, and given the nature of college, the most experienced staffers soon graduate. Print journalism is a poverty-ridden profession, and the student journalist has the worst of a bad lot. Being paid anything is a bonus; minimum wage is a financial fantasy.

Throughout most of its history, the college student press has enjoyed less First Amendment protection than commercial newspapers. Sometimes college administrators have forced the student paper to publish their own political views. Other times the administration silences the student press from reporting on controversial topics. Often the threats to journalistic independence are disguised as concerns about "responsible" reporting or about the paper's connections to the university. As UT Regent Frank Erwin once warned, "We don't fund anything that we don't control."

Despite these special difficulties, the student journalists must deal with the same issues as their commercial counterparts. They face the same libel laws, the same risk of an invasion of privacy suit, and the same copyright considerations as does a commercial newspaper advised by experienced legal counsel. They face the same political pressures, the need to please readers and placate the special interest groups that try to manipulate media coverage. They often cover the same story, whether it be a large fire in the campus area or the mayor's budget proposal or the activities of the state legislature.

For a century now, the staff of *The Daily Texan* has engaged in this audacious task of publishing a student newspaper. This book is their story.

Their story is about America. These students have reported, analyzed, and in many cases witnessed the historical events of the twentieth century. From Prohibition to the Great Depression, from World War I to Vietnam to the Persian Gulf, from the Apollo landing to Bill Clinton's impeachment trial, the history of this century is in the paper's pages.

Their story is about Texas. Located in the state capital, these students see firsthand the success and failings of the state legislature and governor. They watched as Governor Jim Ferguson attacked the University. They reported as oil spurted out of the West Texas desert. They commented as Texas abandoned its segregationist past for a more inclusive future.

Their story is about the University of Texas. These students kept the record as the University grew from a few ramshackle buildings in a former cow pasture into the head of a massive UT System. They saw it become one of the leading public universities in the nation. They watched as UT presidents fought with regents, as regents fought with politicians, and as students protested everything. From the visit of prohibitionist Carry Nation in the early 1900s to the aftermath of the *Hopwood* court decision in the late 1990s, these students have observed and recorded life on the Forty Acres. For a century, they have served as the unofficial UT historians, creating the rough draft of the events that will comprise the University's yet-to-be-written account of its past.

Finally, their story is our story. We each served a year as the paper's editor. We know what it is to give yourself to the paper, and the rewards and costs *The Texan* offers in return. We know about the adrenaline rush of deadline, the excitement of breaking a story, the pressure of being at Ground Zero of an event like the *Hopwood* decision, and the satisfaction of watching an editorial prompt necessary reform. We also know about unappreciative readers, the fears of irrelevance, the gnawing stress of dealing with horribly complex problems, and the realization that a single mistake can be eternally preserved in print to the paper's harm. Perhaps worst of all, we know about those times when editors—as all good editors do—sit alone in their offices late at night and wonder if the job is too much for them. We understand what being *Texan* editor entails, and that personal experience flavors the story.

The paper's story has been five years in the making. We, the authors, submitted the drafts to satisfy our Plan II theses requirements. Rogers wrote the first half about the paper's history from 1900 to 1950; Copp took up the story from 1950 to 1999. We each would like to thank our thesis advisor Mike Quinn—himself a former *Texan* managing editor and long-time friend of the paper.

In addition, Rogers would like to thank Professor Lewis Gould, who did his best to introduce a young student to the rigors of historical research. Copp would like to thank her dad, her family, and Dave for years of ideas and support.

We are grateful for the staff of the University's Center for American History, who have archived the paper's trail for history and who were very helpful in tracking the paper's historical photos.

We both thank Texas Student Publications and TSP General Manager Kathy Lawrence for access to its archives and the release of its copyright on all *Texan*-related material and photographs. Not all of what we found reflects favorably on TSP, but its commitment to an accurate history of the paper helped our research considerably. Special thanks is due TSP photo editor John Foxworth for his invaluable work in gathering and preparing the book's photographs. All photographs in this book are courtesy of Texas Student Publications, unless otherwise indicated.

Finally, we would also like to thank our publisher, Eakin Press, and our editor, Melissa Locke Roberts. We wrote this story at least partly for ourselves, but because of Ed Eakin and his colleagues, it now can be shared with others. It is especially gratifying to us that we were able to publish the book within the *Texan* family. Ed Eakin's son Michael served as *Daily Texan* editor from 1973 to 1974, and his actions during the struggle between the paper and Frank Erwin are described inside these pages.

This book is the *Daily Texan's* story. We hope you enjoy it.

THE UNIVERSITY OPENING.

FOOTBALL PROSPECTS.

The very first Texan, *Vol. 1, No. 1, October 8, 1900.*

CHAPTER 1

A NEW WEEKLY: 1900–1910

The University of Texas was still young in 1900. Only seventeen years had passed since its official opening, when the Texas Legislature at last had undertaken the constitutional mandate to create a "university of the first class." In 1900 the number of students had risen dramatically from the year before, allowing the campus to reach the unprecedented enrollment of 582 students.[1]

Students in 2000 will travel to the University by car or plane. In 1900 they took the train or even rode on horseback. The library lacked electric lights.[2] In 1900 penicillin was decades away; childhood vaccines for polio were unknown; air conditioners were a science-fiction fantasy. Instead of shorts and T-shirts, male students wore coats and ties. Female students wore ankle-length dresses; a UT student in biking shorts would have been expelled if not incarcerated.

One professor described the campus "for the most part a thicket of weeds and trees with here and there a cow trail marked by the north Austin bovines."[3] Many students carried guns, and the bark of six-shooters could disturb the quiet of a campus night. One student even used his gun during a grade dispute with a professor. The student, apparently ill with the flu, had missed a homework assignment. The skeptical professor insinuated that the student had fabricated the excuse. As the student described his reaction, "Well, what could I do? I drawed my gun and said, 'Professor, you take that back.' He took it back but reported me, and now they won't let me have my degree."[4]

One early UT president glumly summarized

the situation: "In the last analysis, Texas is governed by hookworm and malaria; there's no hope for the university."[5]

Into this time, *The Texan* was born.

The Texan had two nineteenth-century predecessors, *The Ranger* and the *University Calendar*.[6] *The Ranger*, usually around four pages, was the larger and more established; the *Calendar* had much smaller pages but still had a healthy base of advertisers.

One *Texan* editorial later would say that *The Texan* was the "result of an effort to harmonize the two political factions existing at the time. The idea of two papers was abandoned, and the *Calendar* and the old *Ranger* united forces, forming *The Texan*."[7] This explanation, while given only three years after the fact, has some weaknesses. Neither the *Calendar* nor *The Ranger* seem highly political papers; if there were factions, they weren't very factious, at least compared with later political feuds that would roil the Forty Acres. More important, Fritz G. Lanham, *The Texan*'s first editor, claimed the reasons for combining the two papers were more about economics than ideology: The small student body could not support both newspapers.[8]

Unfortunately, the exact reasons behind *The Texan*'s founding are lost. The first *Texan* makes no mention of why it was created. *The Ranger* ends without a farewell, leaving no indication that the editors thought their paper was closing. UT archives contain only three copies of the *University Calendar*, none of which are the final issues that might mention the paper's demise. Whatever the

View of Texas State Capitol, looking north from Congress Avenue.

full story behind *The Texan's* birth, it does not appear in the paper trail.

The first *Texan* was published on October 8, 1900. It was a weekly paper, published every Saturday morning. The *"Daily"* in the title was still thirteen years away. On its first day, the paper had four pages. Page 1 displayed two news stories; page 2 had editorials next to a notice about the meeting of the Glee Club; page 3 contained "Locals and Personals," such as "McCullough has recovered from injuries sustained in a recent practice game"; page 4 had notes about the gym, literary magazine, and law school. Advertisers included the City National Bank (which boasted a capital of $150,000), a barber offering Turkish baths, and the Driskill Hotel, a long-time Austin landmark.[9]

The paper was a private enterprise. The subscription rate was $1.25 a year, payable to the two business managers. (The paper reported that all students had a "patriotic duty" to subscribe,[10] and a few years later began to publish the names of students who had not bought a subscription.[11])

The Texan billed itself as "a weekly newspaper, published in the interest of the students and alumni of the University of Texas."[12]

The lead story on Day One was the return of students to campus for the fall semester. It was the eighteenth annual session of the University of Texas, and the enrollment had risen from 483 students to 582 students. The news story advised students to follow the "rules of gentlemanly conduct," achieve "complete thoroughness in your work," and preserve a "close application and attention to duty." "Remember always," Lanham's story advised, "that gentlemanly conduct is what is expected of you, and by the standards of gentlemen you will be measured, and by them you must stand or fall."

In *The Texan's* first editorial, editor Fritz G. Lanham wrote, "It is our object primarily and ultimately to please the student body," and he labeled that goal "the only requisite for a good college paper." Lanham believed that there were "two sides to every issue" but thought *The Texan* should present only "the proper one."

Who was Fritz Lanham? How was he able to found a now century-old institution? Lanham was both academically accomplished and socially popular. Although the University did not have a formal valedictorian and salutatorian, Lanham was chosen as one of two faculty representatives at graduation, an honor *The Ranger* said went to the "most worthy men in their classes." *The Ranger* reported that Lanham was "probably one of the best all-around men Varsity has ever produced, being orator, athlete, scholar, writer, and musician. . . . Mr. Lanham has just turned twenty, and the taking off of those high honors at so early an age is a source of gratification to his numerous friends."[13]

If *The Texan* in fact was founded as a compromise between two political factions, Lanham's intelligence and social popularity would have made him the natural choice to lead the new paper. In addition to his journalism experience, he was president of the senior class and highly respected on campus. Having worked on both *The Ranger* and the *Calendar,* he would have known the parties on both sides and would have been in a position to bring them together.

As editor, Lanham defended UT students from other publications, blasting the "ravings of irresponsible newspapers" that published allegedly sensational accounts of a civil disturbance involving UT students.[14] Apparently whenever UT students caused a ruckus in town, Lanham and his paper came to their defense. This does not mean, however, that Lanham favored student frivolity. He criticized the University for having a study room in the library because it caused too much noise. "The library should be as quiet as a tomb," Lanham wrote. "It is an enormous crime to even whisper to your dearest friend in such precincts."[15]

Some later editors would be rebels and alienated outsiders, attacking both the University and the student body. Lanham, in contrast, personified conventional views, whether it was in admonishing students to fulfill their duties or urging them to remain silent in the library. He did not shun editorials that were essentially public service announcements. But Lanham's conventional writings always seemed devoted to the UT students. He was their class president, their paper's editor, their voice, and their defender.

His job kept him busy. Although the paper had a contribution box for articles of a "newsy nature," Lanham often found the box empty. He would then stay up all night to write everything (except advertisements) that would appear in the paper.[16]

Lanham did not serve his full term as editor. He resigned in early January 1901 because of illness. In his departing editorial, he wrote, "You can hardly understand or appreciate the numerous trials of an editor until clothed with his responsibility. Criticism is an extremely easy task —especially in this day when men's standards of propriety differ so materially. Be not too hasty in your denunciation of principles advocated or sentiments expressed by the editors of your college publications."[17]

Many talented and ambitious students have discovered, as Lanham did, that editing *The Texan* is an extremely difficult and demanding job. To students accustomed mainly to praise, the recognition that any difficult editorial decision will produce vehement criticism can be an unpleasant realization. That Lanham might have found this difficult does not detract from his considerable accomplishments in journalism. He founded the paper, creating it when perhaps no other student on campus could have done so. Because of his efforts, an institution was created, and in that sense, all *Texan* staffers have followed after him.

After leaving *The Texan,* Lanham stayed busy, in both journalism and politics. He edited *Alcalde,* the UT alumni magazine, for four years.[18] He also wrote "Putting Troy in the Sack," a spoof of Homer's *Iliad.* In his spare time, he wrote and acted in plays[19] and became an accomplished amateur magician.[20] His father took office as governor of Texas in 1903, and Lanham served as the governor's stenographer while attending law school at the University.[21] In 1919 Lanham was elected to the U.S. House of Representatives, where he remained for decades. During his time in Congress, he supported helium research, opposed the Hawley-Smoot tariff, and called for a U.S. military build-up to counter Adolf Hitler. Lanham also wanted to deport all "persons who were preaching doctrines that tended to undermine the fundamentals upon which the American government was established."[22]

Lanham currently does not enjoy the fame of such *Texan* editors as Willie Morris or Ronnie Dugger. But his name receives a frequent (albeit

THE TEXAN

A SEMI-WEEKLY NEWSPAPER PUBLISHED EVERY WEDNESDAY AND SATURDAY BY THE STUDENTS OF THE UNIVERSITY.

VOL. IX   AUSTIN, TEXAS, WEDNESDAY, OCTOBER 14, 1908   No. 7

OTHER BRANCHES IN ATHLETEDOM

BASKETBALL A PERFECT DEAD ONE—NO POSPECTS OF THE GAME HERE THIS YEAR—TENNIS ASSOCIATION FLOURISHING—GYMNASTS HANDICAPPED.

SOME INTEREST IN FENCING

Basketball seems to be a "dead one" at Texas for a while at least. At a recent meeting of that august board the Athletic Council—many plans of resurrection were discussed, but none even showed the semblance of success.

(Continued on page 2.)

LONGHORNS 11; CHRISTIANS 6

The Plucky T. C. U. Bunch Defeated by Texas in a Middling Game—All Plays in Detail.

The Game in Detail.

IN THE DIFFERENT DEPARTMENTS

NOTES GATHERED FROM TALKING WITH THE HEADS OF THE DIFFERENT SCHOOLS — ALL CLAIM TO BE FLOURISHING — BETTER TIMES COMING.

PROMINENT SPEAKERS EXPECTED

Engineering Department.

The Department of Education.

There will be a meeting of the De-
(Continued on page 3.)

(Continued on page 3.)

Y. W. AND Y. M. C. A. TO GIVE A PICNIC

FALL AFFAIR TO TAKE PLACE IN EAST WOODS TOMORROW AFTERNOON — ROASTED BACON PICKLES, CAMP-FIRE TALKS.

STUDENTS INVITED TO ATTEND

(Continued on page 3.)

MANY INITIATIONS ARE ALREADY OVER

SACRED GOAT RIDING AN EVERY NIGHT EVENT IN GREEKDOM. MANY INITIATES "GET WISE" WHILE SEVERAL ARE YET TO GET "INSIDE DOPE."

SEVERAL ARE NOT ANNOUNCING

(Continued on page 2.)

unknowing) tribute. While in the House of Representatives, Lanham sponsored a bill to establish trademark protection for the United States. The resulting legislation became known as the "Lanham Act," and it still governs the federal law of trademark and deceptive trade practices. Any lawyer dealing with intellectual property thus will frequently invoke the name of this national leader from Weatherford, Texas.

Lanham was *The Texan's* first editor; he was also one of its most impressive. He probably would not have envisioned how his considerable labors in founding the paper would pay compounded interest over the twentieth century, but the paper's subsequent successes undoubtedly would please this remarkable man who gave so much to *The Texan*, to the University, and to the United States.

Growth and Student Government

The momentum Lanham gave to the young paper helped it continue to grow after his departure. The next year, the paper took another baby step forward by publishing its first photography. In 1901 the first pictures—of the Alamo and Galveston Bay[23]—appeared, and the paper thereafter published photographs on a sporadic basis.

In 1903 *The Texan* passed into the hands of the recently established Students' Association. The paper's staff approved, saying that *"The Texan* has ever favored student management of student interests. It feels that the students can matter their affair than the faculty or any private interest."[24]

In 1904 the paper doubled in size to eight pages. The editor credited the "energy and push" of advertising manager James E. Mitchell.[25] In 1905 the paper began a tradition of allowing the different classes (freshman, sophomore, junior, and senior) to publish an edition of *The Texan*. Class rivalry was greater then, and the different grade levels insulted one another fiercely in their special editions.

The paper's size increased again in 1907, so much so that it started publishing biweekly. The editor called the increase "a bold move on the part of management."[26] A special graduation edition appeared called *The Peripatos*, edited by "I. Peripitate" and "I. Walk Slowly."[27]

The Texan began a special section in 1909 to feature readers' letters. Called "Firing Line," it

eventually would become one of the paper's most popular sections. The title box stated, "In this column, space will be given to contributions, preferably under 200 words in length, from the faculty, students, and alumni concerning any matter of general interest they choose. *The Texan* will never express its approval or disapproval of opinions given under the header."[28]

"Suppose the Legislature should take offense!"

But what were the issues? How did *The Texan* respond to the political questions of the day? By and large, the paper ignored national issues. Although Lanham had given a commencement speech on the topic,[29] the United States' military involvement in the Philippines during the early 1900s received no mention in the paper. Nor did any of the national political conventions. The 1904 election of President Theodore Roosevelt was ignored. President William McKinley visited Austin in May 1901, but even the president's arrival did not spark any discussion of his policies.[30] In short, *The Texan's* editorial coverage was local to the point of being provincial.

Some of this neglect of politics was deliberate. Editor after editor pledged to keep *The Texan* free from partisan battles. Editor Clinton G. Brown wrote in 1904 that "*The Texan* will contain lots of news and very little expression of opinion. If an opinion is necessary, we shall seek to make it the thought and feeling of the students and shall not tire you with telling what we think about anything."[31] Editor William A. Philpott wrote in 1908 that "This column is no place to air our own views. If an opinion is necessary, we shall seek to make it the thought and feeling of the student body."[32]

Perhaps *The Texan's* divorce from politics was completely voluntary, but good evidence suggests it was not. After a year of writing editorials about the need for school spirit, William A. Philpott (who had previously claimed the paper was no place for his views) said in his last editorial what he really believed. "We have felt cramped all the session—" Philpott revealed. "Suppose the legislature should be afforded reasons for taking offense! Our allowance would have been reduced to $12.73 per [student], and a college without funds is more ghastly than a college newspaper without freedom.

"Consequently," Philpott continued, "our editorial columns have expressed everything except sentiments and opinions. Often times 'continued from page 1' articles have harmlessly greeted the reader, when a half dozen seething, sizzling editorials have met a relentless fate in the much talked-of waste basket. The result has been rehashed editorials on timely topics of the 'we need a gym,' 'college spirit' caliber."[33]

This reluctance to engage controversial topics is far from the courageous, incisive commentary that later characterized *The Daily Texan*. But these early *Texan* editors worked under significant limitations. The First Amendment originally prohibited only the federal government from censoring the press, and the Supreme Court's first step in applying those restrictions to the states would not occur until 1931 in *Near v. Minnesota*. Thus the early *Texan* editors had grounds to fear the Legislature and UT administrators. Both groups could punish the editors for their political opinions, and the First Amendment would not stand in the way.

But if *Texan* editors could not risk the ire of the Texas Legislature by incisive commentary, they could still write editorials on less controversial topics. One such topic was the creation of a journalism school at the University. *The Texan* called for a journalism school "to meet the needs of this increasing class of students who are interested in or engaged in newspaper correspondence."[34] As practicing journalists, the *Texan* staff no doubt recognized some of the benefit that formal instruction might provide. Nevertheless, some tension existed between the paper and the early journalism department. Editor F. Edward Walker remembered that "There was no official connection between *The Texan* and the journalism school. In fact, there was a general resentment in the student body that the journalism school might try and run *The Texan*."[35] Almost a century later, some of this suspicion and mistrust between the paper and the Department of Journalism still exists—often to the detriment of both institutions.

In its first decade, *The Texan* had two major disagreements with the Students' Association. The first was over whether the Students' Association should buy a telephone for *The Texan*. *The Texan* claimed the phone would help in news collection, pointing out that the phone was a small token when "the only compensation received by the editorial staff is ingratitude and honor, the honor always being questionable."[36] The Students' Association, probably having the better

argument, responded that as the phone was a cost of business, *The Texan* should pay for it out of the paper's operating revenue.[37]

The second disagreement, concerning the influence of Student Association politicians, was more important. Apparently, the student government officials would try to select *Texan* editors who would endorse certain positions. As D. A. Frank, editor in 1904, remembered, "I feel quite certain that the Student's Council had control of the paper before I became editor-in-chief, because I recall that about a year before I became editor-in-chief, I was approached by someone with the proposition that I would be made editor-in-chief if I would take orders from certain parties as to the manner of running the paper. This I refused to do unless I had a free hand in running it the way I thought it ought to be run."[38]

In the spring of 1910, editor George A. Hill published an editorial calling for a change in the process of selecting *The Texan's* editor. Hill wrote, "We feel confident that the student body firmly believes that *The Texan* should be absolutely removed from politics. . . . The political system, now existing, of selecting the editor and associates is inherently faulty, unstable, the creature of the spoils system as a pie distributor, and nonrepresentative."[39] Hill called for a merit-based selection of editors by a non-partisan board—and then for weeks ran letters from other college newspapers on the merits of that system. Under this press barrage, the Students' Association gave Hill what he wanted.[40]

One famous campus event of the decade was the 1902 visit of Carry Nation. Nation, a zealous crusader against booze, arrived in Austin and marched over to the University. Denied the chance to lead the University's chapel service, Nation held her own, causing the students to flock from the official chapel to see the show. UT President William L. Prather tried to break up the meeting, telling Nation that her conduct was unlawful. Nation responded that "The Bible is my law."

The Texan's news coverage of the ruckus was ambivalent. Part of the news story suggested the students were mocking Nation, yet the story also said there was "manifest approval of her address." The editorial, however, was clear. "Could anything but an abnormal craving for notoriety carry her to the extremes she goes?" the editor asked. The editor wondered if she was really sincere and then concluded that Nation was "undoubtedly daffy."[41]

THE TEXAN

A SEMI-WEEKLY NEWSPAPER PUBLISHED EVERY WEDNESDAY AND SATURDAY BY THE STUDENTS OF THE UNIVERSITY

VOL. IX   AUSTIN, TEXAS, SATURDAY, DECEMBER 12, 1908   NO. 24

LEAP YEAR EDITION

HELEN MARR KIRBY DEAN OF WOMEN

A FEW FACTS CONCERNING THE WOMAN DEAR TO THE HEARTS OF ALL WOMEN STUDENTS OF THE UNIVERSITY

WITH VARSITY CO-EDS SINCE '84

HELEN MARR KIRBY, DEAN OF WOMEN.

The Ballad of Passing Loves.

Meditation.

LITERARY SOCIETIES AMONG THE GIRLS

A FEW STATISTICS RELATIVE TO THE GROWTH AND PRESENT WORK OF THE CO-ED LITERARY ORGANIZATIONS.

NOW FOUR ACTIVE SOCIETIES

THE Y. W. C. A. OF THE UNIVERSITY

GREAT WORK HAS BEEN GOING ON THIS FALL AMONG THE CHRISTIAN GIRLS — BIBLE STUDY IMPORTANT FACTOR

MANY NEW MEMBERS ADDED

WOMAN'S COUNCIL NOVELLY ENTERTAINED

GREAT SOCIAL MEETING IN HONOR OF THE WOMAN'S COUNCIL HELD SATURDAY LAST IN MRS. KIRBY'S ROOM.

THE ASHBEL SEMINARY

A Unique and Up-to-Date Finishing School for Ambitious Co-eds— Proved a Producer of Great Minds.

INTERESTING NOTES OF THE VARSITY ALUMNAE

WHAT THE AMBITIOUS WOMAN IS DOING IN THE MANY FIELDS —SCATTERED FROM AUSTIN TO INDIA.

MISSIONARIES, DOCTORS, ETC.

The Texan's editor, D. A. Frank, had some cause to question Nation's sanity, having experienced her temper firsthand as the butt of a practical joke by the residents of B Hall. Historian Joe B. Frantz told the story:[42] Frank was a church-going Methodist, not given to drink. Before Nation's speech, several of the residents had told her that Frank, a teaching assistant at the law school, demanded that students drink with him as a class requirement. As Nation said, "Them boys told me with tears in their eyes that unless they went with him to drink booze that he would give them poor grades, but that the fellows who drank always got good grades." Frank rose to protest, but when Nation asked the audience whether it believed his denials, the dining hall resounded with noes. She then yelled, "Oh, young man, it's bad enough to be a rounder and a drunkard, but it's worse to be a hypocrite."

Nation later was told by the students that Frank had gotten drunk after her speech. She grabbed him, demanding that he blow his breath in her face. He did, but then one of the students reached into Frank's coat pocket and produced a planted whiskey bottle. At that point, Frank gave up and walked away.

Calling Carry Nation "daffy" was nothing compared to how *The Texan* treated one departing professor. In the harshest editorial of the decade, editor Mark McGee said of this professor that "In the classroom his attitude was not that of the average instructor toward students but more nearly that of a dictator toward his subjects."[43] The editorial continued in that vein for many paragraphs.

Such a fierce denunciation of a UT professor was out of character. Usually, *The Texan* was respectful to the point of being deferential. Any criticism of faculty practices was usually made in a polite manner and was never a scathing personal attack. The difference in this situation might have been that this professor was leaving the University; perhaps the administrators and other professors disliked him and he was fair game for *The Texan*. Regardless, this type of personal attack on a UT professor would not again appear for years.

ADMINISTRATION, RACE, AND GENDER

These, then, were the issues specific to the first decade. But in addition to those, there were some perennial issues that began in 1900 which have lasted to the current day. Tracing these themes through the century can reveal both how much or how little the University has changed.

One such perennial issue was the relationship between the paper and the UT administration. By most indications, the relationship was cordial during the first decade. The degree of deference varied from editor to editor, but all stayed within certain bounds. *The Texan* printed no strident editorials denouncing the administration, as it would in later decades. When the paper did criticize the administration, it was usually about matters such as allowing garbage to collect on campus or not opening the library at night. Of course, more time in the library is hardly a revolutionary demand. In the first decade, *The Texan* might complain about the administration's occasional failing, but it never challenged its fundamental authority.

Another perennial issue in *The Texan's* history was race and gender. In gender matters during its first decade, *The Texan* was advanced for its time. Yes, one editorial quoted approvingly a woman who thought that marrying a good man was more important than her education.[44] But from the beginning, the paper hired a sizable number of women, and those women worked in important editorial positions. None were chief editor in the first decade, but they played an important role in producing the paper. In fact, the paper's editors on several occasions turned the entire *Texan* over to women for special issues.[45]

In racial matters, however, *The Texan's* coverage during its first decade was more shameful. Editor Frank T. West wrote that "The students are rebelling at the use of our athletic field by a gang of sportive coons who make the neighborhood hideous with screams and yells every Sabbath morning. . . . Can not those who have our athletic field in charge ask the police to compel those coons to move on?"[46]

The paper's treatment of Hispanics was also derogatory. In a news story under editor Frank T. West about Texas Independence Day, *The Texan* revealed this view: "The great chief reason why Texas separated from Mexico was because the people of Texas refused to be governed by an inferior race. The moral superiority of the Texan would not bow to the moral inferiority of the Mexican."[47]

These views sound repugnant to modern ears, but it must be remembered that those *Texan* staffers, like all of us, were products of their times.

They grew up in a racist society. Their fathers and grandfathers had fought for the Confederacy. To expect *Texan* editors of the 1900s to hold the racial views of the 1990s would be unfairly anachronistic.

Nevertheless, these types of racist stories (both produced under the same editor) were not common. For the most part, *The Texan* wrote little about minority issues, probably in large part because the campus was not yet integrated. For a paper confining itself to campus events, racial issues did not frequently appear.

In sum, *The Texan's* first decade was marked by steady growth without overwhelming controversy. The paper appeared only weekly, and the student editors seemed to avoid trouble. The decade ahead would prove far more contentious.

The Daily Texan

FIRST COLLEGE DAILY IN THE SOUTH

AUSTIN, TEXAS, SUNDAY, JANUARY 14, 1917.

No. 78

UNIVERSITY MEN WILL VOTE FOR CACTUS BEAUTIES

MEN FOR DEBATING TEAM CHOSEN SOON

TEXAS MARKSMEN WILL GET LETTERS

TRAYWICK HERE THIS WEEK.

SENIOR ACADEMS ELECT.

YALE PROFESSOR HERE THIS WEEK

DR. MABEL ULRICH TO SPEAK BEFORE UNIVERSITY GIRLS

PRESIDENT FAVORS MILITARY TRAINING

MAY HAVE MUSEUM IN NEW BUILDING

BOSTON TECHNOLOGY PROFESSOR TALKS TO ARCHITECT STUDENTS

LANDSLIDES IN TWO INTRAMURAL GAMES SATURDAY

EMPLOYMENT BUREAU ACTIVE.

BEAUTY BALLOT.

TEXAN STAFF, 1916-17.

CHAPTER 2

A Daily *Texan*: 1910–1920

Throughout *The Texan's* history, great controversies seem to occur in batches. The paper will go for years without any momentous events, then suddenly it will be embroiled in critical controversies. One such momentous period was the paper's second decade, particularly the time between 1913 and 1918. In these years, the paper would grow to a daily, participate in the fight between the University and Gov. James Ferguson, comment on World War I, see one editor fired by the administration, and suffer military censorship.

The First College Daily in the South

This decade began with the paper's movement toward becoming a daily. (In 1910 it would be published only twice a week.) After the introduction of a summer issue, *The Texan* began to plan the shift to a daily paper.

To a reader, the prospect of a daily seemed to appear on *The Texan's* pages suddenly. Editor George Wythe later recalled, "The idea of a daily newspaper at the University of Texas . . . was conceived by a group of us, and the idea was put into effect within a surprisingly short time."[1] On January 22, 1913, the president of the Students' Association proposed a daily, saying that bulletin boards did not suffice to inform students and that a daily paper could unify a divided student body.[2] A few weeks later, Wythe wrote, "The question of a daily *Texan* is now definitely before the student body. A daily for the University of Texas is no longer a dream; it has become a necessity."

Despite the claim of necessity, Wythe quickly added, "It will not be necessary to make subscription compulsory. . . . Every student will have the privilege of casting a vote either for or against the entire scheme."[3]

Every student would have the privilege of voting, but *The Texan* tried to ensure that they voted the right way. For weeks, the paper ran lengthy front-page articles about the need for a daily. "Whenever there is government by the popular vote," one article said, "newspapers are indispensable." The UT student body needed an "opportunity for forming intelligent opinions concerning matters brought before them for settlement by vote."[4] "A daily newspaper offers the only means of effectively informing students so that they may vote intelligently." "You ought to have a daily newspaper at the University of Texas."[5]

Some students had reservations, however. Some feared that they would be forced to buy the paper, which then was purchased with voluntary subscriptions. *The Texan* emphatically assured students that this would not happen. Others worried that such a dramatic increase from a semi-weekly to a daily paper would leave *The Texan* in weakened financial status. The paper assured readers that "if the financial basis for a daily is lacking," *The Texan* could go back to a semi-weekly.[6] But students could never know if a daily was possible, the editors encouraged, unless they voted to try the experiment.

On Saturday, April 19, students went to the polls to decide the status of *The Texan*. That morning, the paper urged everyone to vote on the issue, saying "A stay-at-home vote is a vote against the amendment."

"Compulsory subscription is NOT an issue," *The Texan* declared. "It is expressly prohibited by section 18 of the amendment. . . . If you want the news while it is news; if you want all the news; if you want to enlarge the capacity of your paper and make it commensurate with the size of the student body; if you want a decent and convenient and efficient means of making the announcements of the day; if you want progress all along the line—cast your ballot for a *Daily Texan*. Let's have the first college daily in the South."[7]

And students agreed. The measure to have a *Daily Texan* passed overwhelmingly. Of the voting students, 986 supported it; only 47 voted against the proposal.[8] *The Texan* was now *The Daily Texan*.

The first issue of *The Daily Texan* appeared on September 24, 1913. *The Texan* reported, "This issue of *The Daily Texan* is free. It is distributed broadcast over the campus. Fifteen hundred copies are being mailed to alumni. Regular deliveries will not be made until Friday. Save this copy."

Editor Ralph B. Feagin wrote, "As the first college daily in the South and the youngest of all college dailies, we humbly enter the arena of college dailies and extend greetings. Please bear with us in our first attempts and give us your assistance and cooperation."[9]

The eight-page paper was published every morning except Monday. Being produced six days a week, the 1913 *Texan* came out more frequently than the 1996 *Texan*. The masthead proudly proclaimed *The Texan* to be "The First College Daily in the South."

"THE BLANKET TAX HAS SO MUCH TO RECOMMEND IT"

One issue of the campaign to create a daily *Texan* was whether students would pay a mandatory fee. The paper had promised emphatically that would not happen, but the prospect was revisited a mere two years later.

In the fall of 1915, editor Daniel Williams began calling for a blanket tax to fund athletic programs and student publications. "Too long already," Williams wrote, "have a relatively small number year after year paid for that which the entire student body consumed and profited by."[10] In the spring of 1916, the call became a cam-

paign. Williams devoted a lengthy editorial responding to an objection that poor students could not afford such a blanket tax. "But this argument, however, is advanced by anyone except the poor student himself. In the first place, he is too proud to declare his inability to pay his part of the expenses of the student body. In the second place, if he thinks carefully regarding the plan, he will see that it is an admirable cooperative plan whereby athletic contests and the publications can be brought within reach." Furthermore, Williams continued, "By paying for the activities, the students would be more uniformly interested in them."[11]

The campaign continued throughout the spring semester. "The blanket tax has so much to recommend it," the paper advised, "that the students have not so much to consider the advisability of adopting it as to rebuke themselves for neglecting to adopt it long ago."

When put to the ballot in May, the blanket tax passed easily, with 1,307 students voting in favor and 213 voting against. The mandatory fee that two years earlier had been proclaimed an impossibility was now a fact.

The long-term implications of the mandatory student tax were mixed. On the one hand, the tax guaranteed *The Texan* a source of revenue independent of fluctuations in the advertising market. On the other hand, it gave the Students' Association (which controlled the distribution of the student services fee) some financial leverage over the paper. In 1916 this was not an issue because the Students' Association controlled the paper more directly, but future *Texan* editors would have to consider the SA's power over student services fees.

"THE MAN WHO MADE *THE DAILY TEXAN*"

The second editor of the newly established daily was Lynn Landrum. Although most *Texan* editors tried to avoid highly controversial issues and biting editorials, Landrum did not. In this he was influenced by his predecessor Ralph B. Feagin. Landrum wrote that "Feagin's editorials took hold of contemporary conditions with an incisive fearlessness and open-minded common sense that constituted a departure in college journalism."[12] While this was an accurate description of Feagin, it was also extremely true of Landrum himself.

Landrum blasted the University for its foreign language instruction, calling for more training in conversation. "Speed the day," he wrote, "when the University is in a position to turn out linguists as well as lame-duck philologists."[13] Landrum also singled out a certain UT professor for attack. In a harsh denunciation, he wrote that the professor "conceives of classwork as a sort of hide-and-seek game with the students against the professor." At a time when students were expected to wear suits to class, Landrum wrote, "The necktie is the symbol of tyranny."[14]

Landrum also attacked the Students' Association for preventing a *Texan* reporter from attending its meetings. He criticized the SA leaders, likening them to a "man who tells you that he wants a place as your servant but on the condition that you keep your nose out of your own business."[15] Landrum wrote more than five editorials on the subject, making him one of the pioneers of opening campus activities to the public. Some criticized *The Texan's* strong advocacy on the issue, but Landrum curtly replied, "We have no apologies for the part of *The Texan* in the discussion."

Such boldness was characteristic. As Landrum once wrote, "When a newspaper man has got to the point where he is threatened with a good sound thrashing, he has arrived at the dignity of being a real journalist. According to this view, *The Texan* has more than one journalist on the job."[16]

Landrum left office early because he didn't have enough time to keep up with his schoolwork. His successor praised Landrum, saying that "During his editorship, his policy has been twofold: First, tell the truth; and second, when a thing is wrong, swat it."[17]

After Landrum left office, his predecessor Ralph B. Feagin wrote in to say that Landrum was "the man who made *The Daily Texan*." Landrum would go on to a long, distinguished career at the *Dallas Morning News*. Already, the paper was producing a distinguished group of professional journalists.[18]

THE BIGGEST BEAR FIGHT IN THE HISTORY OF THE UNIVERSITY

In all the University's tumultuous history, perhaps the greatest fight was with Gov. James E. Ferguson. Ferguson was suspicious of the University in general and of its accounting system in particular. Eventually, Ferguson's dislike bloomed into a full-scale war when he vetoed the University's appropriations bill and made speeches around the state denouncing the school.

One would expect *The Texan* to play a major role in the conflict. As the University's newspaper, it would be expected to comment heavily on such a momentous event as a battle between the University and the governor.

Such involvement would be even more likely given that a major tactic of Ferguson's foes, such as UT regent Will C. Hogg, was to use the press. In a letter sent to alumni, Hogg urged them to "address an open letter to your home paper."[19] Hogg wrote, "In order to get before the public of Texas complete and accurate information concerning the issues of the controversy between Governor James E. Ferguson and the University of Texas, involving the very existence of a free University for all the people, it is absolutely necessary to have the aid of the press."[20]

In July of 1917, Hogg wrote, "We have been conducting a diligent and, I believe, effectual campaign on behalf of the University—effectual in the sense that we have spread a knowledge of the falsehood and frivolity of the Governor's charges among the intelligent reading people of Texas."[21]

Governor Ferguson agreed with Hogg that the publicity campaign was "effectual." When he wrote a pamphlet explaining his decision to veto the University's appropriations bill, Ferguson said, "Most of the editors of the big daily newspapers of the state are working overtime in their effort to misrepresent and unfairly criticize my action in vetoing the appropriations for the State University."[22]

Although Ferguson's claims of misrepresentation may be debatable, he was correct that this became a major issue in newspapers statewide. The *Dallas Morning News* published no less than twenty-one editorials on the subject.[23] In fact, one member of the *Dallas News* (who was so familiar with John A. Lomax, a major Ferguson opponent who Ferguson successfully fired, that he signed his letter only "Bru") wrote to Lomax saying, "I wish you would write me specifically how I can help you most."[24]

Curiously enough, however, *The Texan* did not appear to play a major role in the controversy with its editorials and news coverage. Will C. Hogg compiled a scrapbook of newspaper articles on the topic from many papers, both large and small, around the state.[25] It would have been natural to clip any editorials or stories on the subject from *The Texan*, which was, after all, the University's own newspaper. Yet nothing from *The Texan* appeared.

Nor do the microfiche collections of *The Texans* from those years yield evidence to support a substantial *Texan* role in the conflict. While a few issues are missing, the ones present contain few if any strong editorials or news stories on the topic.

This was likely deliberate. In October 1916, editor Roy E. Hawk mentioned a dispute between the governor and UT officials but then emphatically stated, "*The Texan* will KEEP OUT OF POLITICS. . . . It must be remembered that the paper is a student paper, representing student opinion, and that opinion varies as does the Texas weather."[26] It seems, then, that *The Texan* under the leadership of Hawk deliberately chose to stay out of the Ferguson controversy.

Why? The subject was obviously newsworthy, and one might logically assume that it should have been covered in the UT paper. Why did Hawk choose to remain neutral?

One answer might be that the University wanted him to do so. The issue was complex, and if the UT newspaper was deemed irresponsible on the controversy, it might have undermined the University's position. Indeed, evidence exists that similar fears were present with the alumni magazine *Texas Alcalde*. John A. Lomax, the University secretary, wrote to Will Hogg: "*The Alcalde*, as the mouthpiece of alumni opinion, will always be a source of danger, for it can be quoted effectively against the Alumni in a crisis, should its pages give a particular version therefore. While he was Editor-in-Chief of the *Alcalde*, I had more than once to eliminate Ben's [Ben White's] editorials because they touched on political questions and would certainly have harmed and not helped the cause of the University."[27] If UT officials were worried about editorials in the *Alcalde* (traditionally a far less controversial publication than the student paper) harming the University, they must have been even more concerned about *The Texan*. It seems likely that they might have encouraged or ordered the *Texan* editors to avoid the Ferguson issue.

This may have been to the editors' liking. *The Texan*, it seems, had already had to apologize to Governor Ferguson at least once. In November 1916, the paper reported that a black postal worker received several votes for governor over Ferguson.[28] This infuriated Ferguson, and the paper later apologized.[29]

Furthermore, it seems Governor Ferguson was prone to filing libel suits when he felt defamed. Will C. Hogg wrote a memo to the Finance Committee of the Ex-Students' Association trying to find out the "name and number of libel suits and where filed by him [Ferguson] since he became governor."[30] Given Ferguson's apparent proclivity for suing newspapers, the student editors may have decided to avoid the issue.

While the paper's editors may have dodged the issue in print, some evidence suggests that they still may have been involved surreptitiously. On May 28 a major student rally took place. A large group of students headed by a student leader in a military uniform marched on the capitol and denounced Ferguson.[31] Ferguson was upset, referring to the protesters as "hoodlums." But UT officials claimed that they had no responsibility for the actions of the students.[32] The students were just acting on their own.

Twenty-three years later, a different story would emerge. In his essay "Random Recollections of the University 'Bear Fight,'" John A. Lomax described the campus reaction to the alleged plans of Ferguson to fire UT President Robert Ernest Vinson: "At the University, the repercussions bioled [*sic*] into quick actions. Dan Williams, the dynamic *Texan* editor, had student committees at work before the day was an hour old. 'No classes tomorrow. An early morning mass-meeting of protest, George Peddy, chief speaker. A parade to the capitol and around it. Banners galore: DOWN WITH KAISER JIM (Hitler was yet a corporal!); NO AUTOCRACY IN THE UNIVERSITY, etc.!'" Lomax related a story from Judge Robert Batts, "It seemed that President Vinson and Dan Williams had met with him [Batts] at his house to arrange details of the student parade, an episode so important, that it set the tide definitely away from the autocratic domination of the University of Texas by a Governor."[33]

If Lomax's account is correct, the *Texan* editor and the UT president met covertly to organize a student protest against the Texas governor. Not only was the *Texan* editor involved in the controversy, he may have played a critical part. Lomax seemed to believe that the student protest was pivotal in turning public opinion against the governor. If so, *Texan* editor Dan Williams deserves much credit for organizing the protest so quickly and contributing to the University's ultimate victory against Governor Ferguson.

Perhaps editor Roy Hawk was reluctant to become involved in politics (at least in print), but it appears that his immediate predecessor had no such hesitations.

WORLD WAR I

The Ferguson war was not the only fight in which *The Texan* would soon find itself involved. At the same time the University was fighting at home, the European nations were fighting in World War I. After the war began in 1914, the *Texan*'s news coverage of it was sparse. Occasionally, a letter from a UT alumnus would mention the "European war," but the issue was not given significant news coverage. Part of the reason for this, of course, may have been the absence of a wire service. Even if it had wanted to report more extensively on the war, *The Texan* had little way to acquire the information.

Then, after years of scant coverage, the war broke into the paper's consciousness. In February 1917 a huge headline blared, "WAR SEEMS IMMINENT; MERCHANT LINER SUNK." Another read: "NAVAL RESERVES OF THREE STATES MOBILIZED FOLLOWING SINKING OF AMERICAN STEAMSHIP HOUSATONIC OFF SCILLY ISLANDS—VON BERNSTOFF [THE GERMAN AMBASSADOR] ORDERED HOME." One story was titled, "PROFESSORS THINK WILSON IS RIGHT; PROMINENT FACULTY MEN BELIEVE UNITED STATES HAS TAKEN ONLY HONORABLE COURSE LEFT." A chemistry professor said, "Each and every citizen of the United States should stand behind the government, no matter what his inward feelings might be on the matter."[34]

The campus then voted on whether to institute optional military training for students. Editor Roy E. Hawk (who had so earnestly wished to avoid politics) supported the measure, though with a curious disclaimer: "We will vote for optional military training, but as to what the will of the student body should be, we know not, nor do we care."[35] In fact, the "will of the student body" coincided with Hawk's. Students favored optional military training by a 3–1 majority.[36]

After this extensive coverage in February, the issue disappeared for more than two months. There were no accounts of the European battles

or the national policy debates over whether to enter the war. *The Texan* had one news story about demonstrations being planned to "show loyalty in crisis," but that was the extent of the reporting.

When war did break out in April, the paper responded with a display of patriotism. A huge headline proclaimed "UNIVERSITY PREPARES FOR WAR; INSTITUTION TO BECOME MILITARY TRAINING CAMP." The news story continued, "America's declaration of war upon Germany yesterday was the signal for the University, both faculty and students, to begin preparation for the conflict that appears to be at hand. . . . Companies have already been formed by members of the Law Department, the Engineering Department, the faculty, and University Hall. Drilling has already begun." An editorial urged all students to attend a loyalty parade. "Every loyal citizen and every student of the University of Texas who is backing the government will be given the opportunity to openly display his willingness. Full-grown, able-bodied Americans of Austin should be found in the parade Monday."[37]

A week later, *The Texan* printed all the verses to "The Star-Spangled Banner" on page 1.[38]

Not everyone supported the war rush, but dissident voices would not be heard in *The Texan*. One editorial after the war's outbreak announced, "Our pacifist friends have little to say now."[39] A week later, the attack on pacifists grew fiercer: "They have to be handled with gloves, for in many cases they don't know the war is on, and when they are made aware of the fact, they always insist that they can best fill the positions of the 'thinking' man rather than the solider. The woods are full of such animals. They will always be with us as long as they can afford to publicly make known their policies. They have been against the new drill scheme from the start are still opposed to it. This group has in its organization both students and faculty members who care little for things other than those concerning or benefiting self."

That *The Texan* would devote an entire editorial to attacking these dissidents suggests that student unease over the possibility of a foreign war may have been greater than *The Texan*'s news stories would indicate. *The Texan* may have supported war, but the need to bash opponents so fiercely suggests that at least some students may have thought otherwise.

Some of those dissident voices found room in

The Daily Texan

FIRST COLLEGE DAILY IN THE SOUTH

AUSTIN, TEXAS, SATURDAY, APRIL 7, 1917.

No. 143

UNIVERSITY PREPARES FOR WAR

FRANK BAKER IS CAUSE OF DANIEL BAKER'S DEFEAT

TEXAS BEATEN IN DEBATE; 2 TO 1

TRACK TEAM HAS SLIGHT HOPE FOR VICTORY TODAY

CLASS BASEBALL TO OPEN TODAY

INSTITUTION TO BECOME MILITARY TRAINING CAMP

FACULTY AND STUDENTS FORM COMPANIES—MASS MEETING SET FOR TODAY TO ARRANGE FOR LOYALTY DAY PARADE.

Political Rally Law Auditorium 7:30 O'clock Tonight

THE DAILY TEXAN

FIRST COLLEGE DAILY IN THE SOUTH

AUSTIN, TEXAS, MONDAY, NOVEMBER 11, 1918.

NO. 22

UNIVERSITY CELEBRATES PEACE

CROWD OF 2500 ATTENDS WAR FUND CONVOCATION

ARMISTICE SIGNED MONDAY MORNING STOPS HOSTILITIES

TEXAS WALLOPS OKLA. AGGIES IN FAST GAME

TEAM PLAYS GOOD GAME

STUDENTS IN MONSTER VICTORY CELEBRATION

BROWN APPOINTS POLL OFFICIALS FOR ELECTION

ENTIRE REGIMENT AND GIRLS MARCH

BELIEVE VARSITY QUOTA SUBSCRIBED

MARINES TO LEAVE FOR GEORGIA TECH THURSDAY NIGHT

The Texan's "Co-ed edition," an issue published by only women students. At the start of the war, *The Texan's* male editor was strongly enthusiastic about the war. A female editorial writer was much less enthused. An editorial entitled "THE WOMAN'S PRAYER FOR PEACE" asked, "What attitude does the woman of the University take toward the war question? It is the woman who must sacrifice those nearest and best loved. . . . In the heart of every woman of the University who is guilty of any thought whatsoever . . . there is a prayer. . . . That prayer is for peace."

But "we stand opposed to militarism," the editorial continued. "We fight that fighting may be done away with forever and ever. . . . We women of Texas pray for peace, and at the same time we resolve to throw every atom of selfishness, every personal interest that may conflict with the general good into the melting pot. We will send our men to fight if the need comes. Would that we might go ourselves."[40]

Despite the patriotically correct ending, this editorial was one of the strongest anti-war sentiments published in *The Texan* at the time. The male editor was strongly pro-war, and no other alternative perspectives appeared. In this case, the tradition of a co-ed edition allowed a meaningful expression of diverse opinion.

Those with dissident views, however, would be left with little choice in supporting the war effort. On April 25, 1917, UT President Robert Ernest Vinson announced, "All students who, by five o'clock Wednesday afternoon, April 25, have failed to register for a course in Military Science, unless excused by the president, will be dropped from the rolls of the University."[41] (This was months before Congress passed an official draft.) On April 27 *The Texan* reported that 400 students had been dropped from the rolls.[42] That number was more than 15 percent of the male students.

While war fervor seized both the campus and the paper, *The Texan* argued against hysteria on some issues. One editor wrote, "It is the earnest hope of *The Texan* that the Board of Regents at their meeting in Galveston will reconsider the act that made it impossible for aliens—friendly or otherwise—to serve the University in any capacity. The declaration of war is old enough now to enable everyone to act more normally on matters that are distorted considerably by war's first glamour."[43]

The paper suffered because of the draft of male students. Editor Silas B. Ragsdale wrote that staffers were either "physical wrecks, women, or youths, so prepare for the worst. . . . The staff is slim as well as wrecked and youthful, so forbear again."[44]

To make matters worse, the campus was hit with an influenza epidemic. In October 1918 *The Texan* suspended publication for almost two weeks with the explanation that "because of the influenza situation, the delivery department is very inadequate and uncertain."[45] That was not surprising. Going house to house exposing oneself to the epidemic would be enough to make anyone "uncertain" about the job. The 1918 flu outbreak was one of the worst in history, killing an estimated twenty to forty million people worldwide.[46]

Finally, peace had arrived worldwide. "UNIVERSITY CELEBRATES PEACE," said the headline. "STUDENTS IN MONSTER VICTORY CELEBRATION."[47] The new victory celebration made a fitting counterpart to the earlier parades of patriotism. At the University, World War I both began and ended in a celebration. At this second celebration, however, fifty-one UT students would be missing.[48] They had died during the war, and the University marked their loss with gold stars on a special flag commemorating war dead.

The Texan's problems, however, did not end with the war. Starting on November 15, the paper was published in abbreviated form. There was a national paper shortage, and the federal government wanted to "conserve the paper stock resources of the country."[49]

In addition to the paper shortage, *The Texan* faced censorship from military authorities. On November 19, almost a week after the end of the war, editor F. Edward Walker wrote an editorial on "lessening the restrictions" about the military controls imposed on UT students. "Some reasoning," he wrote, "seems to point toward the lessening of the restrictions on the students in the Students' Army Training Corps if they are to effectually accomplish the work that the University requires them to do. . . . The military duties of the student soldiers have occupied practically all of the time not spent in class and very frequently most of this time also." There wasn't enough time to study.

Furthermore, students had to have a pass signed by a military commander to leave campus, even if it was to go across the street to buy a bottle of ink at the Co-Op during their free time. Walker wrote, "Why not give freedom during their spare hours to leave the campus if necessary to accomplish the ordinary little things that they must leave to do?"[50]

The military was not pleased, and it did not want such criticism to reoccur. At first, Walker tried to accommodate them. On November 20 he wrote, "We have inaugurated a department for news about the Students' Army Training Corps, and all of this material will be censored by the post headquarters. This censorship was not imposed on us, but we are asking for it in order that we will not inconvenience the military authorities by printing inaccurate or misleading news, and so as not to publish any stories before the time is ripe."[51]

But this was not enough for the military. A day later, *The Texan* reported, "Yesterday, the editor of *The Texan* was told in effect that he had no right as a member of the naval section of the Students' Army Training Corps to publish anything in the columns of the paper without submitting same to the censorship of the military authorities."[52]

Walker was in a bind. Being under draft, he could not leave the military, nor would the First Amendment have then protected him. So to preserve the independence of *The Texan*, Edward Walker resigned as editor and was replaced by Stanley Walker, presumably someone not under military control.

An editorial read, "His resignation will therefore enable *The Texan* to resume its place as the independent organ of the student body. . . . *The Texan* is the paper of the students of the University. . . . As such, it feels that it has a right to champion the cause of the student body."[53] The price of being able to champion the students' cause, however, was the resignation of a *Texan* editor.

Edward Walker was not gone for good. Although he stayed out for the rest of the fall semester, Walker returned as *Texan* editor in the spring semester. In an editorial entitled "THE VANISHED S.A.T.C.," Walker labeled the military program "a failure" and said "that a very large percentage of the opinions have at any time been favorable is not very likely."[54]

So Walker had the last word, after all. The military could issue its orders, but in the end, *The Texan* survived this attempt to destroy its independence.

RAGSDALE AND THE *BLUNDERBUSS*

In the midst of the tension caused by the war, *The Texan* was experiencing serious problems with the UT administration. In the spring of 1918, editor Silas B. Ragsdale, along with the paper's managing editor Edward Walker and two other prominent student leaders, had produced an April Fool's Day newsletter called the *Blunderbuss*. The *Blunderbuss* was not affiliated with *The Daily Texan*; Ragsdale acted as a private student and not as *Texan* editor.

For their roles in publishing the *Blunderbuss*, all four students were ordered expelled from the University. A front-page *Texan* news story reported, "Four of the most prominent University students have been suspended from the University by the disciplinary committee because they were connected with the issuing of the *Blunderbuss*, which is a humorous, anonymously published publication making its appearance on April first of each year."[55]

An uproar ensued. Both *The Texan* and the student body opposed the decision, which was made by a disciplinary committee lacking student members. One "Firing Line" letter suggested that the suspension was "causing many of us to doubt whether we have any vestige of our boasted student self government left at our University."[56] Another letter said, "Now in 1918, when our country is fighting 'to make the world safe for democracy,' we are forced to admit that democracy and student self-government have proved an abject failure in the government of the student body of the University of Texas."[57]

A *Texan* editorial (somewhat melodramatically) warned, "Just what will happen to *The Daily Texan* if the discipline committee holds to its original decision is not known. . . . Apparently the only thing that can be done will be to close up the office and suspend publication until one of the two [editors] are reinstated in the University.

"The decision seems to be the result of a consideration that does not take into account the good of the entire University."[58]

In an editorial titled "SWAN SONG PRECURSOR," Ragsdale wrote, "*The Texan*, speaking as the student organ and not as the individual mouthpiece of one of the so-called culprits, believes that it expresses student opinion when it says that the action of the discipline committee is held in disfavor. The petitions declaring the penalties too severe show this to be a fact.

"Leniency is therefore asked and expected," Ragsdale continued. "*The Texan*, as do hundreds of students, asks that such action be taken at the committee meeting."[59]

Ragsdale was correct about student opinion. All four students were respected campus leaders, and hundreds of students signed petitions asking the UT administration for leniency.

The students' voices, however, went unheard. UT President Robert Ernest Vinson wrote in a general announcement that "I find these petitions seriously defective. . . . The petitions are, properly speaking, not petitions at all but simply protests and expressions of opinion."[60]

Having declared "expressions of opinion" an invalid form of petition, Vinson then asked the Students' Association to pass a resolution on the suspensions. In a unanimous vote, the Assembly responded by calling the penalties "too severe."[61]

Nevertheless, the discipline committee still handed down a harsh sentence. *The Texan* wrote, "Ragsdale's sentence for his White Sox editorial is a choice between suspension for the rest of the main session and resignation from his office of editor-in-chief of *The Daily Texan*."

Ragsdale, needing to finish his degree before entering the military for World War I, chose to resign. In his departing editorial, he wrote, "So goodbye. In future wanderings over the world, we will think about the University, and we will grieve for the University, and we will love the University —but in all cases we will want our University to be like that one we went to back in our frosh, soph, junior, and the first two-thirds of our senior years."[62]

In an editorial titled "A TRIBUTE," Ragsdale's successor F. Edward Walker wrote, "*The Texan* has lost its leader, and the loss is a great and irreparable one. . . . All of us recognized him as a leader. Those of us who knew him recognized him, above everything else, as a loyal friend; as a man with an irreproachable sense of morals and of justice; as a brilliant student; as one who could, and who now still can, face his fellowmen with a knowledge that his character is above reproach. Greatest of all, we knew him as a thorough gentleman."[63]

Expelling an editor for the content of an editorial is one of the greatest blows a university can deal to press freedom. That action, however, is now largely prohibited by the U.S. Constitution. But in Ragsdale's time, the First Amendment ap-plied only to the federal government and not to the states. Later, its prohibition against "abridging the freedom of the press" would allow *Texan* editors to criticize the administration without fear of expulsion.

Such legal protection, however, came too late for Silas Ragsdale.

A perennial issue with *The Texan* has been how it gets along with the administration. In this area, *The Texan* from 1910 to 1920 fared far worse than *The Texan* from 1900 to 1910. Having Silas B. Ragsdale expelled was a major defeat for the paper.

Much of this strained relationship might have been avoided had UT President Robert Ernest Vinson been more flexible. Vinson, who refused to pardon Ragsdale and declared the students' petitions invalid, acted in the face of widespread student opposition.

Whatever Vinson's personal characteristics, *The Texan* was not as opposed to the administration as it would be in later decades. There were no editorials attacking Vinson by name, for instance, and certainly the paper's editorials were not fiercely hostile toward the administrators. Relations might not have been as cordial as they were in the previous decade, but *The Texan* and the Main Building were still basically on the same side (if only because the paper did not have much choice in the matter).

In some cases, the student journalists in this decade may have accepted the administration's restrictions without much opposition. Editor George Wythe recalled one incident:

> One of the troubles of a student editor is to avoid offending the sensibilities of the Texas legislators upon whom we depend for our sustenance. One Tuesday afternoon an issue editor of *The Texan*, who had just seen his issue go to press, appeared on the campus, and encountering by chance the late Dr. Sydney Mezes, who was then President of the University, handed him an advance copy of the paper, on which the ink was still fresh. As it happened, my editorial in that issue made some reference to the legislature. Owing to the delicate situation then pending, Dr. Mezes feared that any reference might be misunderstood. He got in touch with me and asked me to delete the editorial in question. Unfortunately, by that time practically the entire issue had been run off, and there was some question as

to how the additional expense would be met, but Dr. Mezes undertook to see to that. I thought then, and I think now, that Dr. Mezes was unduly alarmed, but I had no desire to rock the boat, and therefore submitted an innocuous editorial on the subject "The Blue Bonnets on the Campus."[64]

Yet no amount of editorializing about bluebonnets could hide the controversy of this decade. *The Texan*'s second decade was tumultuous, full of both achievement and defeats. The paper had expanded to a daily, and by buying access to a wire service, it was poised to devote more attention to national issues. Yet it had suffered through the Ferguson controversy, the expulsion of one editor, and the forced resignation of another. It was a difficult period. Fortunately, the Roaring Twenties would prove less taxing.

CHAPTER 3

TEXAS STUDENT PUBLICATIONS: 1920–1930

The 1920s would prove to be a far less controversial decade for the paper. No editors would be expelled, and the years would be more placid than those of the previous decade. Nevertheless, from dealing with a dean upset over lingerie ads to incorporating Texas Student Publications to hiding in a coat closet to spy on the UT Board of Regents, *Texan* staffers would find plenty to occupy themselves.

The Daily Texan began the decade of the Roaring Twenties by observing the election of Warren G. Harding as president. "HARDING SCORES LANDSLIDE VOTE," the headline read. "INDICATIONS POINT TO THE GREATEST REPUBLICAN VICTORY IN HISTORY."[1]

Voting in campus elections, however, was not producing landslides, and *The Texan* wrote a concerned editorial decrying the low voter turnout in Student Association elections.[2] More than one-third of the student body voted, however. (The usual turnout in the 1990s was about 7 percent of the student population.)

The change in fashions did arouse some consternation. In 1920 a *Texan* editorial bemoaned what it viewed as cultural degradation: "The true gentleman is a person who is becoming rarer and rarer as the craze for jazz and a good time continues to grow in favor."[3]

In 1921 the University began to discuss the possibility of moving off the original Forty Acres to obtain more space. "REGENTS ADVOCATE TRANSFER OF UNIVERSITY SITE," the headline blared.[4] A *Texan* editorial approved, saying, "It appears that the Board has adopted the wisest and most sensible plan in its recommendations,

namely picking up the University and placing it upon a site at least as desirable as the one now occupied."[5] The proposed location was known as the Brackenridge site and constituted 500 acres on the Colorado River.

The proposal enjoyed significant support. UT students approved the change by a 12-to-1 margin in a student referendum,[6] and UT President Robert Ernest Vinson supported the move.[7] Texas newspapers from the *San Antonio Express* to the *Dallas Morning News* endorsed the proposal.

Politics intervened, however. The Austin Chamber of Commerce opposed the move,[8] and the Texas Legislature adopted a compromise that would give the University more space but not permit it to leave its current site.[9]

The year 1921 marked several firsts for the paper. On May 31 the paper announced, "*Texan* to have wireless news during summer. . . . For the first time in the history of the school newspaper, use will be made of wireless reports."[10]

TEXAS STUDENT PUBLICATIONS

It was also in 1921 that Texas Student Publications, the agency that handles the paper's business affairs, was founded. According to *Daily Texan* editor Mike Godwin, who wrote an essay on the paper's history:

By 1916, it was apparent that *The Texan* and the other student publications, for all their competence at journalism, were beginning to suffer from financial mismanagement. So the Students'

In the 1920s, liquor could be obtained with a prescription, for "medical purposes."

Association decided to unite the various student publications under a "Board of United Publications of the University of Texas," which would hire a general manager to handle the publications' business affairs.

Five years later, the Students' Association incorporated the publications board as an independent entity that would eventually be called "Texas Student Publications, Inc." The new corporation was placed in charge of publishing *The Texan*, the *Cactus*, the *Longhorn* (a literary magazine), and, later, the *Texas Ranger*, which reigned for decades as one of the nation's leading college humor magazines.[11]

As J. W. Calhoun, a faculty member on the TSP Board, would write in 1928:

Previous to the incorporation of the publications there was no system, no policy, no continuity. Each publication was in the hands of a separate manager. The manager was elective and changed every year. He left no record of income and expenditures, there was no accumulation of experience or assets. Each manager faced anew all the problems of previous managers and had no record of how the problems had been met, what had been the failures and the successes of his predecessors. It was inevitable, therefore, that the same blunders were made year after year and doubtless new ones were added from time to time. Incorporation may have introduced some troubles that did not exist before, but it has cured the ones mentioned above. There are complete and comprehensive records, there is continuity of management, and there is accumulation of experience. The organization is now in a position to improve progressively.[12]

The minutes from the first meeting of the Board of United Publications of the University of Texas still exist. The date is May 19, 1916, and the minutes are kept in hand, presumably by the secretary Ray Sherrile. A motion passed "that the Secretary advertise daily in *The Texan* for bids for the management of any or all of the University publications."[13] The board continued to deal with the paper's financial affairs for the next five years, discussing such things as salaries and preventing the unauthorized sale of *Cactus* ads. At the May 25, 1921, meeting, the board's minutes noted, "Bennett L. Wooley selected to manage publications under incorporation, on a $2,000 salary." The last minutes recorded for the Board of United Publications are for the meeting of April 28, 1922. The board fixed the salary of the supervising business manager at $2,400 for the entire year and placed all financial affairs under the direction of the board.[14]

The first recorded meetings of the Texas Student Publication Board of Operating Trustees occurred on June 30, 1922. The board addressed the question of advertising, saying, "No advertising contrary to the policy of the University of Texas shall be accepted by the business manager. Dances not on the Social Calender and advertisements of Chiropractors were mentioned as being contrary to the policy of the University of Texas."[15] The total TSP budget for 1922 was $30,905.96.[16]

Although Texas Student Publications had arisen from the Students' Association, the UT administration still exercised considerable control. On November 5, 1924, UT President W. M. W. Splawn told the TSP Board about the conclusions of a special committee that he had appointed: "You will observe that the committee recommends that the Board of Directors of the Students' Publications be advised to establish some form of efficient censorship of the *Longhorn*. The committee also recommends that the Board of Regents withdraw their subsidy unless they have definite assurance of a change of policy on the part of the *Longhorn*."[17]

On December 20, 1924, President Splawn told the TSP Board about a request of the Discipline Committee that he had approved: "It therefore recommends that the Publications Board be requested to define the nature and degree of editorial responsibility for the appearance in University publications of unfounded attacks or criticisms of the University or of any of its activities."[18] Who would determine if the criticisms were "unfounded" was not specified, but it seems clear that the UT administration was exercising editorial control over the student media through the TSP Board.

In June 1925 the controls were tightened. The TSP Board created an "Editorial Advisory Board" for *The Daily Texan*. The committee was composed of the *Texan* editor and managing edi-

tor, the TSP manager of publications, and the two faculty members of the TSP Board. The students were outnumbered on the committee, although *Texan* editors did have the right to appeal to the entire TSP Board. The committee was to meet weekly during the school year. It was instructed "to formulate general policies for the *Daily Texan* news columns," "to formulate general policies for the *Daily Texan*'s editorial columns," and "to coordinate activities along editorial lines with those long advertising lines, in order that the newspaper shall be as evenly balanced as possible."[19] In short, while the elected student editor was nominally in charge, the faculty and administration had substantial control over the paper. That the committee met weekly shows how great the administration's control was. As a *Texan* editorial assessed in 1924, the authorized student publications "are subjected to the most severe restrictions."[20]

LINGERIE, CLOSETS, AND CENSORSHIP

After the formation of TSP in 1921, *The Texan* continued along with little noticeable change. In November 1921 the staff had to decide between putting out a paper and observing the venerable tradition of attending the UT-Texas A&M football game. Their choice? "Today being Thanksgiving, the *Texan* staff will take a holiday and go to College Station with the rest of the bunch. Consequently, there will be no paper issued Friday morning."[21]

In 1922 *The Daily Texan* found itself in trouble with the dean of women. An angry Lucy Newton marched down to the office of the TSP business manager to complain about a risqué advertisement.[22] The ad, published on Sunday, October 9, advertised "Jersey Silk Lingerie." The lingerie in controversy—modest by current standards—reached down to the knees.

In October 1922 the UT Board of Regents banned the student ownership of automobiles. The reasons were that cars were "detrimental to scholarship and conducive to the creation of social distinctions."[23] The regents may have been right about social distinctions, but *The Texan* dissented, arguing that UT students should be able to own cars.

A daring incident of investigative reporting took place in 1924. Pat M. Neff, then governor of Texas, had expressed an interest in becoming UT

The 1924 staff of The Daily Texan.

president. At the time, the regents' meetings were closed to the public, and this meeting was especially sensitive.

Many years later, *The Texan* recounted what happened:

> The nerve of a freshman reporter on *The Daily Texan* helped inform the public of what went on behind closed doors at the May 16, 1924 meeting of the Board of Regents, reported *The Texan* May 18, 1924.
>
> At that time, too, meetings were closed to the public, but this freshman, among the reporters to whom the regents turned a deaf ear, had an idea, suggested by none other than Dr. W. S. Sutton, then acting president, who told this freshman reporter to hide under the table if he wanted to "get the dope."
>
> While the Regents went out to dinner, he hid in a closet in the Regents' meeting room, concealing himself behind maps and charts.
>
> The regents returned from dinner. Will C. Hogg of Houston, heading a delegation of ex-students to protest the election of Neff, took the floor.
>
> "Wait a minute, wait a minute," said Lutcher Stark, then chairman of the board. "I want to caution every one of you to absolute secrecy about what goes on in this meeting. No word

must get out to the newspapers. Will you pledge absolute secrecy?"

> They all pledged.
>
> Hogg started to speak again.
>
> "Sh-h-h," said one regent. "Let's lock all the doors."
>
> All the doors were duly locked.
>
> "Better close the windows, too," said another regent.
>
> The windows were closed and bolted, and the meeting was on.
>
> Members of the ex-students committee severely criticized the board for interference in faculty control of the University. Hogg, speaking for the ex-students at their suggestion, urged that the board take plenty of time and get the right man. He protested the consideration of Neff.
>
> When Hogg finished his speech, a voice, which the freshman reporter in the closet identified as that of Regent Frank Jones, gave his pledge to Hogg as representative of the ex-students:
>
> "Well, you have sufficient confidence in us to believe that we won't elect Neff, haven't you? Well, Neff is not the first governor of Texas who has wanted the presidency of the University. We won't give it to him."
>
> The meeting then took up the discussion of the qualifications of Dr. Ford and Dr. H. E. Bol-

Here Is Inside Dope on How Regents Selected President

❖ ❖ ❖ ❖ ❖ ❖ ❖ ❖ ❖ ❖ ❖ ❖ ❖ ❖

The nerve of a freshman reporter on The Daily Texan, university of Texas campus newspaper, Friday morning, made it possible for the student paper to give part of the "inside" story on the election of Governor Pat M. Neff as president of the University, which was followed by his refusal to accept the subsequent election of Dr. Guy Stanton Ford and the resignation of Regents Frank C. Jones and Sam P. Cochran from the board.

This freshman's story indicates also that the decision of the board of regents to elect Neff president was not made until Friday after protesting ex-students had been assured Thursday by members of the board that this would not be done.

The Daily Texan has many reporters and it sent some half a dozen over to cover the meeting of the regents on Thursday. To these awe-stricken youngsters the regents turned a deaf ear, they thought. But one reporter had an idea, suggested by no other than Dr. W. S. Sutton, Acting President, who told one of The Texan

men to hide under the table if he wanted to "get the dope."

The boy reporter, hearing this suggestion made to one of his fellows, took Sutton at his word. While the Regents went to dinner he hid in a closet in the Regent's meeting room, concealing himself behind sundry maps and outlines, drawn by no other authority than Herbert M. Greene of Dallas, University architect.

The Regents returned from dinner. Will C. Hogg of Houston, heading a delegation of ex-students to protest the election of Neff, took the floor.

"Not a Word to Newspapers"

"Wait a minute, wait a minute," said Lutcher Stark, chairman. "I want to caution everyone of you to absolute secrecy about what goes on in this meeting. No word must get out to the newspapers. Will you all pledge absolute secrecy?"

They all pledged.

Hogg started to speak again.

Doors Locked, Windows Closed

"Sh-h-h," said one regent. "Let's

lock all the doors."

All the doors were duly locked.

"Better close the windows, too," said another Regent.

The windows were closed and bolted. And the meeting was on.

Members of the ex-student committee severely criticized the board for interference in faculty control of the University. Hogg, speaking for the ex-students at their suggestion, urged that the board take plenty of time and get the right man. He protested the consideration of Neff.

When Hogg finished his speech a voice which the freshman reporter in the closet identified as that of Regent Frank Jones gave this pledge to Hogg as representative of the ex-students:

Jones Promises

"Well, you have sufficient confidence in us to believe that we won't select Neff, haven't you? Well, Neff is not the first governor of Texas who has wanted the presidency of the University.

(Continued on page four)

ton of California. All during the meeting the ex-students were assured that Neff would not be selected. During this time, the reporter, with his ear to the closet door, took notes. The regents said that only Bolton and Ford were being considered. The ex-students took trains out of town, satisfied.

Friday Neff was elected. Following his election Chairman Stark said: "No, Neff's election was not a complimentary one. If it was, why did two regents resign as protest? We wanted him to be president of the University."

This ends the story of the freshman reporter, whose name was kept secret for the sake of his university career.[24]

Although Neff later turned down the job as UT president, he at least was fairly friendly toward the University. Later governors were not. In April of 1924, *The Texan* reported, "With one stroke of the executive tomahawk, Governor Miriam Ferguson abolished the University summer school, the Department of Journalism, the School of Music, the Department of Library Science, and the office of Business Manager."[25] (Miriam Ferguson was the wife of former Texas Governor Jim Ferguson, who had attacked the University in the last decade.) *The Texan* re-

sponded that the Department of Journalism might be a good thing to keep around.

In January 1926 editor Stewart Harkrider announced *The Texan*'s program for the new year: "1. Cleaner and more beautiful campus. 2. Launching of a 'better grades' campaign. 3. Creation of a real 'friendly spirit' among the students. 4. Closer cooperation between the students and the faculty. 5. More useful service of *The Daily Texan* to the students." Controversial it was not.

A far more controversial year, however, would be 1927, which involved a fight between the *Texan* editor and the Faculty Disciplinary Committee. Editor Sam Johnson charged the Faculty Disciplinary Committee with attempted censorship of *The Texan*. He accused them of trying to suppress the student side of campus political questions, and then he resigned in protest.[26]

On January 10, 1927, the TSP Board accepted the resignation of Sam Johnson. Johnson wrote to the board, "Gentlemen: Please accept this as formal notice of my resignation from the editorship of *The Daily Texan*. I assure you that it has been a pleasure for me to have been associated with you and an honor to have served on this board. I have only the best of feelings toward the members of the present board—students and faculty. Wishing for your continued success, I am Sincerely, Sam C. Johnson."[27]

A few years later, editor Jimmie Payne would write, "The University of Texas rejoices in a journalistic freedom that is paralleled very rarely in American collegiate studies. . . . Here, the faculty, wisely it would seem to us, withholds its censorial yea or nay."[28] Payne may have been being speaking sarcastically, but if not, fellow editors like Sam Johnson would disagree about the paper's "journalistic freedom."

And whatever the degree of censorship imposed by the Faculty Disciplinary Committee, the professors on the TSP Board continued to exercise significant control over the paper. In April 1927 the TSP Board passed the following resolution:

> Resolved that it is the sense of the Board that *The Daily Texan* in its news and editorial columns should not carry material supporting or opposing any candidate for student office, except that material commonly called the "formal announcement," which is given free to each candidate
>
> That the staff of *The Daily Texan*, as an official body, should refrain from taking sides in any political controversy.

This rule would prevent the paper from thoroughly investigating any issues in the government race because that material could be construed as supporting or opposing a candidate. The result was that *The Texan* generally limited its election coverage to an announcement that candidate X was running for office Y.

In 1927 the *Texan*'s offices moved. For years, the paper had been published in the Main Building. Now, however, all the TSP publications would be located in Brackenridge Hall, or as it was more commonly known, B. Hall. The TSP manager of publications, William L. McGill, said, "This is the first time in the history of Texas Student Publications that all of its various interests have been brought together in suitable quarters."[29]

A disturbing allegation surfaced that year about the integrity of the *Daily Texan* staff. In a letter to R. L. Batts, John A. Lomax, the secretary of the Ex-Students' Association, wrote to attack the conduct of UT's athletic director, Theo Bellmont. Lomax wrote:

> He [Bellmont] has acquired an unwarranted opinion of his importance in University life. Through the use of money of which he has had control to hand out to athletes, to pay direct to editors of *The Texan*, and through other means, he has become a dominating influence in student life, and has used this influence not only to discredit his own immediate associates in the athletic department, but also members of the faculty from the President on down.[30]

If it were true that *Texan* editors were accepting bribes in return for favorable coverage, it would be a disgraceful episode in the paper's history. Bellmont apparently was also paying the athletes impermissibly (allegedly with money received

from Lutcher Stark, chair of the UT Board of Regents).

On February 4, 1928, the TSP Board met to consider a request from the *Texan* editor for a salary increase for the editor, managing editor, and chief editorial writer. The editor wrote that the current salary "is not a living wage for a student; that to do the work of editing *The Texan* or writing its editorials properly requires most of a student's time not devoted to his courses in the University; that few, if any, of the students usually seeking either of the three offices are independent, but must depend largely on what they earn to pay expenses."[31] Some things never change.

VAUGHAN V. TSP

Another perennial issue involved internal conflicts between different members of *The Texan* staff. Usually, such quarrels are hushed up and settled internally—but not this one.

On February 29, 1928, editor Trueman O'Quinn wrote to the TSP Board to complain about his managing editor. He wrote:

> There is a need for someone who will perform the duties which ordinarily fall to the managing editor. I have been unable to prevail upon the present managing editor [Richard Vaughan] to supervise the night work more closely, and I am informed by the issue editors and other members of the staff that they can never depend upon the managing editor for advice and assistance because he does not frequent J. Hall enough to lend such aids as editing the paper, nor can he be located always over the telephone when an emergency arises.[32]

The TSP Board formed a "Special Committee to investigate the charges of neglect of duty brought by Mr. Trueman O'Quinn, Editor-in-Chief of *The Daily Texan*, against Mr. Richard Vaughan, Managing Editor." The committee concluded that "Mr. Vaughan has failed to organize the night staff properly," "has failed for various reasons to keep the respect of some of his staff members and has maintained at times only a rather loose discipline among the staff," and "has not given at the most more than an average of two hours a night (and hardly any time during the day) to the performance of his duties. This time has been insufficient."

The committee also concluded that Vaughan had "exhibited a lack of interest in his work on the occasion of the special edition of *The Texan* dealing with the opening of the Littlefield Dormitory. . . . Mr. Vaughan has exercised only a rather careless supervision of the issue editors. . . . In conclusion, we find Mr. Vaughan guilty of the general charge of neglect of duty. Extenuating circumstances, however, lead us to recommend only severe reprimand as the most logical penalty for this negligence."

Vaughan was reprimanded and suspended without salary for three weeks.[33]

Unfortunately, that did not resolve the problem. The TSP Board subsequently stopped paying the managing editor and assigned his responsibilities to the editor. Rather than bring in student assistance, the TSP manager of publications, William L. McGill—an administrator and not a student—took responsibility for producing the paper. When four issue editors resigned in protest over the TSP Board's treatment of Vaughan, the TSP manager not only supervised but actually produced the paper for two nights.[34]

Richard Vaughan, the ousted managing editor, went to the Men's Council, which ruled on April 3 that the TSP Board could not transfer away all of the duties of an elected official. (The managing editor at the time was elected and not appointed.) Vaughan stomped down to *The Texan* with the ruling. McGill recognized Vaughan as *The Texan's* managing editor, "but informed him that under instructions from the Board, the managing editor of *The Texan* did not have any duties."[35]

On the same night of April 3, the UT Students' Association also passed a "Resolution Concerning *The Daily Texan*":

> Whereas the Editor-in-chief of *The Daily Texan*, Trueman O'Quinn, has been grossly negligent in the performance of his duties, and
>
> Whereas he has proven himself incompetent to hold office as Editor-in-chief of *The Daily Texan*, and
>
> Whereas he has permitted personal animosities to interfere in the execution of his official duties, and
>
> Whereas without justification or authority he has taken it upon himself to usurp powers that do not belong to him, and
>
> Whereas he has used his position for the purpose of individual political interests rather than the interests of the student body, therefore

We move that Mr. O'Quinn be impeached.

McGill refused to publish the SA resolution because it might be libelous. He wrote to the TSP Board, "I therefore sought legal aid on this particular matter, and was advised by Mr. J. H. Hart of Hart, Patterson & Hart, attorneys and counselors of law of Austin, Texas, that it would be dangerous for *The Daily Texan* to publish the statements referred to above." Of course, the only libeled party would have been Trueman O'Quinn, but perhaps there was a genuine fear that the editor would sue his own paper for libel. There is also the chance, however, that McGill (then acting as *de facto* managing editor) was trying to protect O'Quinn.

Vaughan came back to McGill and said that it was a "legitimate news item" that the Students' Association had impeached the editor of *The Daily Texan*. Vaughan requested that McGill publish that information.

McGill refused. He argued that: 1. The material tended to expose O'Quinn to public hatred, contempt, and ridicule and thus could be libelous; 2. *The Texan* had a policy of not publishing names of those convicted by the Honor Council; 3. In addition to not publishing libel, *The Texan* was required by TSP to "protect the rights of our readers and the persons mentioned in the news; and to play fair and be just in handling all news"; 4. The TSP Board had ordered that the findings of the investigation of the managing editor not be published.

Thus occurred the unusual situation where the Students' Association had impeached *The Texan* editor—but the paper did not tell anyone.

The whole mess went to the TSP Board, and the board reached a compromise. The SA resolution attacking O'Quinn would not be printed, but *The Texan* could report on the actions of the Men's Council, Students' Association, and TSP Board.[36]

This compromise still did not settle the fight. Vaughan sued Texas Student Publications for his back pay for the period when he had been suspended. The TSP Board met again on April 13, 1928, and "the Manager of Publications was authorized to retain the firm of Woodward & Gay to represent Texas Student Publications, Inc., in a suit filed against that body by Richard Vaughan."[37]

When the case *Richard Vaughan v. Texas Students Publications* went to trial, TSP lost. TSP's attorney wrote to the board, "I discussed the jury's

The 1925 "Girls' Edition" of The Texan. *Pledges for Theta Sigma Pi, a female journalism fraternity, traditionally took over "all editorial positions, including the all-male sports office," for one night each year.*

verdict in the above case with one of the jurors, and he told me that while the jury was satisfied that the plaintiff had been derelict in the discharge of his duties, he was nevertheless entitled to his compensation because the Board of Publications had made a contract with him and had not had him impeached by the proper tribunal."[38]

The case had come to trial in the Justice of the Peace Court. TSP appealed to the County Court, but the two sides settled out of court before the appellate hearing. TSP paid $50 to Richard Vaughan, $14.90 in court costs, and $10 for its attorney. The original verdict was $99.99 for Vaughan, plus court costs.[39]

After this, matters settled down for a few months, but then the administration removed *The Daily Texan's* editor from office for a few weeks. Arno Nowotny, assistant dean of men, placed several key *Texan* staffers, including editor Jimmie Payne, on disciplinary probation. The paper reported that the editor's office was vacant because of "scholastic difficulties."[40] Nowotny then informed TSP that two students "will be barred from serving in their present editorial activities until the end of the long session."[41] The TSP min-

utes later record that "The Manager announced the receipt of a letter from the Dean of Student Life's office reinstating Mr. Jimmie S. Payne as editor-in-chief of *The Daily Texan* as of Feb. 5th."[42] That such an action by the administration was possible shows how much power the University had to control the leadership of the paper.

In May 1929, as a result of the litigation with Richard Vaughan, TSP developed a new contract for the publication editors. It spelled out that editors would be paid only upon the performance of their duties. The contract also stated, "It is understood and agreed by the parties to this contract that no editor shall be deprived of his salary by reason of statement of any editorial opinion, unless such statement is in conflict with the established rules and regulations of the University, in regard to decency and propriety, or except when said editor is impeached by the duly-constituted agencies of the Students' Association."[43] Of course, "decency and propriety" were vague words that could mean almost whatever the University wished, but the TSP Board seems to have tried to give the editors at least some protection against being punished for their political views.

ON STRONGER GROUND

The issues of race and gender did not appear in *The Texan* often during the 1920s. Occasionally, however, a brief statement would reveal the general attitudes of the time. In 1921, for instance, *The Texan* covered a crime story in which a black man had wounded a white man. The headline was "MAN WOUNDED BY NEGRO MONDAY IS IMPROVING LITTLE." The story stated, "The negro was taken to an adjoining town for safe keeping."[44] That such action would be necessary to protect the man from a lynch mob is powerful testimony to the state of race relations in the 1920s.

The relation between *The Texan* and the Students' Association was generally good during this decade. Although the SA had tried and failed to impeach a *Daily Texan* editor, *The Texan* usually was not critical of the SA, as it had been in previous decades. And the incorporation of TSP set up a structure that in the future would help to isolate *The Texan* from the power of student government.

The relationship between the administration and the paper was also better than it had been in the previous decade and would be in the 1930s. Although editor Sam Johnson did resign over the faculty's attempts at control, the faculty's efforts at censorship were relatively mild compared with what the regents would do in the late 1930s.

The biggest milestone for the paper during the 1920s was probably the incorporation of TSP. Although this created some problems by allowing the University to claim to act as *The Texan*'s publisher, incorporation undeniably helped the paper financially and gave it the professional support staff (such as business managers) that it needed to grow.

In sum, the 1920s was a good decade for *The Daily Texan*. Although censorship existed and the internecine conflict in 1928 was damaging, the paper in 1930 rested on a stronger foundation than it had in 1920.

CHAPTER 4

THE ROOSEVELT ERA: 1930–1940

The 1930s would prove to be difficult for the paper. Censorship increased significantly, and *The Texan* saw its first highly publicized battle with the UT administration. Yet amid the turmoil, the paper weathered the Great Depression, commented on the New Deal, and began to devote more attention to the growing threat from Nazi Germany. And it continued to produce large numbers of future journalists—including a certain Walter Cronkite.

Student registration in 1930 had reached 4,118.[1] The editorials often reflected the tone of the first part of the century, dealing with non-controversial campus topics and public service announcements. One editorial, for example, included this comment: "One cannot help noticing the Main Building bulletin boards, supposedly there for University announcements, but covered with every conceivable sort and form of advertising which has no relation whatever to University affairs."[2] A news story reported that, "One student has been dropped from the rolls of the University by action of the Faculty Discipline Committee for appearing at the University dance drunk."[3]

"THE BUDGET MORE NEARLY RESEMBLES A PRAYER"

The Great Depression took its financial toll on the paper. The budget for 1928 was $37,150.[4] In 1943, the budget reached a low of $29,259.[5] In 1930, TSP manager William McGill (on *The Texan*'s thirtieth birthday) told the TSP Board about "the serious effect on the Publications of the business depression during the past year."

The publications had a net operating loss of $189.89 for fiscal year 1930. *The Texan* was taking a slight loss, but the main problem was with *The Cactus*, the UT yearbook.[6] The TSP Board reported, "The total revenue from the three publications dropped 5 percent during the past year."[7]

Traditionally, TSP had a policy of planning to spend only 85 percent of anticipated revenue, allowing a 15 percent margin for "unforeseen emergencies." In 1930 McGill said, "Your manager advises you, however, that it is impossible to set up the budgets this year with that 15 percent margin. If he should arbitrarily fix the expenditure budgets at 85 percent of the revenue expected, those budgets would not be comprehensive, complete, nor accurate. He would know and the Board would know that the budgets were meaningless and that expenditures would exceed the figures set down."[8] McGill suggested that TSP budget only a 2 percent cushion between revenue and expenditures.

A big decision was whether to continue printing *The Summer Texan*, a smaller summer edition of the paper. The 1930 *Summer Texan* sustained a net loss of $948.47, and printing the paper five times a week for the summer of 1931 would create an estimated loss of $2,652.[9] The manager of the University Press, which was printing the paper, complained of his net loss and warned, "I don't know who is responsible for the deplorable situation existing the past three years between the Summer Session authorities, the Student Publications and the University Press, but I do know that if the *Summer Texan* is printed by the University

The Texan *newsroom, 1930.*

Press next summer, it will not be at a loss."[10] The press manager later agreed to keep the lower rates, but *The Summer Texan* was still cut back to two issues a week.[11] McGill wrote to TSP in July 1931 that "The budget of last year was hardly a budget at all—it more nearly resembled a prayer."[12]

The Texan continued to summarize world and national news, but the TSP Board wanted *The Texan* to deal primarily with college affairs. It passed a policy saying, "In authorizing a contract whereby the Texas Student Publications, Inc. will be furnished daily with copy of news reports coming to the *American-Statesman* over the United Press wires, the Board of Directors does not contemplate a radically different news policy for *The Daily Texan*. The Board expects *The Daily Texan* to continue as a strictly college newspaper, serving the students primarily with University news."[13]

This policy did have certain benefits. It kept *The Texan* focused on the UT market, providing news that students were unable to obtain elsewhere. To a large extent, *The Daily Texan* survives by serving a niche market, and this resolution kept the paper focused on its target audience.

The perennial problem, however, has been in striking a balance that does not exclude significant national and world news. A focus on campus news risks producing a parochial paper that avoids state, national, and international issues. And as fascism appeared in Italy, Germany and Japan during the 1930s, the paper's staff would often have to revisit the tradeoff between printing UT news and reporting on world events.

In January 1932, however, *The Texan* was justified in printing local news about an international figure. The UT scientist H. J. Muller, who would win a Nobel Prize for his experiments with radiation and genetics, disappeared. *The Texan* printed an extra edition, which said that Muller was lost because of a "highly nervous condition brought on by overwork in his laboratory."[14] The next day, *The Texan* printed yet another extra. "DR. MULLER FOUND," the headline blared. The good scientist was in a "dazed, delirious condition." He was found "sitting on rocks looking blankly into space."[15]

A few months later, the focus shifted away from Dr. Muller to a more embarrassing subject— bribery. One student was suspended after trying to bribe a TSP Board member. The editor of *The Cactus* was suspended from the University for two years for taking bribes. An Austin businessman was also convicted by the Faculty Committee and denied readmission to the University.[16] The TSP Board adopted a detailed procedure for dealing with contracts in hopes of reducing bribery. UT President Harry Y. Benedict wrote to a friend about the matter:

> Two curious things are to be mentioned: (a) the bribery has been without effect in landing the contracts—they are paid on the erroneous theory that they are effective agents; (b) the downfall of student government seems to be almost complete. Starting without formality on the honor system and gradually including student publications, etc., the honor system has been abandoned and student publications on the financial side especially have to be run by faculty. O tempora, o mores![17]

Growing Tension with the Regents

In 1932 *The Texan* clashed with the UT Board of Regents. An editorial pointed out that the laborers on campus had no wage clauses in their contracts and were being paid less than the minimum wage suggested by the Texas labor commissioner. The editorial reported that so far the regents maintained a hands-off attitude, "but in view of the direct challenge thrown down by Mr. Gragg [Texas labor commissioner], they owe it to themselves and to the University to define their position."[18] A campus petition asked the regents to help the laborers. "We find industrial slavery and misery," the petition stated.[19]

The regents responded by attacking the paper. Judge R. L. Batts, chair of the Board of Regents, stated that the student petition "was in pursuance of a policy of *The Texan* to occasionally attack the Regents." A *Texan* editorial responded that calling on the regents to define their position was not an attack. "*The Texan* feels that the state labor laws, if ruled constitutional, should be enforced. . . . A statement of this belief was not an attack on the Regents."[20] Perhaps not, but it seems that the regents thought otherwise, and four years later they would decide to do something about *The Texan*. But for now, at least, the paper was safe.

Meanwhile, the New Deal was arriving. On November 9, 1932, *The Texan* announced: "Roosevelt and Garner win by a large majority."[21] Austin banks took out a full page ad to announce that there was no need for fear after the "banking holiday."[22]

On the whole, *The Texan* was a pro-Roosevelt paper. One editorial in 1934 stated, "Recovery can never be attained by the continuation of the plutocratic system that led to the crash of 1929."[23] Of the National Recovery Act, a *Texan* editorial said, "NRA is here to stay, notwithstanding the fact that there are frequent controversies as to the constitutionalities of its many phases. A constitution is merely a guide, an omnipresent road mark which is useful so long as it takes us in the right direction, but when it fails us, it must be changed or interpreted in such a manner that it will continue to serve its purpose."[24]

In 1932 the TSP Board had to deal with a problem involving the residents of Brackenridge Hall who wished to publish a newsletter. Unfortunately, the constitution of the Students' Assembly stated, "It shall be unlawful for any student to publish any publication for distribution to students unless such publication be under the supervision of the Board of Publications of the Students' Publications, Incorporated." The TSP Board, however, did not wish to supervise the additional publication, so it ordered *The Texan* to give Brackenridge Hall even more coverage.[25]

The 1933 election for editor was one of the closest and most contested in the paper's history. D. B. Hardeman edged out Joe Hornaday by six votes. Hornaday asked for a recount, but V. I. Moore, dean of student life, refused.[26] Hornaday appealed to the regents for a recount. A *Texan* editorial agreed, saying, "When a small group take it upon themselves to run the government as they see fit, against the will of a majority of the students, it is time for someone to step in."[27] The regents did step in and granted Hornaday a recount.[28] Hornaday won, as an error of 46 votes was found in the recount.[29]

During Hornaday's tenure as editor, *The Texan* published an editorial commenting on a Nazi policy to allow mental patients to be put to death if three doctors recommended it and the patient requested it. The editorial said, "It is an idea that we might use in our attempt to solve a similar problem that faces us in the United States, namely, the problem of the mentally defective person."[30] The editorial writer probably did not know that the "euthanasia" often was not voluntary at all, but that editorial does not represent one of the paper's finer moments.

At the start of the spring semester of 1934, *The Texan* suddenly found itself in a censorship fight with the University. UT President Harry Y. Benedict was going to hold a special conference on the status of the student editors.[31] Much of the administration's concern seems prompted less by *The Texan* than by *The Cactus* and a humor magazine called *The Ranger,* but the issue also affected the paper.

A *Texan* editorial entitled "Censorship" responded to the Benedict conference: "The way to meet the problem of supervision of student publications is, in short, to repeal faculty supervision as such. . . . It is the editor's job to decide for himself what he may publish with [legal] impunity and what he may not. . . . The issues comes finally to this: Should student publications be edited by students, or should they be edited by members of the faculty?"[32] "Censorship even in its most minute form is undesirable."[33]

Benedict was not swayed by the editorial. A new committee was created, with members to be appointed by the president, "to assist in safeguarding the finances and character of student publications."[34] The committee on "editorial propriety" was to exclude material not only deemed libelous but anything considered "false, improper, or detrimental to good conduct and reputation. . . . Failure to exclude material regarded by this subcommittee as objectionable shall be reported by the subcommittee to the Dean of Student Life for appropriate action by a Discipline Committee."[35]

TSP manager William McGill wanted to comment "on the general subject of the proposed 'Censorship.' . . . I believe that the danger to student editorial independence is not as great as some of the discussion on this subject would indicate. The word 'censorship' is a harsh word and I do not believe gives the proper description of the relation which could be expected to exist between the proposed Committee on Editorial Propriety and the editors."[36]

There may have been some merit to this claim. In his departing message to the TSP Board, editor D. B. Hardeman (who had finally won election) wrote:

I want to extend my thanks and express my appreciation to the Board for the freedom which they have allowed me this year. This freedom from censorship in any form which prevails on *The Daily Texan* is an encouragement and a very admirable situation. I cannot conceive of a worse situation than a college paper which exists under strict censorship. While a paper may make mistakes and to some people may be a constant threat to their security, a free paper inspires the confidence of its readers and gains a reputation for honesty and courage which is worth a great deal. I want to say again how much I have appreciated the tolerance and the freedom from censorship which have prevailed this year.[37]

Hardeman may have been comfortable with the board's restrictions, but *The Texan* was about to get two editors who would push the limits. Traditionally, *The Texan* did not comment extensively on state, national, and world affairs, and when it did, the editorials were usually temperate. Editor Joe Storm departed from that tradition. His editorials were fiery, and he did not shy away from strong positions.

Consider, for example, his argument on whether the United States should participate in the 1936 Olympics in Berlin: "If the Nazi government chooses to refuse Jewish participation on their own Nazi team, that is their right; and bluntly, none of our business."[38]

Storm also waged a vitriolic campaign against the creation of a Reserve Officer Training Corps at the University. He wrote, "The hungry eyes of fascism bulged toward the University Saturday as Texas reserve officers met in Austin and resolved not to abandon efforts to establish a ROTC unit on campus." He labeled the ROTC "another Hitleristic shocktroop to throttle freedom of thinking, discussion, and organization."[39]

Editorializing in this tone provoked a reaction. On November 5 the TSP manager reported "that a member of the Board of Regents had transmitted to him certain protests received from members of the Texas Legislature against the policy of *The Texan* in discussing partisan political issues."[40]

On November 7 the TSP Board met to deal with the issue. After a thorough discussion, the following resolution passed unanimously:

The Board of Directors of the Texas Student Publications believes that *The Daily Texan* should be edited with zeal for building respect and friendship for the University and with a factual, analytical, and unbiased attitude toward current problems.

The Daily Texan

EXTRA! **EXTRA!**

The First College Daily in the South

Vol. XXXIV

AUSTIN, TEXAS, SUNDAY, FEBRUARY 26, 1933

No. 127

T. W. GREGORY IS DEAD

Gregory Father of Union Plan

UNIVERSITY'S PATRON TO BE BURIED HERE

Campaign Among Students and Exes Conducted by Him

Dreams Realized When He Breaks Ground For Men's Gym

Thomas Watt Gregory and Building Named for Him

Campus Groups Unanimous In Asking Fund Trustees To Place Medallion in Building

Gregory's Interest Dates from Day He Took Degree

Diligence and Devotion Are Best Characteristics Of His Work

By E. L. BATTS
Former Chairman, Board of Regents

'Influence Will Live'—Battle

'Best Friend Lost'—Shivers

'Inspiration,' Says McGill

Faculty Members Look Forward To Talk by Spencer

Huge Gap Left in Ranks Of Exes, President Benedict Says

Gregory and Batts Form Law Firm

One of University's Great Men

The Board feels that the news and editorials on these problems can be presented without antagonizing state officials and without stirring up controversies which give misleading impressions to the people of the state. The Board hereby expresses its confidence in the ability of the present Editor to conduct *The Daily Texan* in this manner.

Further, the Board reaffirms its approval of the editorial policies that have been formulated for *The Daily Texan* and directs the Editor to endeavor to abide by those policies.

In making this request, the Board is fully aware of the cooperation that is needed from the Editor and his staff if the spirit as well as the letter of the rules is to be observed.[41]

Storm's immediate reaction is not recorded. But in his departing message to the TSP Board, he spoke in detail about his thoughts on the censorship:

As for the policy of the Board itself, I think it is entirely too conservative. You expected that. But I do not say that to ask more freedom for editors; only for more responsibility.

The Board has prided itself with being liberal with editors. I think it has kidded itself quite a bit in this respect. As you remember, when a particularly important issue came up last year, there was a little alarm about my having been too outspoken editorially. I mention it only to throw light on a certain situation.

When I retaliated editorially against a news story in the *Star-Telegram* concerning "schoolboys" falling for the "hot oil crowd," the editorial was so effective that some legislators concerned in the issue went to Regent Parten asking him to have me hushed. The Board learning this, immediately proceeded to hush me. I don't think you realized what you were doing, and you wanted to go further; but a hot-headed editor would have pressed his point and given you plenty of trouble. Major Parten would have been mixed up in the trouble to his neck, and the University would have received more of that harmful publicity we hear so much talk about than you could imagine. As a matter of fact in that case, the editor was within his specified rights. The Board acted on the assumption that the handbook gives it power to set the policies of *The Texan*. The policies have been set, and they do not need changing. But I think it should be a fundamental policy of the Board to stand by editorial courage, and not to assume that it must protect the University (in that case it was an oil interest or two) from an editor

who is acting within the spirit as well as the letter of his contract. If you disagree with me on my analysis of the aforementioned specific issue, that is not important. The general idea still holds good that the board should refrain from quieting the editor on any topic of discussion within the realms of common decency and beyond the application of the libel laws. It will work out to the best interests in the long run, even if it might embarrass someone for a short time. An editor properly impressed with his responsibilities will rarely abuse them, and he is best fitted to judge as to the abuse, being amenable to criticism and the natural reproaches, as any other human being.

The Board need not apologize for the editor in any case. That is his business. The Board does not choose him, and it should not control him—only set the basic policies by which he is to operate and then stick by them. If an editor ever gets the impression that the Board does not trust him, be assured that he will do everything in his power to justify that mistrust. The opposite is true. If the editor feels that the Board is trying to censure him either openly, mentally, or through his staff, be equally assured that you are in for more trouble than if you left him alone, regardless of his whims. He has certain rights which he feels should not be trampled upon. If they should be, he will plan a retaliation, and do not assume that you have the power or ingenuity to stop him. His powers are boundless, if he is in the right. He can break you, the Publications, or the President of the University if he has a mind to. It is not for you to turn his mind in that direction.

Probably we all have our own little circle of friends, advisors, admirers, and criticizers. But it has been on the outside of my circle that I learned of more criticism of *The Texan* because it was thought to be edited by the Board of Directors than because it was thought to be insufficiently directed by it or any of its members.

The Board may not gain as much applause from its circle by a complete hands-off policy in regard to editors, but it can gain in respect whatever it loses in applause. If the editor is made responsible for his acts (he is elected by the students and may be withdrawn by them), the Board has only to refer any dissatisfaction to him, openly and frankly. He will probably appreciate it.[42]

The TSP Board did not appear persuaded.

Before leaving, Storm saw *The Texan* obtain its first printing press. On April 26 *The Texan*'s front page boasted, "DUPLEX TUBULAR PRESS FOR *THE DAILY TEXAN* ASSURED BY JUNE 15."[43] An editorial stated, "That the University should maintain on the campus its own printing establishment is unusual. That it should be the only school in the South with such high-speed machinery, and be able to operate one of the most highly developed presses in the country for the printing of college publications is quite out of the ordinary."[44]

The Texan's current press is much better than the one acquired in 1935, but Storm's words still remain true. *The Daily Texan* is still one of the few college newspapers in the nation to own its own printing press.

Storm's departing editorial was as strong as ever; however, this time his words were not criticism but praise. He lauded his staff, saying, "They neglected courses, endangered health, forsook many pleasures to serve well—to share their burden of a responsibility for little more than that they thought it was right."[45]

Storm also had a few departing words to the TSP Board about the editor's low pay. He talked about how much the editor was overworked in relation to his salary. "The editor spends most of his 'idle' time on organization work, letter writing, and in catching up on his work generally. . . . The ordinary editor puts in an average of eight hours on *The Texan* a day. Sometimes he is up until 3 and 4 o'clock in the morning. His time is irregular, and his work is often very tiresome. The actual labor is worth more than the salary; and the worry, strain and responsibility is worth much more than the labor. For the time put in, you pay the delivery boys more than the editor."

Once again, some things never change.

No "Political Questions"

Ed Hodge, *The Texan*'s next editor, would deal with the consequences of Joe Storm. On July 28, 1936, the UT Board of Regents issued a new rule for the paper. The order stated:

> The Editorial Advisory Committee is directed also to employ an agent to examine prior to publication all proposed non-advertising contents of each issue of *The Daily Texan*. The Committee or the Committee's agent shall have the power to exclude libelous material, improper personal attacks, reckless accusations, opinions not based on fact, inaccurate statements, articles on national, state and local political questions, indecencies, material detrimental to good conduct on the stu-

dent body, and material prejudicial to the best interests of the University; and any material in conflict with good taste or wise editorial management; and shall enforce such other policies as are formulated by the Board of Directors of the Texas Student Publications, Incorporated.[46]

UT President Harry Y. Benedict, who had proposed such a rule to the UT regents, called Hodge into his office and broke the news. "You must have known this was coming," Benedict said.

Hodge may have suspected it was coming, but he would not accept such censorship without a fight. In his departing message to the TSP Board, Joe Storm had prophesied that "a hot-headed editor would have pressed his point and given you plenty of trouble. . . . The University would have received more of that harmful publicity we hear so much talk about than you could imagine."[47]

Whether Ed Hodge was "hot-headed" is not clear. What is clear is that he would give the University plenty of trouble.

Hodge immediately went public about the censorship. In fact, he wrote about the issue for months. Every day, a prominent box in the masthead continued two statements and asked, "Which Is the American Way?"

The first statement was from the University of Wisconsin regents: "Whatever may be the limitations which trammel inquiry elsewhere, we believe that the great State University of Wisconsin should encourage the continual and fearless shifting and winnowing by which alone the truth can be found."

The second statement was the UT regents' rule forbidding *The Texan* from discussing any matter of national, state, or local politics.

Later, Hodge created another box to run daily on the editorial page:

> The editor-in-chief of *The Daily Texan* is elected under the rules of the Students' Association to assume responsibility for all editorial opinions expressed in the paper, and is subject to the rules and regulations of the Handbook of Texas Student Publications, Inc., a private corporation chartered under the laws of the State of Texas and controlled jointly by the faculty and the student body of The University of Texas.

On July 27, 1936, a censor was placed on *The Texan* to examine prior to publication "all proposed non-advertising contents of each issue," and the censor's powers are set out in Section 38 of the Sixth Edition of the Rules and Regulations of the Board of Regents. Since that action, the opinions expressed in the editorial columns of *The Texan* are not necessarily the unmodified opinions of the students nor of the editor-in-chief.

Any reader disagreeing with *The Texan's* policies, as censored, is invited to submit articles to the open forum columns.

At least one professor on the TSP Board disliked this box. The TSP minutes record that "Dr. Fitzgerald moved that the boxed statement now running at the head of the editorial column of *The Daily Texan* be removed. This matter was discussed informally by members of the board, but no action was taken."[48]

Usually, student protests soon fade away. Fighting the system is exhausting, and this battle probably consumed Hodge's entire life. Yet Hodge refused to give up. By placing these boxes on the editorial page daily, he never let the issue die.

Hodge also used humor against the regents. For example, he once wrote editorials on national political topics, knowing they would be suppressed. After they were withheld, he then left the space blank except for a statement explaining that the editorials had been censored.

Another time, Hodge printed a satirical editorial entitled "DON'T WALK ON THE GRASS (A MODEL EDITORIAL)."[49] The point was to dramatize the trivial subjects the regents' rule would force *The Texan* to comment upon. (Decades later, editor Willie Morris would write a similar editorial about grass to protest censorship.) Hodge also editorialized on the ideal campus flower.[50]

Hodge's use of humor was a sophisticated form of political jujitsu. The regents were given exactly what they asked for—a *Texan* that stuck to campus events. In fulfilling their demands, however, Hodge made the regents appear ridiculous.

Hodge found allies in his fight against censorship. Newspapers around the state, such as the *Houston Post*, attacked the censorship at the University.[51] Hodge then reprinted all the supporting editorials in *The Texan*. The "harmful publicity" that Joe Storm had prophesied was now reality.

On September 28, 1936, the full TSP Board met for the first time since the controversy had exploded. At the time, the TSP Board had nine voting members: the editors of the three student publications, three professors appointed by the

UT president, two students from the Students' Association, and the president of the Students' Association.[52] *Texan* editor Ed Hodge moved that this meeting be open to members of the press. Some professors fought to keep the meeting secret, but the students outvoted them, and the press was admitted.[53]

The TSP Board was presented with the following resolution:

> Be it resolved that this body, the Board of Directors of the Texas Student Publications, Inc., go on record as opposing any control by way or direction of policy, censorship, or any other method which has been or shall be exerted by any person, group of persons, or organization to which such power (that of censorship, direction of policy, etc.) has not been specifically designated by our Charter.
>
> Our reasons for adopting this resolution are as follows:
>
> 1. that without reference to what should be the policy of any of the publications, we believe that the Board of Directors is fully qualified to determine such policy,
>
> 2. that we recognize the fact that the Texas Student Publications, Inc., was founded by the authority of the student body by popular vote,
>
> 3. that we recognize that said Board of Directors as the authorized agent of the student body, and of the student body alone,
>
> 4. that we, the members of the said Board of Directors, cannot, in the light of honesty and fairness, recognize any control exercised by any person or group of persons other than those authorized by the student body of The University of Texas in the Charter of the Texas Student Publications, Inc.,
>
> Therefore, be it further resolved that we, the members of the Board of Directors of the Texas Student Publications, Inc., respectfully petition the Board of Regents of The University of Texas to remove their agent or agents and that said agent or agents cease to exercise censorial powers over the said publications.

By this time, one of the professors had left. Another professor offered a tamer substitute, but that was voted down. The original resolution passed 5-to-1.[54] All the student board members were united.

The board was then faced with the decision about paying the censor. The board went through much discussion and several resolutions, the discussion of one of which was ordered stricken from the record. Finally, by the same 5-to-1 margin, the board passed a resolution that refused to pay the censor.[55]

At the next board meeting, the professors tried to regain control. One professor challenged the legality of the appointments of two of the student board members. He moved and another professor seconded the motion that the board not recognize the two student members. Two students then moved that the board adjourn to submit the dispute to the proper tribunal. The motion passed, and the TSP Board adjourned.[56]

At the October 16 meeting, the faculty on the TSP Board once again tried to pay the censor. Professor Paul J. Thompson pointed out that the TSP Board had authorized the payment of the censor on August 28. The professors moved to pay the censor $50 a month. The students tabled the motion. As one of the students stated, "I vote for the motion to table the proposal to compensate the editorial agent because I feel that to favor the proposal would be to ratify the principle of censorship of *The Texan*."[57]

While the professors on the TSP Board were struggling to pay the censor, Hodge was busy on other fronts. The Students' Association had decided to submit the question of *Texan* censorship to a student referendum.[58] The students voted against censorship by margin of 3-to-1.[59]

The Students' Association was about to go into its fall elections, and Hodge turned the censorship issue into a litmus test for the candidates. *The Texan* produced a questionnaire to determine the position of all SA candidates on the censorship.[60] Not surprisingly, the candidates—all seeking the paper's endorsement—opposed censorship.

Although he was successful in winning allies in the Students' Association, Hodge did not fare so well among the faculty. The General Faculty met on October 13; following are excerpts from UT President Harry Benedict's remarks, perhaps the strongest case yet made for the administration's control of *The Texan*:

> Since the action of the Board of Regents was taken upon my recommendation, since *The Texan* has not printed my statement regarding this action made to the Students' Assembly and the Board of Directors of the Student Publications in meeting assembled, and since the Handbook of Student Publications is not so easily accessible to you as to make you familiar with its contents, it seems to be desirable to outline to you the cir-

> cumstances and reasons upon which the action was based. . . .

> It is the desire of the Regents to leave the Student Publications as free as possible, at least as free as they are in the average state university, and the Regents would much prefer a fine sense of editorial propriety to any set of regulations whatsoever. *The Texan* at present affords evidence of the strictness of the alleged censorship.

> *The Texan* is not an ordinary newspaper entitled to liberty of the press; neither the Regents nor the Faculty nor the Students being newspaper corporations. Still less has the staff of *The Texan* a right to publish an ordinary newspaper. It is a very rare thing for the staff of a paper, with no financial investment therein, to control a paper. The class rooms of the University are not political rostrums, its dormitories are not public hotels, its cafeterias are not public restaurants, and its student publications are likewise activities with limited objectives.

> The public very generally holds the Faculty and Regents responsible for what appears in the Student Publications. Everybody knows that they have flourished under University protection, that apart from the University they have no reason for existence, that usefulness rather than harm to the University is their function.

> In my opinion, to allow *The Texan* to become almost a political organ is in the long run impossible. People will not, if they can prevent it, allow themselves and their views to be attacked by a partly state-supported publication. . . .

> Censorship is not involved in the action of the Regents. Censorship means control from the outside. The Regents are a part of the inside control of *The Texan*, and unless the editor owns a publication and is personally responsible for libel suits he has to comply with the policies fixed by the authorities in his organization.

> It is the University that is entitled to freedom from being entangled with the controversial opinions of the student editor, not the editor of a University publication to freedom from responsibility to the University. As an individual he is free; as an editor he is not.[61]

After hearing Benedict's speech, the faculty agreed. *The Texan*'s headline the next day stated: "Faculty Unanimous for Censorship, Though 'Regretful.'"[62]

On November 7 the TSP Board met again. This time, the professors finally passed a resolution to pay the censor. The resolution was adopted "with the understanding that this motion is not to be considered an approval of 'censorship' and does not mean the committee goes on record as approving the payment of said funds for the purpose."[63]

Then former *Texan* editor D. B. Hardeman wrote a letter to the TSP Board president about the current controversy. At a previous board meeting, he had tried to make what he considered to be an important point but had discovered that his remarks had somehow failed to appear in the official minutes. The letter was meant to have his statement formally recorded.

> In the course of my remarks I stated, not once but several times, that during my tenure of office as editor of *The Daily Texan*, Mr. William L. McGill, director of student publications and adviser to President Benedict, not only did not ask or warn me to refrain from editorializing on controversial political questions, but actively encouraged me in such a course by submitting to me for publication editorials on such controversial matters.
>
> In my remarks, I cited three specific controversial political questions on which *The Texan* took a partisan stand. The report contains mention of these instances, but it fails to put in one vital point—that Mr. McGill, of his own volition, submitted such partisan editorials to me for publication. These three instances are the fights against the West Texas land tax amendment, against the overall tax limitation amendment, and the fight for lump sum appropriations. . . .
>
> It has been repeatedly charged that the past few editors of *The Daily Texan* have been violating the established policies of *The Daily Texan* as drawn by the Board of Directors. What I sought to point out in the September 28 Board meeting is the fact that if these policies have been violated in past years, it has been with the assistance and acquiescence of the director, who not only is concerned with publication affairs, but is well known as public relations adviser to President Benedict.[64]

TSP Manager McGill denied that his editorials were what the regents meant to prohibit. But it did appear that in the past it was acceptable for *The Texan* to print partisan editorials—as long as UT administrators wrote them.

Hodge next tried to reach a compromise with the University that could remove the censorship. One such compromise went to the regents in January 1937. The censor would be abolished, but the TSP Board could remove the editor for repeated violations of UT policy and more journalism courses would be required of editor candidates.[65] The regents took no action on the proposal.[66]

A few months later, however, the regents adopted Hodge's compromise.[67] The censor would go, but the editor could be fired for violating the regents' policies. The plan would go into effect and the censor would leave on June 1—the day after Ed Hodge left office.

The new rule about removing the editor stated:

> The non-editorial members of the Board of Directors of the Texas Student Publications, Inc. acting as a separate committee, shall have the power to take disciplinary action against the editors and may remove any editor after due notice for violation of the policies set up by the Board of Directors or for non-performance of duties. In trials for removal the Dean of Student Life shall preside and, in case of a tie, shall cast the deciding vote.[68]

The new rules about content loosened some of the restrictions:

> The news and editorial policies of the *Daily Texan* shall exclude from its columns libelous material; improper personal attacks; reckless accusations; opinions not based on fact; inaccurate statements; indecencies; material detrimental to the good conduct of the student body; unduly violent and partisan material on national, state and local political questions, and material too prejudicial to the best interests of the University; or speaking generally, any material in conflict with good taste or wise editorial management; and the Board of Directors of the Texas Student Publications, Inc., shall adopt such affirmative policies as will make *The Texan* one of the best college dailies in the nation.[69]

Now the paper could editorialize on politics, as long as the editorials were not "unduly violent and partisan." It could present negative information as long as it was not "too prejudicial" to the best interests of the University.

What were the results of this year-long fight between the paper and the administration? In many respects, the outcome was favorable for *The Texan*. Hodge had won. The censor would go, and the paper could discuss political issues. Beyond the immediate victory, Hodge's actions set an important precedent. *The Texan* could fight the University and win. It was a precedent that would

The Longhorn Band entertains UT students and fans, 1930s.

inspire caution in UT administrators and hope in future editors.

Hodge had won a victory but not the war. The TSP Board and the University still retained the right to exclude material they disliked, and the board now had the explicit power to fire an editor who disobeyed the UT administration. In addition, the regents asserted the power to change the TSP charter, prevented the TSP Board from changing its charter without the regents' consent, limited the Students' Association power to change the TSP rules, and required *Texan* editors to have taken certain journalism courses.[70] But given the regents and the limited First Amendment protection applied to the college press at the time, Hodge obtained about what he could.

At the end of Hodge's tenure, UT President Harry Benedict died suddenly of a stroke. To put it mildly, Benedict had been under great stress. Besides the fight with *The Texan*, Benedict was answering questions about communism from a Texas Legislature experiencing one of its all-too-frequent Red Scares. He was also in the midst of fighting for the University's annual appropria-

tion. On April 29, Benedict wrote to a friend, "We are now right in the midst of a closing legislative session—the Educational Appropriation Bill is up in the air, and so am I. Even when it comes down, I may still be up!"[71]

Benedict's words proved prophetic, as he died a few days later. *The Texan* published a special Benedict edition commemorating the popular UT president who had served for ten years. No mention was made of Benedict's attempts to censor *The Texan*. *De mortuis nil nisi bonum.*

SYPHILIS AND DIRTY KITCHENS

After Ed Syers succeeded Hodge as editor, affairs quieted down tremendously. The TSP Board minutes, recorded by a certain Jake Pickle (then student body president and later Austin congressman), reflected the quiet consideration of financial matters reminiscent of the pre-Hodge era.

In September 1937, Ed Syers wrote an editorial titled "*The Texan* Isn't Censored." He wrote, "Both sides now agree that *Texan* policy is subject to reasonable direction from a board of directors to function as the name implies. All agree that nothing approaching heresy, idiocy, or the obscene should be forced down the campus throat."[72]

In October, Syers launched a major campaign to improve the sanitary conditions of local kitchens. "Students' Food Cooked in Unsanitary Kitchens," read the headline. "Eating Places Told to Clean Up or Face Court Charges," read another. *The Texan* ran a huge front-page photo showing the filthy kitchen of one local restaurant.[73] A few days later the paper reported that "better sanitary conditions greet new inspection tour."[74]

In the spring semester, Syers launched a major—indeed, perhaps obsessive—editorial campaign against syphilis. The headlines marched in progression: "America finds Syphilis Real Problem, Proceeds to Take Steps Against It"[75]; "Syphilis Film to be Shown by MICA, Health Board"[76]; "Dr. Cox Sees Syphilis as Outstanding Social Responsibility"[77]; "Film to be Shown for Women Today. Orange Jackets to Sponsor Lecture With Mortar Board"[78]; "94 Percent of Students Willing to Take Wassermann Tests."[79] And on, and on, and on.

Syers tried to explain his obsession with syphilis. In an editorial titled "The Reason for Sensationalism," he wrote, "*The Texan* is fully cognizant of the fact that for almost a month it has bombarded the campus with an uninhibited and extreme discussion of a disease" that usually is not discussed.[80] Why? Syers claimed it was because the student body was adult, that America must attack the disease on every front, that the paper could provide an educational channel, and that the campaign would promote the well-being of students.

Syers' college medical records are not obtainable.

During that semester, however, *The Texan* did publish a poll that revealed "More Sex Education Wanted In UT."[81] Apparently the only course dealing with sex was Bible 317: "The Family as a Moral and Religious Agency in Religious Education."

By and large, *The Texan* and the Students' Association got along fairly well during the 1930s. The SA president sat on the TSP Board and thus was closely involved with the paper. The support of the SA was also helpful in Ed Hodge's fight against the regents.

Significant discussions of race and gender did not often appear in the paper during the 1930s. They would increase in the coming decade, but for now those issues were not at the forefront.

The Texan's relationship with the UT administration during the 1930s was contentious. UT President Harry Benedict had proposed the strict censorship rules to the regents, and some *Texan* editors returned his suspicion.

Overall, the decade of the 1930s was less about growth than about endurance. The paper survived the Great Depression. It survived an assault from the regents. Having weathered these difficulties, *The Daily Texan* was prepared to move into the 1940s.

CHAPTER 5

HOMER RAINEY AND HEMAN SWEATT: 1940–1950

The 1940s would prove to be the University's most turbulent years since the Ferguson conflict in 1917. The campus would struggle through World War II. The Board of Regents would fire UT President Homer Rainey for his defense of academic freedom. The Texas Legislature would investigate communism at the University. Heman Sweatt, a black student, would sue for admission into the University's all-white law school. And through it all, *The Daily Texan* would be at the center.

The paper began the decade by dealing with a less momentous issue—alcohol.[1] An amendment was added to the TSP Handbook that stated, "Liquor shall not be drunk in any of the offices occupied by the Texas Student Publications, Inc. . . . Any person under the influence of liquor shall not be permitted to work on a student publication while in that condition. . . . Funds of Texas Student Publications, Inc., shall not be spent for liquor." Wise policies, indeed, but ones that future staffers would not always follow.

WORLD WAR II

The troubles with booze were soon replaced by the far more substantial difficulties of World War II. Although war raged around the globe, *The Texan* had remained hopeful that the United States might remain unscathed. On November 11, 1941, an editorial stated, "On this sad Armistice Day, we should be thinking of peace, and we should be concentrating upon achieving that peace in the quickest and surest manner."[2]

It was not to be. In the early hours of December 7, 1941, Japan attacked the U.S. fleet at Pearl Harbor. That Sunday's paper, printed the night before the attack, stated, "The news coming in off the wire is still dire with regard to Japan, but bright in lots of other ways. President Roosevelt has appealed directly to the Japanese Emperor, after government spokesmen again called the U.S. names."[3]

The December 8 issue describing the attack on Pearl Harbor is missing from the UT archives. On December 9 a *Texan* editorial advised: "Do not distinguish enemies by colors. . . . There are a number of Americans on our campus who are 100 percent Japanese in heredity. Our natural tendency will be to treat them unfairly, unkindly, and unsympathetically. . . . Let us remember always that in the veins of Americans flows the blood of English, French, Mexicans, Germans, Scotch, Irish, JAPANESE, and many other races. There are white men, brown men, and black men. There are Americans who are YELLOW only in the color of their skin."[4]

The Texan resisted some of the war propaganda. One editorial denounced "one of the crudest forms of war propaganda to which this city—or national audience—has been subject to in recent years." (The propaganda meant to imply that the Japanese were "little yellow bastards.") "Don't insult our intelligence with this sort of stuff," the editorial stated.[5]

The Daily Texan was involved in the war effort immediately. Free copies of the paper were sent to all army camps that had UT alumni.[6] In an editorial entitled "*DAILY TEXAN* IN TIME OF WAR," the

editor announced that the paper would include better summaries of world events, show paths of service for students, and explain how the University was helping the war effort.[7]

Meanwhile, the war continued to occupy the staff. In August 1942 the paper had a special edition "about the war and how it affects the citizen, especially the campus citizen."[8] Earlier, an editorial had blasted a perceived lack of commitment. "Do Students Know There's a War?" the editorial asked after a survey found that 30 percent of students surveyed did not want to donate blood for the war effort.[9] The August 16 special edition carried instructions on how to kill a Japanese soldier barehanded. That information was balanced by some advice from J. Frank Dobie: "It is the duty of every citizen now, as it has never been before, to lay aside prejudices and to think."[10]

The paper published some nationally produced advertisements for war propaganda. One advertisement showed a prominent noose and warned of mass hangings of dissidents if the Nazis won. Another told people that the Nazis would rape their daughters.[11]

In July 1943 a headline stated, "Girls Predominate on *Texan* staff, as Boys Go to War."[12] The large number of draftees had left the paper with shortages, and that gave women even greater opportunities to participate at *The Texan*.

In fact, it was an accomplishment that the paper was able to continue publication at all. Both the *Harvard Crimson* and the *Yale Daily News* closed down during the war years. Still, *The Daily Texan* was hard pressed. In January 1944 the editor complained, "Our staff is so depleted that it is hard to get the most important events covered and doubly hard even to find out about the others."[13] Though reduced in size, *The Texan* continued publishing.

The Texan would contribute not only to the home front but to the battlefield as well. Significant numbers of former *Texan* staffers served in the military, and three editors—Joe Storm, Jack Howard, and Robert Owens—died in action.

On May 8 *The Texan*'s main headline read, "Nazis Surrender Unconditionally; Chimes Will Call Students to V-E Program."[14] *The Texan* was not publishing on the day that the United States dropped the first atomic bomb on Japan. But on August 9 the paper reported, "2nd Atomic Bomb Hits Nagasaki."[15] Apparently some UT professors were involved in the research, for

the paper reported that previously, "Federal secret service agents visited the campus to warn friends of the missing men that nothing should be said nor even 'speculated on' about the work of the men who were busy over the atomic bomb."

On August 14 *The Texan* produced a Victory extra. "Peace!!" the headline blared. "Japanese surrender." The lead of the news story read, "History's most devastating conflict was at an end Tuesday afternoon, and for the first time in almost a decade the world was at peace." A smaller story titled "Campus goes wild at news of peace" discussed the University's reaction: "A whooping, honking, hugging crowd of campusites poured out of afternoon labs and away from supper tables to storm the Drag Tuesday afternoon as news of war's end spread like a prairie fire across the Forty Acres."[16]

A few days later in an editorial titled "Peace," editor Horace Busby linked the war's end to domestic affairs: "If the nation forgoes the opportunity to solve the problems of its own land to indulge in the lethargy of reminiscence, then the evils most dangerous to the nation will not be corrected. The war that was fought to put down the evils of the enemy may then prove to be a war that protected the evils and fostered them for the peace."[17]

Rainey and the Regents

Busby probably was thinking about the UT Board of Regents. Throughout World War II, *The Texan* had been deeply involved in a battle between UT President Homer P. Rainey and the Board of Regents. In summer 1942 the Board of Regents refused to reappoint economics instructor J. Fagg Foster, allegedly because of his political views.[18] A front-page editorial titled "Academic Freedom" was published. "Academic freedom is greatly threatened here on our own 40 Acres," the editorial stated. "If this right is not enjoyed, then our great institution of higher learning is degenerated to valueless finishing school. . . . Academic Freedom must be preserved. To this end *The Daily Texan* will fight—until the day when it is denied Freedom of the Press."[19]

At the top of page 1, the paper ran the famous statement attributed to Voltaire: "I may not agree with a word you say, but I will defend to the death your right to say it." More than 500 people signed a petition asking the regents to explain the firing of Foster.[20]

The Texan managing editor did more than sign a petition, however. On June 11, Walter E. Nixon wrote on *Daily Texan* letterhead to a Texas legislator:

> Feeling that The University of Texas is today faced with a grave and far-reaching problem, *The Texan* is appealing to you as a public official concerned with the interests of the University.
>
> Only a week ago we here on campus learned that the Board of Regents declined to appoint Mr. John Fagg Foster as instructor in economics for no expressed reason. His appointment had been recommended by the departmental faculty, the dean, and the president.
>
> Presumably, the reason is the one which the enclosed *Texan* clipping suggests: that he, along with three colleagues, expressed an opinion contrary to that of the Regents. We hope this is not the correct explanation, but since the Regents have declined to offer a statement of their reasons, we are forced to accept this conclusion. If this be true, then the Board of Regents is throttling free speech and abridging academic freedom, and thus may soon place The University of Texas in the same class with Gene Talmadge's University of Georgia.
>
> Should this happen, our degrees would be worthless.
>
> It is not the opinions of these men with which we are concerned, but only their right to express them.
>
> By registering a letter of protest with the Board of Regents, you can help maintain the continued prestige and well-being of the University. We students are trying, but we need your support.[21]

Three days later, the editor published a prominent notice titled "LETTERS NOT AUTHORIZED." Although one staff member sent out a letter purporting to represent the paper, "*The Texan* has authorized no such letters and is not partial in this case. Any such letter is not to be regarded as reflecting the sentiments of *The Texan*."[22] By July 9, Walter Nixon's name was no longer in the staff box.

In July, the Board of Regents struck again. It dismissed three more professors, allegedly for their political views. An editorial denounced the firing but then stated, "We are still free—and silent."[23]

When fall came, the coverage of the regents'

actions decreased noticeably. No explanation was given, but *The Texan* did make the general observation that "where the press is free, it can function as a protector of the rights of our people and of our free democratic institutions."[24]

In January 1943 the Board of Regents turned from the professors to their reading lists. "ENGLISH READING BOOK BANNED FOR 'LEWDNESS,'" the headline read. "REGENTS, INSTRUCTORS CREDITED WITH ACTION."[25] The book in question was *U.S.A.* by John Dos Passos; sales at local book stores immediately increased.[26] *The Texan* quickly published a book review.[27]

Eugene C. Barker, a professor of American history, admitted taking the initial action in suggesting the book might be a problem.[28] *The Texan* published an anonymous column mocking Professor Barker, joking about how shocked the author was that Barker stared at women's legs during a ballet performance.[29]

Other faculty members were not pleased. Robert A. Law, a professor of English, said that *The Texan*'s coverage of *U.S.A.* was "scurrilous" and constituted "sensational, yellow journalism."[30] *The Texan* played his attack prominently on page 1.

The Texan editor Bob Owens would not have to deal with irate professors for long, as he resigned to enter the Marine Corps. Weldon Brewer took over in summer of 1943. On one of his first days in office, he wrote, "We cannot bang on the keys of the editor's typewriter without sensing an appreciation for free-thinking *Texan* writers of recent years who have made it the outstanding college newspaper in the nation."

The conflict between the regents and UT President Homer P. Rainey continued. The regents demoted Arthur L. Brandon from his job with the University's public relations department. Brandon was described as Rainey's "right-hand man," and no explanation was given for the demotion.[31] *The Texan* featured several editorials calling on the regents to explain, but no answer came. Brandon resigned from the faculty in September, saying "to remain here under the conditions imposed by the Board of Regents would be for me to compromise several principles that are dear to me and for which millions of men are now fighting."[32] An editorial stated, "Too many firings, transferals, and forced resignations have occurred at The University of Texas."[33]

The Texan's support of these professors did not meet with universal approval. A *Houston Post* editorial stated, "*The Daily Texan* has swung back to the left again—back to the pink-hued cloud-lands where the embryonic fellow travelers love to soar and regurgitate their predigested pablum from the Marxian dietary." *The Texan* editor replied, "There is nothing un-American about *Texan* editorials. Our Houston editor seems to have a chronic condition of the reactionary glands."[34]

By this time, the actions of the regents had begun to attract national attention. The American Association of University Professors asked the regents to reconsider the firing of three professors.[35] But while the regents were coming under attack nationally, they found a surprising supporter in Austin. After *Texan* editor Weldon Brewer resigned to join the military, he was replaced by Jack Maguire. The first thing Maguire did was to defend the regents' firing of the three UT professors. "There is no apparent reason why the employees cannot keep their freedom of thought while at the same time keeping within the limits of the policies of their employer," he wrote. "There are cases, however, when a faculty member will go beyond the bounds of good taste. Sometimes faculty members may support ideologies which are directly opposite to those promulgated by the institution they represent. In such cases, shouldn't the Regents be permitted to inquire into the action?"[36]

Nevertheless, the regents felt at least some need to assert that politics was not running the University. Regent John H. Bickett claimed, "The assertion by anyone that there has been any political interference in the affairs of the University or in any way with the present Board of Regents is ridiculous and untrue."[37]

The regents, however, soon lost their apologist at *The Texan*. Maguire left the paper in June 1944. The news story on his departure (written by Horace Busby, a future *Texan* editor) stated, "When Navy-bound Weldon Brewer left *The Texan* last fall, Maguire was appointed editor November 15. Since then, Maguire has been defending the most right-wing editorial policy in *Texan* history against students and alumni alike. . . . In fact, Maguire now modestly rates himself 'the second most hated man on campus.'"[38] Maguire was followed by Helene Wilke, the first woman to edit *The Texan* for an entire year.[39] "The policy of *The Texan*," Wilke stated, "would be fair representation of the thought and activity of those who make up the University."[40]

Wilke would soon find herself under fire. UT President Homer P. Rainey suggested that the Board of Regents move the medical and dental schools (which had experienced administrative problems) from Galveston to UT Austin. *The Texan* under Wilke supported the proposal.[41]

The *Galveston Daily News*, however, did not. It attacked the *Texan* editorial, saying, "*The Texan* represents the academic and quite frequently the College Joe point of view, neither of which can safely be allowed to determine the policies of a professional school."[42] Later, that paper accused *The Texan* of a "smear campaign."[43]

Homer Rainey dropped his proposal to obtain the medical school.[44] But this did not solve his problems with the UT Board of Regents. Rainey's habit of making political speeches out of state annoyed the regents. On October 10 the *Texan* headline warned: "THIS MAY BE RAINEY-REGENT CLIMAX."[45]

This was not yet the climax, but it was coming closer. One reason for the fight between Rainey and the regents, it turned out, was *The Daily Texan*. Paul Bolton, a local journalist and radio commentator, said that a 1940 editorial started the controversy. After one gubernatorial candidate boasted of his war record, *Texan* editor Boyd Sinclair "gave his views about candidates who parade their patriotism." Proponents of that candidate "demanded everything from censorship of *The Texan* down to expulsion of Boyd Sinclair. And Dr. Rainey at that time came to the defense of Editor Sinclair. He defended the young man's right to speak his mind, dismissed the notions that censorship of *The Texan* should be imposed."[46] Apparently this support for *The Texan* caused some legislators to think that Rainey was a communist.

Such support for the paper also may not have sat well with the regents. As Bolton stated, "It's possible, too, that a majority of the Regents, or at least some of them, thought that some sort of halter should be put on *The Texan*."[47] This is confirmed by at least one *Daily Texan* editor, Weldon Brewer, who wrote back from the Navy to say, "The Regents have threatened to censor *The Daily Texan*, student newspaper, upon several occasions, apparently denying freedom of expression, which is a tenet of our American liberties and way of life."[48]

Of course, *The Texan* was not the only reason for Rainey's troubles. Rainey's defense of the fired professors, his attempt to seize the medical school for UT-Austin, and his support for his friend Arthur L. Brandon all contributed to the fight between the UT president and the regents. But it does appear that Rainey's defense of *The Texan* was part of the reason behind the controversy.

Whatever the causes, relations between Rainey and the regents rapidly deteriorated. On October 13, Rainey listed sixteen charges against the regents. *The Texan* printed the text in full. Students gathered to sing "The Eyes of Texas" in support of Rainey.[49]

The Texan leapt to Rainey's defense. "The University of Texas, then, as a university of the state, must maintain the freedom and cooperation of administration essential to progress in research, in teaching, and in service."[50] "This is no time for fence sitting. . . . Seek then the truth. Write home and spread the facts. Much of the power of a voting public is vested in the hands of the students of today and yesterday."[51]

The TSP Board objected to much of this. R. W. Stayton, a faculty member of the TSP Board, opposed *The Texan*'s coverage. He objected to statements quoted from another paper and to a letter in "Firing Line" that criticized the regents.[52] The TSP Board passed a resolution ordering *The Texan* to "avoid aspersions."[53]

Helene Wilke stood firm. In an editorial titled "Can Restraints on College Papers Teach True Reporting or Reading," she wrote, "If *The Daily Texan* is asked to print less than the whole truth, to direct the editorials or the news under the faculty or regential dictates, then there is no reason to print anything at all. This will be the attitude and the policy of the editors and staff."[54]

Nine days later, the Board of Regents met. Because Texas had not yet passed the Open Meetings Law, the board could meet in secret, and no *Texan* reporters were present. (Wilke wrote later how she stood outside the room "waiting for the elevator" to glean any possible information.) On November 1, 1944, the Board of Regents fired UT President Homer Rainey.

The Texan's editorial was remarkably restrained. Under such a situation, the natural impulse is to do or say something dramatic. Wilke, however, though firmly pro-Rainey, seemed to understand the risk of riot under those tense circumstances. *The Texan* ran a small editorial on the front page stating:

Action, not reaction, is needed today from the

student body. Letters home, to friends, to legislators will make student demands heard. Impetuous, hasty disregarding of rules and respect could endanger the cause of the University. The time for waiting is past. STAY OBJECTIVE, STAY ACTIVE, STAND FIRM.[55]

The news of Rainey's firing broke on November 2. The next day, students held a large march on the capital, a "funeral procession for academic freedom."[56] Thousands participated.

An editorial explained *The Texan*'s position in depth:

When the Board of Regents acted behind the closed door of Room 336 in the Rice Hotel at Houston, they tried a man without a public hearing. When they convicted that man of charges they will not list, the Board of Regents sentenced a great University to an infamy that makes meaningless its past and futile its future.[57]

At the time, the exact reasons for Rainey's firing were unclear. In retrospect, the facts came out. Rainey was given a list of liberal professors' names by the regents and told to dismiss them. Rainey protested that he could not do so without some justification. The regents said their order was justification enough. Rainey disagreed, and they fired him.[58]

The Texas Senate educational committee held hearings. Rainey was questioned about allegations of communism at the University and whether he believed in "race equality."[59]

Most students and the faculty seemed pro-Rainey. A student group immediately formed to collect donations for Rainey's defense (which aroused suspicions in the Texas Legislature).[60] A poll in late December found that the faculty overwhelmingly supported Rainey. Only seventeen professors were definitely opposed to him.[61]

Gov. Coke Stevenson was less enthusiastic about Rainey, and *The Texan* proclaimed in a headline: "With the Governor Against Rainey, Senate Must Insure Fair Trial."[62] Naturalist and UT gadfly J. Frank Dobie stated that with the current regents, "no self-respecting, able educator" would be UT president. The regents, however, would have no trouble finding a "bootlicker or a quisling or a Laval. There are plenty of them."[63] UT Vice-President J. Walter Burdine, a professor of government, resigned in protest after the Board of Regents refused to consider petitions about Rainey.[64]

There were a few Rainey detractors, however. About ten people formed an anti-Rainey group and "protested the alleged suppression by *The Daily Texan* of 'news and views which are contrary to its expressed editorial policy.' "[65] They submitted a letter to "Firing Line." Helene Wilke refused to print certain parts because she considered it libelous. The two members, Charles Murphy and Bill Jablonowski, then asked to purchase an advertisement to run the entire statement. The TSP Board upheld Helene Wilke's decision to cut one word and one sentence. One reason given was that Murphy was attempting to "circumvent the responsibility, judgment, and authority of the editor of *The Daily Texan*."[66] The board later decided that the *Texan* editor could edit "Firing Line."[67]

In her thirty-column editorial (written upon leaving the paper), Helene Wilke stated, "Some of my political 'friends' were even inquiring about impeachment methods."[68] Not everyone, it seems, was pleased with the paper, but *The Texan* under Wilke seemed to reflect the opinion of the majority of students.

Wilke said that after the firing of Rainey, she and her managing editor "worked 70 hours a week for much of the month to follow. . . . I guess we've seen more big stories than any other year in *The Texan*'s history—The Rainey controversy, Roosevelt's death, V-E day, the jump from the Tower, and then so many other things."[69]

The Rainey controversy continued as the new *Texan* editor Horace Busby assumed office. Wilke was a strong Rainey supporter, but she was also a moderating influence. Busby was a strong Rainey supporter, but he would show far less restraint than Wilke.

On June 26 the Southern Association of Colleges and Secondary Schools put the University on probation because of the Rainey firing. Busby wrote that "a giant among institutions of higher learning is on probation before the people it was intended to serve."[70] Later he said, "It is the ideal and purpose of a university to afford men seeking the truths a climate in which their thoughts and opinions may be aired, tested, studied, and tempered without fear of the interference of prejudice, intolerance, or ignorance."[71]

In the fall, the regents tried to end its probationary status with the Southern Association of Colleges and Universities, passing rules on tenure and academic freedom.[72] *The Texan* responded, "The Board failed, in some respects, to move with the direction and foresight desired for this period, but, and this should be remembered, it did not materially prejudice its own development in the role of true leadership of the University."[73]

This style of editorializing was typical of Busby. He was firmly against the regents, but his criticisms—often phrased in an appeal for general leadership and expressions of concern for the University's welfare—did not draw an immediate crackdown. He was polite and never attacked people by name. Consider when Busby wrote the following: "The University of Texas sorely needs leadership determined to move forward—not leadership eager to turn back to more tranquil days of other years. The University is maturing now, its ails do not need coddling. They need treatment."[74] The TSP Handbook forbade the editor from making "unfair attacks and injudicious criticisms" of UT administrators, but it was hard to censor a general appeal for leadership.

"THE TEXAN HAS ALWAYS BEEN A PROBLEM . . ."

Eventually, shockwaves from the Rainey firing began to dissipate. The Southern Association of Colleges and Secondary Schools removed the University from the probation list. At the time, *The Texan* blamed the whole mess on the regents, saying, "The University of Texas, as a center of learning, is part of a world wide community of knowledge. Its officials cannot flaunt the traditions and practices of that community without reaping a sad harvest."[75]

Two months later, the regents appointed T. S. Painter, who had been serving as interim president since Rainey's dismissal, to become the UT president. *The Texan* published an extra edition to inform the campus.[76] The decision was extremely unpopular. The Students' Association opposed the choice, and more than one hundred faculty members signed a petition to discuss the issue.[77] Painter was closely tied to the regents, and the general attitude of the campus seemed to be against him.

The Daily Texan tried to criticize the Painter appointment, but the editorial was initially censored. The TSP general manager had withheld the editorial because he felt it might violate several board policies. Professor Paul J. Thompson, one of the faculty members of the TSP Board, agreed. According to the TSP Board minutes, he believed that the editorial was a statement of opinion not based on facts, that it was a personal attack on President Painter and the Board of Regents, and that the editorial was not in good taste. He also said the editor was injudicious and unfair and that *The Texan* was the official organ of the University. Another board member said that the student paper should not launch an attack on the president or the Board of Regents.[78]

Earlier in the meeting, *Texan* editor Horace Busby and managing editor Mildred Nebenzhal had offered their resignations. The board did not wish to accept them, and one professor joined the two students in voting to publish Busby's editorial. The final vote was 3-2 in favor of publication.[79]

The editorial appeared the next day. Titled "ERA OF HOSTILITY," it stated, "So long as Dr. Painter is president, a breach, a suspicion—an 'Era of Hostility'—will exist. . . . A great deal of faith that has been restored so slowly, so tediously, and with such great effort, is now destroyed. Just as surely as the administration once proclaimed an 'Era of Tranquillity,' the action Friday proclaims an 'Era of Hostility.' "[80]

Many faculty members shared the editorial's sentiments. The faculty met to take a vote of confidence in Painter. They said they would support the University but "regretted" Painter's acceptance of the presidency. A *Texan* editorial stated, "Nor can it be expected that the suspicions, animosities, and lack of faith which prevailed during his term as acting president will now suddenly disappear."[81] It was not an auspicious beginning for T. S. Painter.

Then a bad situation became even worse. The American Association of University Professors censured the University of Texas, placing it on their so-called blacklist. *The Texan* editorial stated, "The University's future as an institution of higher learning hangs in the balance."[82]

On this climactic issue, Horace Busby left office. The news story about his departure described a "shy, self-effacing editor [who] stayed close to the office of *The Daily Texan*"; "More often than not, he slept in the office—or stayed up all night writing"; "In future years, *Texan* editors will undoubtedly look back to his fight for the individual student on the gigantic Forty Acres."[83]

After Busby, Bill Noble took over. Within months, he would be involved in a serious strug-

gle with President Painter. Noble wrote an editorial about a UT professor who had been fired. The professor had liberal views, but apparently he was suspected of child molestation. Noble believed that the professor was innocent but for political reasons was coerced into leaving to avoid negative publicity and embarrassment for his family.[84]

Whatever the truth of the matter, T. S. Painter was furious. He wrote to Dudley Woodward, chair of the Board of Regents: "It isn't often that I get thoroughly mad, but I was in this condition last Sunday. The incident which aroused my emotions was two editorials in *The Daily Texan*." Painter had told Noble "background information about things with which he would not ordinarily be acquainted." Yet *The Texan* had taken the opposite position with the incident.[85]

Painter wrote:

> At nine o'clock Monday morning, I called together the faculty advisors for the Texas Student Publications, and laid the plain facts before them that Mr. Noble was starting out on the same tactics as Busby followed last year, and I told them very plainly that the present administration would not tolerate the kind of thing that we have been subjected to for two years and that if we were unable to get decency and accuracy out of the editors of *The Texan*, then other measures might well be forced upon us. In reviewing the rules and regulations of the Regents, I find that we have a method for exercising faculty supervision over the editorial policy. I believe I am correct in saying that this provision has not been in force in the past. At all events, I have appointed two members of the Faculty Advisory Committee to act as an Editorial Advisory Committee, and I urged them to get busy and see what they could do to bring about a change of heart on the part of Mr. Noble and his associates.
>
> *The Texan* has always been a problem, and I suspect that the Department of Journalism is in part responsible for the general attitude which *Texan* editors all to often take with regard to the University.[86]

Painter had an ally in Dudley Woodward, the chair of the Board of Regents. Many people had and would complain to Woodward about *The Texan*. One alumni wrote, "I hear complaints, however, that *The Texan* continues its unrestrained editorial policy of radicalism and hope that some proper action may be devised by the Board to enable the Administrative Officers to keep this irresponsible publication within the bounds of reason and make it a credit to, rather than a liability to the University."[87] Woodward responded by writing the UT administrators, quoting the letter, and saying, "You really have no idea how seriously the University is prejudiced by the situation of which I have so long complained. I am depending on your Committee bringing us a program which will correct it. The Board is not lacking in courage to do whatever will prove effective."[88]

Woodward's plan was to hire a professional journalist to act as a managing editor for all UT publications:

> I have long thought the employment of a competent man in this position is essential to proper training of students in journalism, and I know it is essential to anything approaching decent conduct of student publications. . . . With such a position ably filled our relations with the press would be immeasurably better than they have been at any time in the past, and the University would be saved an incalculable amount of embarrassment. . . . The University has been consistently victimized, misrepresented, and embarrassed by the system which is now the effect.[89]

E. E. Kirkpatrick, another UT regent, wrote to Woodward: "As a governing board we cannot condone nor tolerate the insidious insults which have been thrown at us and the University for the past year."[90]

Complaints about *The Texan*'s liberal views on racial equality and the Rainey firing kept coming. Palmer Bradley, a name partner in a Houston law firm, wrote to Woodward, "I can't help but wonder whether we are ever going to do something about *The Daily Texan*, which is now a cross between the *Daily Worker* and the *Houston Informer*. . . . *The Texan* is calling down a lot of criticism on the University. I do hope something can be done to eliminate it, but am willing to defer to your judgment."[91]

Woodward responded that he had planned for a managing editor to control all the student publications. "I thought definite arrangements to this end had been completed so that it would become effective in September 1947. To my dismay, I learned at the September meeting that the arrangement had not been made because a 'nice boy' had become editor of *The Texan*."[92]

Bradley wrote back:

> You can bet your last dollar that the radicals are going to howl if any censorship is placed on the

paper. It occurs to me that the easiest way to handle the matter is to put some permanent faculty member in as managing editor or business manager, or something of that sort, and the logical time to do this is at the end of the summer school. It will thus be a fait accompli when the students return for the regular fall session.[93]

Chair of Regents Dudley K. Woodward's plan was put into effect. The "competent man" that Woodward found was Harrell E. Lee, a former Associated Press reporter who had covered the Texas Legislature. Paul J. Thompson, a faculty member on the TSP Board, wrote to Lee to tell him how TSP manager William McGill had been directly supervising *The Texan*'s coverage of the Legislature:

> Not only was the work done well from the viewpoint of the Texan readers, but it was noticeably helpful to the interests of the University. During any session of the Legislature, the Daily Texan has dozens of opportunities to co-operate with the President or other administrative officers of the University toward the end of printing news or statements that are helpful to the University.[94]

One of the senior UT administrators primarily involved in handling *The Texan* was Read Granberry. Paul J. Thompson told Harrell Lee to contact Granberry "at least once a month during this school year." Thompson wrote:

> I think it is quite important that we report to him how our new program of editorial supervision of the Daily Texan is progressing. He served last year as chairman of the committee which recommended the plan under which you were employed. The committee, though inactive at the present time, may be called into session at any time during this school year to make recommendations for alterations in our plan. . . . If Mr. Granberry has any suggestions, please pay very close attention to them and let us see how they can be used.[95]

The administration's restriction of free speech was not confined to *The Texan*. Painter also was acting to limit faculty dissent. As Painter told the faculty, "Any further attempts, on the part of individuals or small groups within our staff, unjustly to besmirch the good reputation of the University or to retard its progress will not be allowed to pass unnoticed."[96]

The dissident professors knew what Painter

was saying. A coffee discussion was planned on the topic of "academic freedom," but as *The Texan* reported, "Several professors have declined to attend, or to speak if they do attend, because they don't dare to make their views known."[97] Those professors were wise. One professor did attend another such debate and took the communist position, possibly just for the sake of argument. *The Texan* reported his statements. Chair of the Regents Dudley K. Woodward said that the professor should be denied tenure and fired as soon as practical.[98]

T. S. Painter later tried to portray himself as a friend of the free press. Mere months after he ordered faculty to censor *The Texan* more severely, Painter stated, "We have in our *Texan* a student-controlled and published newspaper which gives anybody and everybody at the University an opportunity to express themselves, or to pop off, as we say. . . . I think The University of Texas has always been operated in a truly democratic manner. We have allowed the students to say and write what they wanted to as long as they did not subject themselves to the libel laws."

A *Texan* editorial, in apparent sincerity, concluded, "It is gratifying to know the University's president is as conscious of the benefits of freedom of the press as the journalist is."[99]

At first glance, the *Texan* staff seemed incredibly naive. But some evidence exists that Painter changed his mind at least somewhat about granting freedom to the paper. On January 9, 1948, after the creation of a liberal political party, Painter wrote to Woodward:

> It is going to be difficult to prevent both students and members of our staff from saying things which will give offense to many citizens of the state who are conservative in their views. . . . In some respects, I felt somewhat reassured yesterday, when a member of the staff who is close to the student body, particularly the journalism students, told me that he thought the forbearance which the administration has shown, especially with regard to The Texan, was having a very beneficial effect and was bringing the students around to a feeling of trust, and maybe of admiration someday, in the fairness and wisdom of the administration, which certainly ought to be the reaction of normal American boys and girls.[100]

Sometime in 1947, Painter even defended

The Texan before the regents when Dudley K. Woodward was plotting how best to seize control. Painter wrote:

> Ten years ago, I think I would have taken the position that certain topics . . . should not be discussed in open meetings because of very wide divergences of opinion and the danger of the press reports giving a wrong slant. But since the war and in view of all of the social unrest which we find in young people, their general world-mindedness, and their open questioning of the wisdom of the older generations, I am inclined to believe that the wisest course of action is to have open discussion of even the most controversial questions which the students wish to be informed about.[101]

But whatever Painter might have wished, the censorship of TSP media was real. In February 1947, one TSP Board member, Stuart A. MacCorkle, stopped publication of an article in *The Ranger,* a campus humor magazine. The article allegedly had "political implications."[102] (It discussed how a student had campaigned for Gov. Beauford Jester.)

The Texan quickly came to *The Ranger's* defense. Editor William Noble wrote:

> When it is denied an editor his right to speak his mind, then the "Freedom of the Press" to which everyone pays lip service becomes a mere mockery. . . . Never was the mandate of the board meant to include censorship of political or controversial material. If that is the case, then Bryson [*The Ranger* editor] has been guilty of subterfuge. For six months, he has been masquerading as editor when in reality the magazine has been "edited" by the three-man committee. . . . Censorship is a terrible thing. It goes hand-in-glove with such things as Fascism and Communism.[103]

Noble knew of what he spoke. In the original *Texan* news story describing the censorship, two paragraphs describing what material was supposedly "political" were removed. *The Texan* stated, "This is not a quarrel over censorship of so-called smutty material. It is a fight for the right of a publication to comment on anything it sees fit, be it political, academic, or what-have-you."[104]

The Texan, however, did not yet have that freedom—whatever T. S. Painter might say to the contrary.

RED SCARES

The firing of UT President Homer Rainey and his replacement by T. S. Painter was one major event in *The Texan*'s life during the 1940s. Another concerned the paper's travails with Red Scares and charges of communism.

The problem began early in the decade. When most people hear the phrase "Red Scare," they think of Joe McCarthy in the 1950s or the Palmer raids after World War I. At the University of Texas, however, Red Scares went on for decades.

The first major Red Scare involving *The Daily Texan* occurred in 1941. In January a bill was proposed in the Texas Legislature that would require all Texas teachers to take a loyalty oath. Under the leadership of editor Boyd Sinclair, *The Texan* opposed the measure.[105]

In March a new book was published by U.S. Congressman Martin Dies attacking communism and accusing some prominent people of communism. Boyd Sinclair reviewed the book and said it was ghost written. He also pointed out that there was little evidence for the charges. "Martin Dies . . . is a worse author than he is an investigator," Sinclair wrote. As for those accused of communist leanings, "If men such as these constitute our Fifth Column, give me a membership card."[106]

A Texas legislator was not pleased. Joe Ed Winfree stood up on the floor of the House and denounced *The Texan* in heated terms. He said that he would rather close the University than "see America ruined from within. . . . If that stuff out there doesn't stop, we'll close her up."[107] The Houston legislator charged that the University was tolerating "crazy ideas" and promoting "the teaching of nazism, communism, and fascism."[108]

Such allegations from the Texas Legislature were not new. UT President Harry Benedict had dealt with similar allegations shortly before his death in 1937. But UT President Homer Rainey took an even harder stance than Benedict. As a *Texan* headline stated, "RAINEY TO RED-BAITERS: 'PUT UP OR SHUT UP.'" (Rainey actually used the phrase "Put Up or Shut Up.") "If anyone has any evidence," Rainey said, "It's about time to produce it."[109]

This was a remarkably blunt public statement for a UT president to make. Rainey was certainly not winning any points for diplomacy. But he did understand the emotions at work. The month

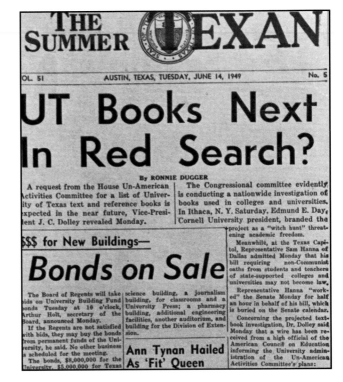

This June 14, 1949, headline warned of the communist scare which was about to strangle academic freedom at UT.

after this outburst, Austin held an "I Am An American Day." Rainey made a big show of encouraging all students to join in the celebration of patriotism.[110]

Another Red Scare would occur in 1943. The new editor, Ralph B. Frede, would be in office only a matter of weeks before he would be attacked by the Texas Legislature. On February 25, *The Texan* published an editorial by Sue Brandt entitled "Russia Is Wiping Out 7 Sins for Bright Future." The editorial referred to seven problems that the new Russian government since the Revolution was trying to fight. It stated:

These sins as enumerated by Josef Stalin are drunkenness, prostitution, poverty, begging, insecurity, race differences, and religion. The progress that has already been made toward the wiping out of these sins has been effective enough to be in part responsible for Russia's current war successes. . . .

Religion the Russians want none of. Their accusation against it seems to be justified when they say that religion in the past has been merely an instrument of force and superstition used by the state on one hand and the church on the other to hoodwink and intimidate the common citizen. When the day comes that education has overcome ignorance and superstition in the Soviet Union, then, Stalin says, religion will again be needed.

If Russia can continue in these paths which she has taken "since the revolution," perhaps America and the rest of the world can see a brighter prospect for post-war relations with the Big Bear of world politics. The seven sins certainly make sense so far.[111]

The editorial did not raise an immediate fuss. (Indeed, the next day a "Firing Line" letter praising the editorial was published.)[112] But this calm was only momentary. On March 2 (Texas Independence Day), *The Houston Post* blasted *The Texan* for publishing the editorial:

The left-wing swing evident among some elements of both faculty and student body of The University of Texas reached the farthest point yet on the road to Moscow—farther than Hitler got —in a recent issue of the University's student newspaper, *The Daily Texan*.

Not satisfied with a three-column spread extolling a Soviet-made documentary file of life in Russia, which the most conservative American would not particularly disapprove and therefore was perhaps too mild, the same issue of *The Texan* featured a four-column signed editorial approving Russia's abolition of religion as a "major sin," along with drunkenness, prostitution, poverty, begging, insecurity and race discrimination. . . .

Communistic sentiments are not strangers to the *Texan* columns, or to some of the faculty articulations, but this is the first time we know of that *The Texan* has gone so far as to hint of doing away with religion as part of our emulation of the Soviet example.

A few years ago there was a lively controversy of whether the faculty should be empowered to censor *The Texan* editorially. The faculty prevailed, and we wonder whether this anti-religion propaganda had faculty approval.

Also we wonder what the fathers and mothers of the University students, as well as the taxpayers who foot the institution's bills, would say of this implied suggestion of the idea of removing religion, the cornerstone of American civilization, from our way of life.[113]

A *Texan* editorial replied:

The *Texan* is not atheistic nor is it communistic. It attempts to discuss the history and life of Russia from an objective viewpoint, admitting its good points and rejecting its bad ones. The author of the editorial, while perfectly sincere in what she said, may have been, perhaps, a bit careless in her manner of listing religion as a major sin. Perhaps she should have explained that religion in Russia before the revolution, according to history books, was closely associated with the czar's tyranny and represented only oppression and despair to the Russian people.

Persons not in the University area frequently misinterpret *Texan* editorials and stories. *The Texan*, it must be remembered, is not the official organ of the University administration or of the Regents. It is a student publication and represents the opinions of the students. . . .

It seems unfair to us for a large city paper to judge a student paper without tolerance and in such a way that it reflects on The University of Texas, an institution of higher learning sacred to the citizens of Texas.

Perhaps a bit more tolerance on the part of the Post and a bit more judicious wording on the *Texan*'s part will prevent misunderstanding.[114]

Fat chance. On March 17 the Texas House of Representatives by a vote of 97 to 25 passed a resolution condemning the editorial. The resolution stated:

. . . Whereas, this is an alarming editorial to appear in any American newspaper, or in a newspaper of any Christian country, much less to appear in the daily student publication of a state-owned and financed University, and expresses and condones theories against religion which are definitely contrary to the principles upon which this State and Nation were founded; and the expression and great prominence of such an editorial in *The Daily Texan* constitute a disgrace and embarrassment to the great University of Texas and to the citizens of this State who support the school with their taxes; and

Whereas, this unfortunate editorial policy and the writing of such atheistic theories cast reflection upon the faculty and the student body, and for fear that similar writings and editorials will again appear in such campus newspapers under the present editorial policy, and that such writing might lead the people of Texas to believe that such views are taught, advocated or fostered by the University or certain members of its faculty:

BE IT RESOLVED by the House of Representatives that the President, Board of Regents and Faculty of The University of Texas be called upon to determine whether this editorial was passed and approved by the faculty censors of *The Daily Texan*; and that faculty supervision and censorship of the editorial policy of the paper either be changed or strengthened so as to prevent another such occurrence and the publication of similar articles advocating beliefs which are contrary to Democracy and religion;

That the editor of *The Daily Texan* be requested to devote at least part of his editorial policy to the principles on which this country was built and for which we fight, and toward a complete understanding of the principles of Democracy and religion, in order that the youth of our State University might read more about God, America, and Democracy, and less about Russia and the destruction of religion in that country.[115]

What had originally appeared to be a simple error in wording was now a major issue. Several local ministers rallied to the paper's support.[116] Regent H. K. Aynesworth disagreed with some of his fellow regents and came to *The Texan*'s defense, saying, "The quotations (from *The Texan*) concerning Russian religion, taken in their context do not, in any sense, justify the conclusions drawn by the editor of the Post. . . . Must these young students, many of whom are making the supreme sacrifice to preserve the American way of life, be prevented from expressing their thoughts about any subject in which the entire American citizenship are vitally interested?"[117]

Gov. Coke Stevenson said that the editorial had created an erroneous impression because of its inadvertent use of language. The governor said he had spoken with the writer and the student editors and believed the problems stemmed from a miswording. He was also reassured by the large number of UT students enrolled in Bible classes.[118]

Stevenson would not always be so tolerant of the University. In 1947 he denounced the teaching of "totalitarian philosophy" at the University. *The Texan* responded, "Let our young people be completely informed concerning these 'isms' and do not worry—they will know which to choose. . . . An uneducated mind is easy prey for evil propaganda."[119]

Later in 1947, a communist speaker was denied the use of a meeting room available to other groups. A *Texan* editorial argued, "Who can learn that truth which is to make him free if only one side of the debate is allowed? Are we afraid of ideas here?"[120]

This was not the last time the paper would tangle with the issue of communism. It would remain to trouble the paper during the McCarthy

decade, but such Red Scares associated with the McCarthy era were faced by *The Texan* years before the 1950s.

SWEATT V. PAINTER

Another major issue of the 1940s that would persist into the next decade was that of race. *The Texan* began its aggressive support of the civil rights movement early in the 1940s, and it continued that support throughout the decade, even under significant attempts at censorship.

The paper supported civil rights in the early years of the 1940s, a time not traditionally associated with the civil rights movement. In January 1942, *The Texan* warned about the dangers of racism: "We must be careful not to assume the racial superiority which we condemn in other people."[121]

This position continued in later years. Before leaving office to enter the military (where he would die in action), editor Bob Owens allowed *The Texan* argue for what was at the time an extremely controversial position—racial equality. On February 6, 1943—the day Owens wrote to the TSP Board to resign as editor—*The Texan* carried an editorial arguing that "Minorities have rights to full citizenship. . . . If we are to win the peace, we must first erase all traces of fascism in this country."[122] It was the strongest pro-civil rights editorial that the paper had yet carried.

Owens published another editorial on February 9, titled, "DR. QUO [STATUS QUO] REJECTS EDITORIAL." This piece compared America's treatment of blacks with Germany's treatment of Jews.[123]

After that, the staff editorials disappeared altogether for a week or two. In their place, the paper reprinted nationally produced war propaganda. It was clear that editorializing about race relations in that manner was not going to continue.

Owens' successors also had progressive views on race relations. Under editor Weldon Brewer, *The Texan* opposed the "race riots" in which mobs of white citizens attacked black Americans. "With the inconsistency that so many nations find hard to understand in us, we have been busy denying at home the very freedoms for which we are fighting abroad." This was a strong civil rights position, but the editorial writer used a clever

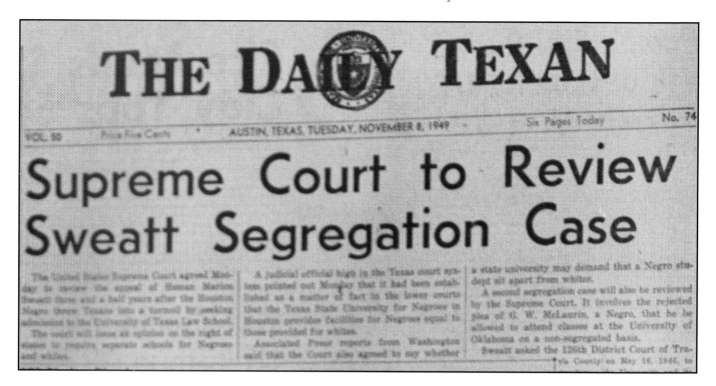

dodge—he blamed the riots on the Nazis, saying, "Mobs led by rabble-rousers and Axis saboteurs are beating and killing Negroes in many cities."[124] This allowed him to criticize racism while still appearing patriotic.

In 1944, *The Texan* gave front-page coverage to allegations that race restrictions kept the committee which organized student dances from finding a nationally recognized band.[125] The committee members accused *The Texan* of "yellow journalism" but formally announced that the committee would consider a band of any race.[126]

But this aggressive coverage did not last. On March 27, 1945, the TSP Board ordered *The Texan* to stop discussing race relations. The resolution stated:

> The subject of race relations having been discussed at length pro and con recently and some of the articles having become inflammatory in tone, the Board of Directors is of the opinion that further discussion of this subject in *The Daily Texan* should be discontinued. This resolution is the unanimous opinion of the members of the Board.[127]

Yet the issue could not be avoided for long. A year later, *The Texan*'s headline read, "NEGRO'S APPLICATION DECLINED PENDING OPINION BY SELLERS." The lead of the news story read:

Heman Marion Sweatt, Negro of Houston, presented a scholastic transcript and filed application for admission as student into the Law School of the University of Texas Tuesday February 26. Register E. J. Matthews, acting under instructions of acting-President Painter, declined the application pending legal opinion by the Texas Attorney-General's Department.[128]

The Texan did not immediately endorse admitting Sweatt, stating instead that graduate schools should be created at Prairie View, a historically black college. But a front-page editorial did say, "If there is a lesson to be taken from this incident, it should be that bigotry and prejudice is the inevitable road to trouble—open-mindedness is the only profitable approach. The bigotry that has retarded the obvious progressive action in this case may, ultimately, prove costly and damaging to the State, the University, and the people of the State."[129]

Heman Sweatt stated, "My sole desire is to occupy one seat in a classroom of a law school, and eventually practice law in Texas."[130] According to a *Texan* news story, Sweatt "doubts that the law school at Prairie View would be equal to that at the University." Texas Attorney General Grover Sellers denied Sweatt's request for admission, citing "the wise and long-considered policy of segregation."[131]

Although there was campus support for integrating the law school, *The Texan* under editor Bill Noble opposed integration. A front-page editorial stated, "No matter how good their intentions, no matter how sincere their actions, the students who met early last week to vote support for the National Association for the Advancement of Colored People skirted dangerously near something for which they and the people they would help may some day be sorry. . . . They cannot advance the Negroes' cause by doing something that would throw back what progress has been made in the last fifty years. No one at the meeting would ever desire this."[132]

What "progress" had been made in the last fifty years was not identified.

But the editorial was not the only perspective that *The Texan* printed. In a debate on the topic "Education for Negroes in UT," Carl Lofstedt wrote, "I advocate opening the doors of every school and college of the University to any person, be he black or white or bright purple, who is academically qualified for admission. . . . We cannot deny a man his legal rights because someone else will take illegal action to prevent him from enjoying those rights—rather should we take steps to prevent contravention of those rights."[133]

Texas eventually established the "Texas State University for Negroes" for Sweatt.[134] In return, the NAACP held a public meeting and demanded integrated schools. The speaker at that meeting, *The Texan* reported, was Thurgood Marshall.[135] In court, Marshall contended that the black school was inferior to the UT School of Law. The dean responded that the Texas State University for Negroes—which lacked a library and was housed in a basement—was "equal, if not superior, in every respect to the University law school."[136]

The Texan, under editor Jo White, disagreed. An editorial titled "Equality for the Negro Race Cannot be Deferred Forever" stated, "The printed text of our Constitution rings out against discrimination, and yet it is far from reality."[137] Another editorial discussed the heavy financial cost of creating separate-but-equal institutions: "We'll pay for our prejudice for a while, but one day we'll wake up and decide against continuing the luxury."[138]

In 1948 editor William H. Smith also took an aggressive stance in favor of civil rights. Upon the formation of a campus NAACP group, an editorial stated, "We welcome the NAACP upon campus. Their work in obtaining the promises of the Constitution for minority groups may some day save the necks of some of our Southern gentlemen, for the NAACP is working against communism in one of the most effective ways."[139]

Some UT students disapproved of *The Texan*'s stance. In September 1948 a "University States' Rights Club was formed." The president condemned the "noisy propaganda of the radical minority through their campus newspaper, *The Daily Texan*."[140] A *Texan* editorial restated the paper's position: "To put our position very plainly, the Negro should be granted full equality or the Constitution amended. We think he should be given full equality."[141]

In October the Texas Supreme Court refused Sweatt a rehearing of the issues. *The Texan* news story stated, "It took two and a half years, but Heman M. Sweatt finally exhausted Wednesday the last legal resort in Texas. . . . Attorneys for Sweatt indicated that they would appeal to the United States Supreme Court." The next day, a *Texan* editorial declared, "Once more the state of Texas, as many other states, has failed to provide for its citizens and in turn has seen its citizens appeal to the federal government for aid."[142]

Sweatt, of course, won his appeal to the Supreme Court, and the 1950 case of *Sweatt v. Painter* later paved the way for the 1954 decision in *Brown v. Topeka* that outlawed racial segregation in public schools.

The Clique

Between World War II, the firing of Rainey, the Red Scares, and the fight over integration, it had been a momentous decade for *The Texan*. But not everything was pitched battles. There was also some of the solid day-to-day journalism that benefits the community. *The Texan* produced a special investigative feature on allegations of beatings and poor conditions at the State School for the Deaf.[143] *The Texan*'s coverage forced the governor to improve conditions at the school, and even Board of Regents Chair Dudley Woodward praised the paper. Another *Texan* investigation revealed the poor conditions in Texas mental institutions. Papers around the state praised *The Texan*, and reforms were passed. Closer to home, the paper's staff waged a fight for fire escapes in the journalism building where they worked. *The Texan* reported that after several editorials were published, "a few days later, fire extinguishers in the building were placed in conspicuous positions and painted a bright red."[144]

Relations with the Students' Association were mixed during this period. The Students' Association and *The Texan* were allies on the Rainey fight. But when it came to integration and liberal views, the more conservative forces in the SA were not pleased.

In 1946 the Students' Association ordered an investigation of "the management, policy, and competency of *The Daily Texan*."[145] A resolution stated that "there now exists on the campus of The University of Texas a manifest undercurrent of dissatisfaction, distrust, and anxiety in regard to the policy of reporting, managing, and editing of *The Daily Texan*."[146]

Three assembly members, however, explained that "the Clique, which is a small but powerful group of fraternity political leaders, is making an all-out bid for power."[147] They then stated, "The editorial policy of *The Daily Texan* is a matter decided by student elections. Bill Noble's campaign was very clear, and his actions and policy have been in accord with that platform. The Clique people who supported him are obviously enraged that he has refused to break his campaign promises and become their tool."[148]

Perhaps the Clique did not expect to find itself on the front page. Nothing ever came of the SA investigation.

Relations with the UT administration were also mixed. UT President Homer Rainey protected the paper, and in return *The Texan* defended him vigorously. President Painter, on the other hand, was no huge friend, but *The Texan* did not suffer the same type of censorship that had been attempted in 1936.

On issues of race and gender, the paper's positions were tolerant for the times. With many men leaving for war, women took senior staff positions such as editor and managing editor. Helene Wilke, for instance, was not only the paper's first female editor, but also one of its best of the decade, skillfully leading the paper through the intense upheaval caused by the Rainey firing.

On racial issues, the paper was also progressive. While the degree of support for integration could vary from editor to editor, *The Texan* consistently supported the civil rights of minorities. In this area, the paper was far ahead of UT administrators like T. S. Painter.

The 1940s was probably the most eventful decade that *The Texan* had yet experienced. The paper defended Homer Rainey, survived Dudley Woodward, weathered Red Scares spawned by the Texas Legislature, and fought for integration. Fifty years after its founding, the paper had grown from Fritz Lanham's small weekly into a strong and significant UT institution.

CHAPTER 6

FIGHTING FOR RIGHTS AND INDEPENDENCE: 1950-1960

I n an old, yellowed building just a stone's throw east of the Tower—which, yes, sparked many a comment about "yellow journalism" —*The Texan* began its most tumultuous decade yet: the 1950s.

Future *Texan* editor Willie Morris later wrote of that decade, "back then, the editorial page could blaspheme the Apostle Paul, but not taxation of the wealthy." In that era, "the contempt for an independent student voice trying to engage itself in important issues in the age of Joe McCarthy and the general 1950s silence was reflected in an effort to do lasting damage to the state universities' most basic civil liberties."[1]

The fight for the 1950s really started in 1949 under editor Dick Elam. That year marked the first new beginning on campus since the war. Summer enrollment was down to 7,850, the lowest since 1941.[2] The drop was attributed to a decline in veterans' enrollment.

On the surface, both in *The Texan's* pages and on campus, things appeared calm. The paper overflowed with reports of beauty pageants, carnivals, weddings, and the occasional Students' Assembly ruckus. Americans had defeated the Axis powers; Americans were ready to play.

The Texan introduced tabloid-size, five-column pages for the summer edition, published Tuesday, Thursday, and Sunday mornings. Students still subscribed to *The Texan*, at $1 for both summer terms. The paper was delivered to students' homes if they were in the carrier zone. If they lived outside that zone, students could pick up papers from the old journalism building by showing their subscription receipts.[3]

The Texan was THE news source for students. As proof of that fact, a small October front-page misprint caused 300 students to hunt for an incorrectly scheduled convocation.

Structurally and socially, the paper reflected the students. It had a society section, a page devoted to intramurals, a world news section, a half page devoted to wedding announcements named "Rings on Their Fingers," and a section about fraternity cavorting called "Greek Gambits."

The University still had a home economics building, and *The Texan* ran articles about housekeeping and opportunities for student wives.

In 1950, Coke was it. That year the University got its first machines. *The Texan* kept close tabs on the drink, reporting the need for more, and recording campus consumption—up to 4,500 Cokes a day. By May 1951, *The Texan* boasted, students had spent $25,000 on two million Cokes.[4]

Barton Springs was a popular place to relax, as staff writer Herby Herbsleb wrote, "All one needs for an afternoon of studying is 20 cents for bus fare, a cute date, 40 cents admission to the pool, a portable radio, swim suit, blanket, Coke money and a book to ease one's conscience."[5]

A POLICY OF BROAD-MINDEDNESS

Under editor Elam, *The Texan* retained its "by and for the students" policy which had been *Texan* tradition for forty-nine years. Elam noted that *The Texan's* policy of "news on the newspage, and editorials on the editorial page" had "become the watchword of *Texan* staffers."[6]

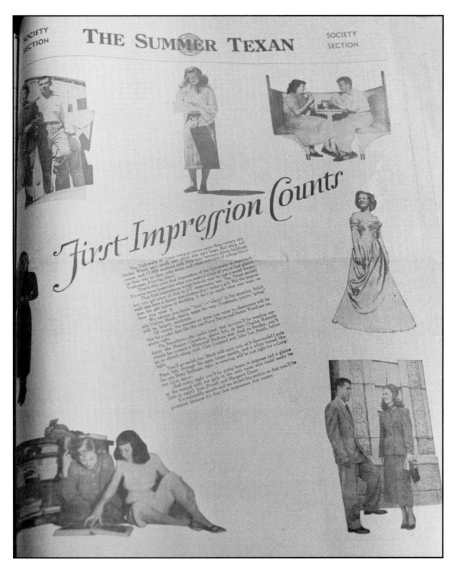

Left: *The 1950s* Texan *pages reflected the student body, with sections titled "Greek Gambits," "Rings on Their Fingers," and the "Society Section."*

Below: *The 1940s and 1950s saw season after season of beauty contests—from Aqua Carnival to Ten Most Beautiful.*

Jan Lander
Alpha Chi
Omega

Mary Lynne Arthur
Alpha Chi Omega

Marsha Grant
Chi Omega

Jackie Booth
Alpha Delta Pi

Judy Camp
Delta Zeta

Laura Lou Goyne
Pi Phi

Fran Leland
Zeta Tau Alpha

Donna Harris
Tri Delt

Yet Elam and all the 1950s editors wrote front-page news. The majority of *Texan* articles were published without bylines. When a major news story broke, however, its byline usually belonged to the editor or managing editor.

Elam began his year as editor, in keeping with the tradition before him, by writing his editorial policy for the upcoming year:

"How far back a liberal approach to campus and world news goes we can not adequately determine. A policy of broad-mindedness seems to have existed through the history of the newspaper; we record a decade of liberalism from investigations. Both labels explain the path of the *Summer* and *Daily Texan*s.

"Specifically, two traditions are to be ignored. The traditional eight column *Summer Texan* format is being replaced with this tabloid size. The change is intended as an aid to staff members and readers on interpreting *Texan* news. The second is a deviation in political stands. For a decade, *The Texan* could have been pigeon holed as a "liberal democrat" publication. This political support was thought-out; it was not inherited. This year's

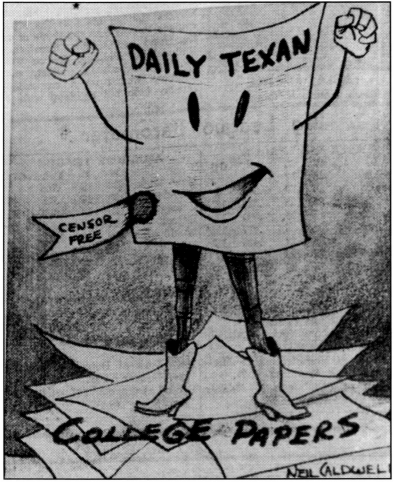

paper (with due apologies to Mr. Pulitzer and the *St. Louis Dispatch*) will study state and national thought process from which [our positions] will be derived."[7]

The first edition under Elam hinted that the calm was not to last. Bannered across the front page was an account of the charge against student body president Ellis Brown for negligent homicide of vice-president Robert Ferguson. The two had been in Brown's car, turning on 29th and Guadalupe, when Brown's car went into a skid. The car hit the curb and struck a metal post, throwing Ferguson into a brick wall.[8]

Elam's political stand was quickly tested. On June 8 the National Education Association announced that communist teachers would be barred from teaching. The House Un-American Activities Committee formally requested a list of UT reference books and texts. Soon, educators nationwide were losing their positions.

Elam and *The Texan* staff came out strongly against teacher dismissal. "Thought control has no place in a democracy," Elam wrote.[9] But the encroachment continued. On July 26 *Texan* reporter Mary Moore broke to students that Gov. Allan Shivers had signed a "loyalty oath" into law. The new law required all University teachers, employees, and students to swear allegiance to the United States in order to be paid or admitted. The bill was sponsored by Rep. Sam Hanna of Dallas, who declared the idea justified because "we oughtn' be spending taxpayer's money to educate such trash. If I had my way, I'd kick 'em all the way to Mexico."[10]

On August 23, when *The Texan* reported that oaths were passed out to UT employees, it implored students to reject the oath.

"The fight to remove the law that is ever a threat to the principle of freedom of thought and action will be spearheaded, we pray, by those who are compelled to sign the oath," Elam wrote.[11]

The 1950–51 editor, Ronnie Dugger, pointed out an obscure clause in the Constitution had barred "red" professors from teaching at UT the whole time anyway. As editor, Dugger vowed that "when we feel that a group is using freedom to injure another group, we'll say so. The Republican slogan, 'liberty vs. socialism,' strikes us as asinine." But, he added, "we are bound to no set of standards."[12]

The oath would be only a small challenge compared to what else lay ahead for the self-proclaimed "fair-deal Democrat" editor.

"Every human being—Christian, Jew, Negro, laborer, executive—is entitled to equal freedom within the democratic structure," Dugger said in his opening editorial.[13] Only a few days after he took office, the Supreme Court ended a four-year battle between UT and Heman Sweatt, a black graduate student who had sued the University of Texas Law School for the right to attend classes. On June 5, 1950, the Court overturned a state law which allowed "separate but equal" graduate institutions for African-Americans.

Students came quickly. On June 9, 1950, *The Texan* bannered the headline, "UT'S FIRST NEGROES MEET REGULAR CLASSES." *The Texan* welcomed the change, but many irate "Firing Line" writers did not, and University Vice-President James Dolley noted in an August article that the twenty-five African-Americans admitted would "cause some students, especially freshmen girls, to stay away. The drop is expected to be very large."[14] That same day, staff writer Charlie Lewis reported on a cross burned near the law school, and that "KKK letters had been found."

But the racial and political tension didn't dampen campus fun. *The Texan* started publishing an extra edition for Saturday home football games which carried full-page ads purchased by restaurants, banks, fraternities, and sororities that supported the Longhorns. Although the paper didn't have full-color capability yet, burnt orange graced the front and inside pages, cheering the team on as they defeated SMU, 23-20, to win the SWC title that year. For the girls, *The Texan* carried articles on proper game attire, suggesting that a suit would be most appropriate, "as it can be worn in hot and cold weather." Dugger also joined the Steer Here committee in championing a boycott against area barbers, who had raised their prices from 85 cents to a dollar. In "Boycott the Barbers," Dugger suggested that students support a "Bushy Bevo month."[15]

On the business side however, declining advertising and increasing printing costs, combined with the meager 1½ cent funding per $15 student blanket tax allotment per issue, forced *The Texan* to cut costs. On October 19 an apologetic editorial announced a reduction in issues. "Problems, some of them serious, face *The Texan*. There is a constant battle for advertising. That's why an occasional paper will only be four pages."[16]

CONFLICT ABROAD—AND CLOSER TO HOME

Internationally, the Korean conflict escalated, and on January 7, 1951, Universal Military Training began. Within two weeks, about 480,000 eighteen-year-olds—including 400 UT students—were enlisted. A sense of unease that America was about to engage its young men in another world war hung in the air.

"*The Texan* is trying hard to believe that its manpower position will not be in the same condition as it was during WWII. But it looks like the campus is in for another female editor. Is that bad?" staffer Charley Trimble wrote.[17]

The Texan ran a Korean War obituary for UT student Thomas P. McClellan on the front page on February 13, 1951. It was the first of many.

Even with students battling communism overseas, Dugger continued *The Texan*'s campaign against the loyalty oath. "If college students must sign the loyalty oath," Dugger wrote, "why not dentists, doctors, lawyers, ditch-diggers, everybody? Why compel loyal college people to swear they are not traitors? The Reds lie anyway. The oath is totally ineffective."[18]

Dugger emphasized, however, in boldface type, that "*The Texan* is against communism. Let there be no mistake about that. We are against its teachings, its lies, its hypocrisy, its brutality, its squelching of the individual."[19]

Soon after, Dugger resigned as editor, but not for political reasons. He had accepted a fellowship to Oxford University, and needed time to finish school and prepare. To fill the rest of Dugger's term, Trimble took over.

During this time, *The Texan* was independent of the Journalism School—journalism students wrote for *The Texan* and received some compensation, but the school did not run *The Texan*. In January, Trimble reported that *Texan* staffers were "hosting" J312 students and inviting students to put the paper to bed. The guests would take over all positions, and *The Texan* would furnish plenty of refreshments and copy paper.[20]

In addition to J students putting out the paper, Theta Sigma Pi pledges, a female journalism fraternity, traditionally took over "all editorial positions, including the all-male sports office" for one night each year. "If a male does get a finger in the production," staff writer Pat Pigman wrote, "his name is changed to a feminine counterpart on the masthead of the issue."[21]

Although *The Texan* continued to boast it was the most unrestricted paper in the world, regulations were encroaching on that claim.

In May 1951, TSP resurrected the "editorial council" consisting of the editor, managing editor, student body president, a cabinet member, and assembly member appointed by TSP to "influence decisions as to policy and technique of presentation by helping the editor to interpret student opinions, interest, and anticipate student reaction." [22]

The committee was "forbidden to determine final policy," Trimble argued, but it was the concrete beginning of a decade-long power struggle for freedom of the press in the '50s. [23]

Other policy changes that restricted *The Texan's* freedom followed under 1951–52 editor Russ Kersten. In 1951 the TSP decided to appoint future managing editors rather allowing them to be elected. That same year, *The Texan* began requiring signatures on "Firing Line" letters. And controversy over a February 21 editorial entitled "MED SCHOOL" heightened the administration's desire to oversee content.

In "MED SCHOOL," the Board of Regents charged *The Texan* "with violation of policy that the author of the editorial had not made careful investigation of the existing med school situation and that the consequential editorial was in error in substance and purpose."[24]

In response to the editorial, President Painter and the Board of Regents recommended moving the editorial deadline up, and moving the editorial director's hours of employment back, so that "conferences could be held by the editorial director and the non-editorial committee with the night supervisor and Texan editors 'with a view to refresh all key personnel in Texan policies and procedures.'"[25]

In other words, to keep criticism out of *The Texan*.

Korea weighed heavily on the campus. As night editor Kelly Crozier noticed, "Summer school will see hurrying males who want to get in a few hours before Uncle Sam puts their skills to use on a different level. The Korean situation and the nearness of the services are topmost in the lives of the average undergraduate male—that's sure. Fear of the Korean situation and the services—no. There is more a feeling of waiting, of uncertainty. Why plan? Why work hard on school? Why seek job interviews? Why Anything?"[26]

Kersten took on topics heavy and light. He started the tradition of making each semester's first *Texan* free. The bi-weekly summer publication would be published on Tuesday and Friday mornings. Kersten continued the battle against the loyalty oath, especially when Governor Shivers increased the pressure by requiring state employees to swear they had never been communist party members, and, for the last ten years, had not been involved in any group labeled subversive by the U.S. Attorney General's office.

"The whole rotten guilt by association and guilt by implication mess, which affects 32,000 state employees, is based on a legislative reasoning that insults the integrity of the UT staff and each of its members," he wrote.[27]

WOMEN AT THE HELM

The Texan's first female editor/female managing editor team took the helm in 1952. Editor Anne Chambers and managing editor Jo Ann Dickerson began their year with the note that "*The Texan* is not on our shoulders, but in our hands."[28]

Under the female leadership, there were noticeably fewer bathing suit photos on the front page. Chambers and Dickerson covered a Women's Issues in Journalism Conference, in which they noted "the need for keeping a local personal touch with readers through club and social news, but giving emphasis to features outside of homemaking." They stressed food and fashion reporting, but reported that "The majority of progressive newspapers today keep wedding and engagement stories on the inside of society pages and put feature stories on the front page."[29]

Another monumental change during Chambers' term was *The Texan's* and J-School's move into the new Journalism Building, located at the corner of 24th and Whitis.

TSP gave a $125,000 grant toward construction of the $635,000 Journalism Building (now

Texan *staffers in the 1950s.*

known as the Geography Building) and spent $14,000 on new furniture, equipment, and supplies.[30] "The new building was on a hill, so that you got to the front door by climbing up concrete steps on either side," remembered 1957-58 editor Bud Mims. "Between the steps the word 'JOURNALISM' had been chiseled in stone. Followed by the legend in Latin, '*Vincet Omnia Veritas,*' which translates into something like 'Truth Conquers All.' Wags on *The Texan* staff, especially those recruits from the English department, like to translate it as 'Journalism conquers all truth.' Or, 'Truth conquers all journalism.'" The grand opening was celebrated by professional journalists, graduates, and a few local celebrities.

In the new building, *Texan* staffers were armed with typewriters, copy paper, a plastic scanner for photos, linotype machines, and hot metal. *The Texan* did run AP wire stories, and although it was still a black and white paper "we

got to run color on special occasions," Mims said. "But it was the type that was in color."

DAILY AT THE *DAILY TEXAN*

Each year brought new personalities and technological developments, but Mims' account generally described *The Texan*'s operations:

On the northeast side of the building, there was a room that served as the newsroom. Picture about five or six rows of continuous table-desks. Each of these furnishings supported some eight to ten typewriters. During the day, it was officially the School of Journalism lab for reporting courses. Texan reporters were free to use the facilities to write their stories during the day, but used it more at night, particularly when few typewriters in the various *Texan* offices were being stroked.

The staff of key departments began work in the late morning. These departments had page

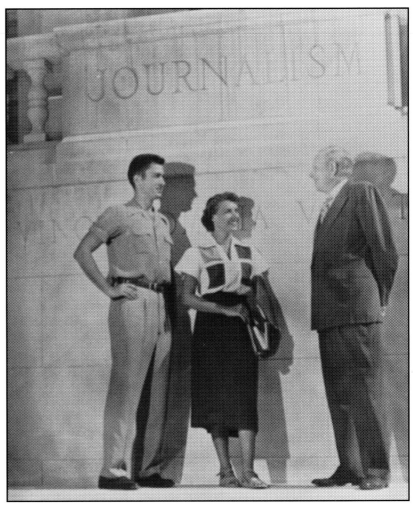

Right and below:
Journalism Building, 1950s.
Bud Mims, 1957-58 editor, remembered, "The new building was on a hill, so that you got to the front door by climbing concrete steps. . . . Between the steps the word 'JOURNALISM' had been chiseled in stone. Followed by the legend in Latin, 'Vincet Omnia Veritas' [Truth Conquers All]. Wags on The Texan *staff, especially recruits from the English Department, liked to translate it as 'Journalism conquers all truth.' Or, 'Truth conquers all journalism.'"*

Texan *press room, 1950s.*

deadlines somewhere around 6:00 P.M., although an editorial could be run through as late as 11:00 P.M.

The key person in charge was known as the night editor, who also ruthlessly recruited new talent by sweet talking and strong arming promising new journalists. The night editor for a particular day would start work somewhere between 6:00 P.M. and 7:00 P.M. He or she would review the list of assigned stories that were expected to come in. We were also free to use any copy that had been written for the School's reporting courses, but usually didn't use very much. We thought it was inferior, so at least 90 percent of what went into the paper was written by *Texan* staff.

As each story was completed, the lowest staffer on the totem pole carried it into the office of the Editorial Director (Censor) whose task was to read it before sending it to the basement composing room via pneumatic tube.

We were repeatedly assured that the censor didn't really "censor." Officially, he was there to read copy and raise questions before it was printed in order to keep bad taste out of the paper. If he objected to something and couldn't work out an immediate compromise with the editor in charge, he could invoke the power of TSP and hold it up for some time.

This arrangement would be challenged by all sides under editor Willie Morris, but *The Texan* ultimately prevailed and survived as an independent voice.

Mims remarked that during his tenure, "the only thing I can remember being held up was an editorial drawing that depicted a lynching; we managed to work out an agreement on how to run it."

Mims recalled the standard procedure of getting out an issue:

All copy was supposed to be downstairs by 11:00 P.M., but sometimes we managed to stretch until midnight. Once the paper was put to bed upstairs, the night staff adjourned to a local bistro—usually Hank's Bar and Grill for coffee. Only one or two on the staff were old enough to drink, so Pete's On-The-Drag for beer for a Lone Star was not possible. After coffee or late supper,

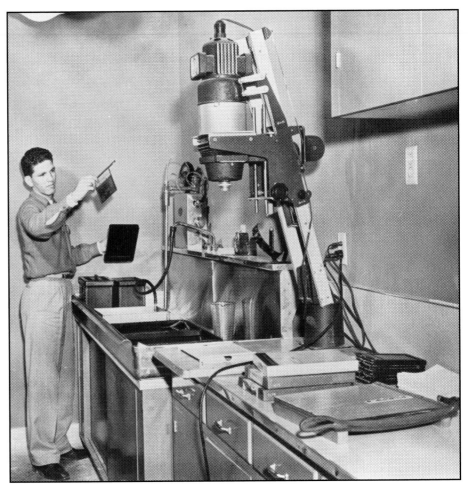

A staffer works on the perfect picture, 1950s.

the Night Editor and his assistant came back to the composing room to oversee the final make up of the front page.

The composing room was a wondrous thing to behold. It occupied the entire east end of the basement, and was ruled by an imposing six-foot-tall foreman named Slim Hays. Linotype operators (who took the paper copy and transformed it into lines of metal type known as "slugs") were typically union people. Of course, there was a love-hate relationship between the older professional men and women, and the raw, young volunteer staff.

Each page was assembled into a metal frame (galley) and when complete, a paper proof was pulled, which had to be read by *The Texan* staffer in charge. To get a head start, editors quickly learned how to mirror-read—from right to left and upside down. After correcting typos spotted at the last minute (rewriting had to be carefully negotiated) a round metal plate of each page was cast to fit on the press and the plastic halftones taped into place. This was between 1:00 A.M. and 2:00 A.M. Then everything was trucked off to the press building on Little Campus. Many nights

The Texan editor, night editor and other staffers would wait around to see the edition come off the press, then adjourn to Night Hawk on Guadalupe for more coffee and breakfast. Then to bed sometime between 4:00 A.M. and 5:00 A.M. *Texan* editors took as few classes as possible—maybe one in late morning and one or two sometime in the afternoon.

EVERYTHING BUT DULL

When Bob Kenny took office for the 1953-54 school year, he lamented that "right now, it looks like this year's *Texan* will run the grave risk of falling prey to creeping dullness, as there will be no ready-made issues."

Kenny underestimated the issues he was dealt, but recognized in his first editorial that "The balance of international relations becomes more and more precarious. . . . The McCarthy hearings will bring out points of lasting importance when the real issues are extracted from time-consuming trivia. The beginnings of a non-segregated school system will bring dramatic incidents."[31]

Kenny's year was everything but dull. The University graduated its first African-American doctoral student in June, and *The Texan* continued pushing for complete integration. UT President Logan Wilson, however, maintained the policy of only admitting African-American graduate students, and only when there were no comparable programs at state "Negro" schools.

The fight against McCarthyism continued as well. *Texan* editors and UT students were fighting to keep McCarthy himself from speaking on campus.

Kenny ran an editorial titled "Not our idea of liberty" in which he wrote, "Let the state know that McCarthy cannot be spokesman for your tradition of liberty; let the world know that McCarthy does not represent you when he speaks of strong arm tactics and shadowy accusations."[32] Kenny and Dugger took the battle a step further, leading a protest rally and circulating a petition which hundreds signed.

The Texan reported that Dugger and Kenny "proudly took a 40-foot list, of 1571 names, to the Sons of the Republic of Texas (who were sponsoring the speech) to reconsider the invitation to McCarthy."[33]

INTEGRATION, AT LAST

On August 24, 1954, it appeared the University was going to finally tear down its racial wall. *The Texan*'s banner headline read: "FIRST NEGRO UNDERGRAD TO ENTER UT THIS FALL." A young Houston woman named Marion Ford had been admitted, and was on her way. But the administration reversed its decision on September 15. President Wilson continued denying African-American undergraduates admission, arguing they had separate and equal institutions to attend—despite the Supreme Court's *Brown v. The Topeka Board of Education* decision rejecting "separate but equal" policies.

Editor Shirley Strum (1954–55) met the integration issue head on. "Desegregation must come," Strum wrote. "The main building lauds that the 'Truth shall make you free.' It does not label this truth 'for whites only.'"[34]

Strum's fight raised administrative eyebrows, as then managing editor Mike Quinn remem-

bered, "Shirley got a call from President Wilson. He told her, 'The Legislature is in town, we have major needs, and I don't want to see anything that would mess this up for us.'"

Yet in July of 1955, the UT Board of Regents declared complete integration of University enrollment, effective September 1956. The decision was too long in coming, but to its credit the University was the first major institution in the South to admit African-American undergraduates.

HUMOR AND HIJINX

As the fourth female *Texan* editor, Strum continued to reduce the endless glamour and bathing suit features from *The Texan*. Each week, it seemed, there was a new contest—whether it was Sweetheart nominations, Aquafest carnival, Varsity Queen, Most Beautiful Freshmen, Ten Most Beautiful, or UT Sweetheart. With each contest, there were ballgown, bathing suit, or portrait shots. In a biting column headed "BACHELOR OF BEAUTY," Strum lamented, "It makes one wonder why we're in the University anyway."[35]

It would take many more years, and many strong-willed women, to fully open the world of journalism. Even the J-School, Mims said, was notorious for sexist attitudes. "The really memorable time was when Paul J. Thompson (founder of the J-School) held forth on the crowning benefit a newspaper career held for young women: 'When you get married,' he told my female colleagues, 'you'll have a write-up in the newspaper as big or bigger than any society girl in town.'"

Strum, and all of the 1950s editors, were pranksters at heart. Strum put together a mock *Texan* calling for the impeachment of then-student body president and her friend Jerry Wilson, for inappropriate, outrageous behavior. "She summoned him to the composing room in the spirit of 'journalistic fairness,'" Mims said, "so he could be prepared for the week ahead. For at least an hour, Jerry knew he was a goner—never doubting the power of *The Texan*."

The Texan's sportswriters were often at the heart of the pranks. They were notorious for their bad grades, readiness to fight, and habit of storing beer in the *Texan*'s Coke machine.

The 1954 Texas-OU Weekend coverage is a unique tribute to two of *The Texan*'s most memorable troublemakers—Mike Quinn and 1955–56

Desegregation in '56 Decreed by Regents

From Heman Sweatt's initial lawsuit to Hopwood in the '90s, The Texan was on the front line of racial issues.

Negroes to Get Suitable Housing

UT's First Negroes Meet Regular Classes

Eby Predicted Segregation End

Brogan Sees Little Effect In Negro Entry

editor Willie Morris. Mims described Morris as having the peculiar talent to "take a puff of his unfiltered Pall Mall, Camel or Lucky Strike, blowing out the smoke, and immediately inhaling it back through his nose."

The October 7 front page carries their bylines, with Quinn lamenting that "most Texans can remember the last time it rained, but few can remember the last time Texas beat Oklahoma." Morris used his space to describe the exodus of UT students to Dallas for the UT–OU game, comparing it to "the pioneer rush days, when the first waves of some 8,000 brash Texans embark on a traditional weekend of society and football."[36]

Unfortunately for Quinn, Morris and 8,000 crazed fans, the Steers lost again, and Sunday's special edition masthead carried the conciliatory phrase: "It was only a game."

Both Morris and Quinn were strongly rooted sports reporters, and, according to Morris, the only two eligible to run for managing editor in the fall of 1954.

"I made a deal with Mike Quinn which may interest you," Morris recounted during a 1997 visit to *The Texan*. "It was the second semester of my junior year, 1955. Mike wanted to be appointed managing editor, but there was a problem because all of the sportswriters were on scholastic probation. None of them were eligible to be appointed sports editor because they were all flunking out and hanging out at Schultz's—except Mike and me. So I made a deal with Mike that I would be sports editor so he could be managing editor, the deal being that when I ran for editor of *The Texan* that semester, he would support me."

The agreement was a success; Willie Morris became editor for 1955–56.

MORRIS' FOCUS ON "THE REAL THINGS"

Morris spent a great deal of his year as editor fighting.

"My sophomore year," Morris said, "the Longhorns were playing the loathsome Aggies in baseball. The Aggies brought over about 3,000 of their cadets. I think it was the last game of the season and the conference championship was on the line. The Longhorns won, and a mass fistfight broke out, that I tell you lasted an hour, and extended from the baseball field, Clark Field, all

the way to the football stadium. I was a reporter and I was covering it, and some Aggie hauled off and knocked the hell out of me. . . . [when the] fistfight subsided, I ran back to *The Texan* and I remember there was blood all over my typewriter."

Morris began his editorship with the following promise: "Joseph Pulitzer once said a newspaper has no friends—to rephrase, *The Texan* has no obligations. . . . *The Daily Texan* is bigger than any one man. We will protect it and its tradition with our youth and our strength, and if necessary, with our personal reputation. You will be jostled, cajoled, embarrassed. Yet, through our telescope of ideas, you will see your life here in much nobler focus. We have been appalled by the tragic shroud which cloaks our undergraduate. This student apathy, this disregard of all save the most material, is a thing of the mid-twentieth century. If we do not kill it now, here on a thousand campuses, it will eventually kill us—an ugly cancer polluting the bloodstream of democracy."[37]

The administration forced *The Texan* to begin running the following disclaimer above its editorials, which it has run ever since: "The opinions expressed in *The Daily Texan* are those of the editor and writer of the article and not necessarily of the University administration."

Morris' first columns are marked by a call to intellectualism and calls for integration. In accordance with the regents' 1955 decree, 104 African-Americans were accepted in September of 1956. And although one barrier was down, others were rapidly created, as regents and legislators looked for ways to keep the University segregated. For example, they forbade integration of UT housing facilities and prevented African-Americans from joining University organizations.

Women were making gradual progress in both *The Texan* and in student government. On September 28, sportswriter Norma Mills became the second UT woman allowed in the Memorial Stadium press box. In that same semester, the students elected a woman, Mary Dannenbaum, as SG president. Sadly, Dannenbaum was killed in a car accident before taking office.[38]

Although the ghosts of McCarthyism still haunted the campus, Morris noted that "five years ago, the loyalty oath was the biggest campus issue. Today it is forgotten, hidden behind a dead principle and a wounded conscience."[39]

Students had other things on their minds,

Right: *Nancy McMeans, Willie Morris, and Jimmie McKinley at a* Texan *party, circa 1955.*

Below right: *Willie Morris, circa 1955.*

Below: *When the censor would not allow some editorials under editor Willie Morris to run, Morris would throw in a blank space labeled* "THIS EDITORIAL WITHHELD."

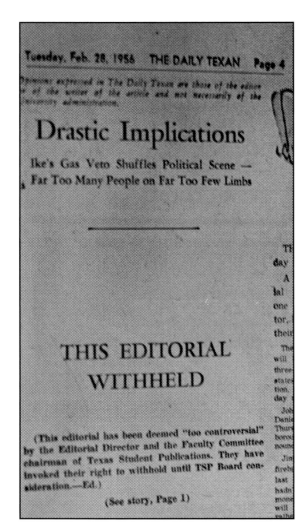

First College Daily in the South
AUSTIN, TEXAS, FRIDAY, SEPTEMBER 23, 1955

Texas in Favorite Role Against Tulane Here

First Female Will Invade UT Press Box

No, the press box elevators aren't ready yet, but the next best thing is.

Writing the Tulane game story for The Daily Texan will be Norma Mills, one of the few females with the nerve to invade the man's world of sports writing. A senior journalism student from San Antonio and a three-year veteran on the sports staff, Norma is poised and eager, but a bit nervous, on the eve of her debut into the Memorial Stadium press box.

What the attitude of her press-box colleagues will be is not known. But many resist stubbornly one of man's last strongholds, sports writing.

NORMA MILLS

Texan *staffer Norma Mills (1955) broke ground as the first female reporter allowed in the UT Press Box at football games.*

and *The Texan* obliged them with greater social coverage, including a front-page story from Yale professor Leon Greenbelt, who "declared beer to be reclassified as non-intoxicating beverage, because stomach doesn't have enough capacity to hold enough beer to cause blood alcohol level to rise to .15 percent, when 'abnormal behavior appears.'"[40] *The Texan* also covered student mischief. On November 3, UT students stole the Baylor Bruin bear cub. And on November 4 *The Texan* announced that Bevo VI had been kidnapped. "[Bevo] is described as dangerous," *The Texan* growled. The warning may have worked, as the steer was soon found wandering in a nearby pasture.[41]

Although Morris supported school spirit, he began to feel *The Texan* wasn't fulfilling the promises he had made when he assumed the editorship. In a November 11 editorial, Morris wrote, "We feel we have reneged. We have done well on the class exteriors—elections, football coverage, administration, but where have we gone from there? The real things have gone unmentioned."[42]

So, much to the regents' chagrin, Morris swiftly changed his focus to a congressional proposal known as the Fulbright-Harris Natural Gas Bill, which had rivers of corrupt Texas money and influence dripping all over it. Regent Claude Voyles said in a February 7 interview, "We feel *The*

Daily Texan is going out of bounds to discuss the Fulbright-Harris gas bill when 66 percent of Texas tax money comes from oil and gas."[43]

Morris' continuous and lengthy criticisms of the bill so irritated Texas legislators and the regents that they decided to shut Morris up. The silencing started slowly, with warnings from President Wilson, whom Morris and others knew as "the great stone face."

"He was a very cold man," Morris said. "I started getting phone calls from his secretary saying, 'Mr. Morris, Dr. Wilson would like to consult with you.' So I'd go over there, and wait the appropriate five minutes. I'd admire the lush carpet that was about six inches deep. I'd go in and he'd offer me menthol cigarettes. And very soothingly he'd say, 'Now, you people at *The Texan*, this is not your role. You shouldn't be involved in state, national and political issues.'"

But Morris didn't budge, so the regents forced the TSP to move up the editorial deadline from 5:30 P.M. to 9:00 A.M. Then, through their appointees in the Department of Journalism, they tried to set a precedent that any controversial editorial or column would have to go to the TSP board for a vote of the eleven members.[44]

The regents also empowered a journalism professor to stay with *The Texan* every night and withhold editorials until the TSP could vote.

Morris reacted by fully defying the rule in every way he could find possible. "I was 20-21, and a little scared—but we really did take our responsibility to *The Daily Texan* tradition seriously, and we simply could not contend with this. No editor worth his salt would live under a rule like this."

So Morris pressed on.

"Several times we ran blank spaces which said 'This editorial is censored.' I had to compromise with them though. They said, 'We have not censored this editorial, we just withheld it.' So in later blank spaces, we ran, 'This editorial withheld.' It was a a pretty efficacious method."

The regents then tried to silence Morris through an unconstitutional interpretation of a rider in Texas law.

"The Board of Regents itself exploded," Morris said. "It handed down an edict, quoting a rather obscure law stating that no state money could be used to improperly influence the outcome of elections. The regents used that as a kind of blanket thing to issue an edict that *The Daily Texan* could not henceforth comment on political issues or state or national issues."

Morris said, "Well, this was quite something. We had the full support of the president of the student body, Ray Farabee, and the student government attorney general came out saying this was unconstitutional."

The battle exploded in February, when, on top of withholding Morris' editorials, editorial director Harrell Lee, supervised by Dewitt C. Reddick (acting director of the School of Journalism), withheld a *New York Times* article critical of the Fulbright-Harris Bill and another of Morris' columns, which contained several paragraphs on press freedom written by Thomas Jefferson.

In defending their decision to withhold the comments, Lee said, "It is my opinion that the regents don't feel *The Texan* is being edited with the zeal which would bring favorable feelings toward the University."[45]

At a five-hour special meeting of the TSP Board, the student majority overturned the editorial manager's decision and granted Morris the power to decide the content of his editorial. The battle was not over, however, as the Board of Regents had final say in the TSP Board's actions. Regent Voyles explained that the administration was not making a big deal over this specific issue, they just wanted to "hold [the editor] to a college yell."[46]

Two days later, Morris analyzed the situation in an editorial titled: "PREROGATIVE OF DISSENT DEFENDED BY *TEXAN*."

"The issue is not how *The Texan* feels on the Fulbright-Harris Gas Bill. To believe so is to cloud reality. The issue is, should not a newspaper have the right to criticize the majority? Cannot a newspaper sometimes be an underdog?"[47]

While the administration enjoyed some success in controlling what could be printed in *The Texan*, several other papers came to Morris' aid to publicize the situation.

"I remember I got a phone call from the editor and publisher of the *Raleigh News Observer*," Morris said. "And he said, 'Brother Morris, I hear you kids at *The Texan* are having a tough time. I'll make a deal with you . . . any time they censor one of your editorials, send it to me, and I'll publish it on my editorial page,' which they did."

Morris also got help from J. Frank Dobie, who penned the now famous phrase in a letter to the editor (well-known despite the fact that the editorial manager deleted this phrase from *The Texan* after Morris had gone home to sleep): "The Board of Regents of The University of Texas are as much concerned with free intellectual enterprise as a Razorback sow would be with Keats' Ode on a Grecian Urn."

Morris also found humor an effective weapon, and famous old articles like "LET'S WATER THE PANSIES," "SCHOOL SPIRIT" and "KEEP OFF THE GRASS" blossomed on the editorial page.

The regents backed off for a while. But it came as no surprise when, in May of 1956, they sought to extend HB 140's restrictions to the faculty, limiting their ability to comment on Texas' politics.

"They extended their decree that no state

Keep Off the Grass
(A MODEL EDITORIAL)

University students this summer are faced with two problems, at least two, in which their cooperation with University landscape experts will help all persons concerned. These two problems deserve every student's careful consideration.

The first problem deals with personal, civic, and University pride. The groundkeepers of the campus are working hard to keep the grass on the campus a pretty green color. In the past, students have disregarded the walks and have walked across the grass making ugly paths, and changing the color of the grass from a beautiful green to an unsightly gray or yellow.

Now, just think: What if every student in the University walked on the grass? The campus would be terribly ugly, even when seen from the ground. But think what it would look like from an airplane! The campus would look like a bunch of cow-paths, all shoved into forty acres.

On first thought this may be silly; but it isn't. It has been said that within the next ten years everyone will be traveling by airplanes. So we must think of the future generation, then, and think of our children who may someday attend this great institution. We shall have consideration for their pride, and if above-the-campus visitors were to see the cow-paths on the campus, what would they think?

The second problem is a bit more personal. The landscape artists have found it necessary to place semi-fences—sticks and wires—on the corners of the walks. This has helped to keep the grass pretty, but it has not entirely eliminated the evils of the grass system.

Some students find it necessary to jump or step over the wires. Now each extra jump and extra step that the student might take over the wires cause strength to be used by the student's body; and overexertion could be the result.

If every student were struck by over-exertion, the hospitals might become crowded and an unheralded panic might reign.

The problems are more serious than they may at first seem, and they deserve the full and careful consideration of students, faculty members, and Regents.

money could be used to forward any kind of political agenda to include the faculty," Morris said. "It had terrifying implications . . . it could have been used to stifle everyday comment."

The decree, described by the administration as "drawing a little circle around political responsibility," was heatedly battled, especially by one young professor who would come to mean so much to the University.

"One of the professors, John Silber, stood up at a general faculty meeting and said 'that little circle happens to comprise 90 percent of my political beliefs,'" Morris said. The faculty resoundingly voted not to bend to the regents, and defeated the decree.

Morris ended his year with a full page of retrospection and pleas to current and future Longhorns to keep up the battle. Years later, he would write in *North Toward Home* that "people would tell me long afterward that this sort of thing could never happen again, in the latter climate of UT. That everything became much better, that academic freedom and freedom of expression had won, that the 1960s were not the 1950s and that at our state university, these issues would become not more straightforward, but more complex, involving the considerations of the very quality of man's society."[48]

However, Morris' battle, although an important editorial victory for the paper, would cost *The Texan*, *The Ranger*, and *The Cactus* editors their votes on the TSP Board for forty years. Even with this snag, Morris' influence on *The Texan* is a large part of why the paper is as free as it is today. He wrote:

> In 1956 the issue was a direct one, and it became larger than *The Daily Texan*, larger than the Board of Regents, larger than the University itself. I've often asked myself in the years that followed, would I do it all over again? And I would be less than honest if I answered that question simply. At the time, as I understood later, the tone, style and context of public discourse meant much more to me than the faculty considerations, of how one arranges complicated matters in feasible, flexible terms. Perhaps I could have been more subtle in dealing with the problem that confronted us—for this kind of personal diplomacy I was probably too immature and too impressionable. Yet I was 20 years old, the real antagonists were in the seats of power. It is legitimate to assume that editors of student papers at any university have a right to arouse that authorities, and within the laws of libel, to bring them down on it. It is right to be able to carry on an aggressive campaign against a matter they consider sterile and contemptuous.

> The attempt to censor *The Daily Texan* in 1956 involved not a displacement of this, but the running roughshod over it by real powers. Perhaps if the student newspaper had not chosen to meet the whole question head on, and in public, the controlling political faction of that day would have thought anything easy and possible. Perhaps we won something more than a battle after all.[49]

STILL PUSHING FOR INTEGRATION

Morris' successor, 1956–57 editor Nancy McMeans, had a full-scale racial battle on her hands, too. A young African-American woman, Barbara Smith, won a starring role in the UT Opera production of "Dido and Aeneas" in the fall of 1956. She was to star opposite a white male, but that was too much for some Texans to bear.

"Just as integration seemed to be proceeding smoothly, the rather eccentric wife of an older faculty member complained to a state legislator that UT was doing a romantic opera with a black woman and a white man in the leading roles," said 1957–58 editor Bud Mims. "The spineless fine arts dean removed Barbara from the part, or pressured her into stepping down. *The Texan* had been involved early on, at first behind the scenes. Some criticized the paper for not coming out in print sooner, and Nancy had to write a long narrative account under the banner headline, 'WHY THE *TEXAN* SAT ON THE STORY.'"

The issue caught the eye of the Texas Legislature, and State Rep. Jerry Sadler went on the record saying he voted against UT appropriations because it had "negro undergraduates." At least two other legislators sponsored bills to strengthen segregation laws. None of them passed.[50]

African-American women were still prohibited from living in the UT dormitories. Often they were kept from even visiting friends there. McMeans attacked this issue incessantly. *The Texan*'s influence in the push for total integration is acknowledged in *Overcoming: A History of Black Integration at the University of Texas at Austin*, by Almetris Marsh Duren.

The staff of *The Texan* made time for "extracurricular" publishing, according to 1956–57 col-

Top left: *Bud Mims running for* Texan *editor, 1957. At right, Carol Hudspeth, Student Assembly candidate.*

Top right: *This photo accompanied a Silver Spurs article in the 75th Anniversary special edition of* The Daily Texan. *From left: Steve Butler, Bevo's keeper; Tim Perkins, student body VP; Bud Toole,* Cactus *editor; and Bud Mims,* Texan *editor.*

Bottom left: *Bud Mims, Christmas 1957.*

Bottom right: *Nancy McMeans circa 1957-58. The photo was taken by Bud Mims for a J-School photography class.*

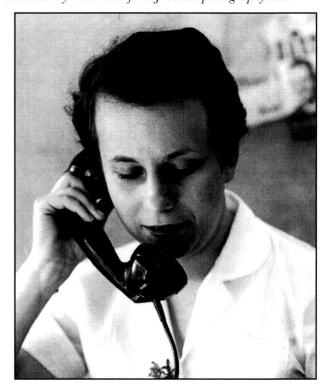

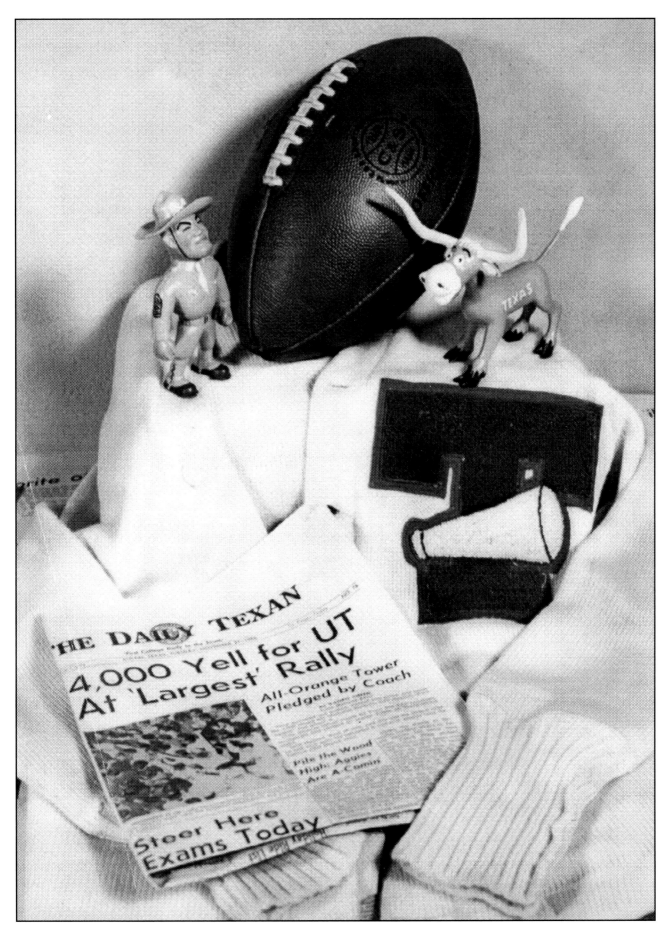

Photo assignment by Bud Mims, circa 1956–58.

umnist Jimmie McKinley. Staffers delved into *The Dilly Texanne, The Picknick Paper,* and *The Texan Hymnal.*

"There was a serious effort at writing that went beyond the requirement of journalism," McKinley said. "This was a time when other outlets for student writing were comparatively few."

The Texan Hymnal was a good-natured publication, which, according to its mission, was "published occasionally by Hall-White, Inc., Miss Wynn's Office, JB, Austin 12, Austin, Texas, Sloppywright 1955 by Hall-White, Inc. Entered as last-class matter December 21, 1955. All rights reserved, all material submitted will probably be lost." Much of the writing centered around *The Texan.* For example:

"THE YELLOW RAG OF TEXAS"

There's a Yellow Rag of Texas,
Its called the TDT
It's run by J. C. Goulden
With Help of TSP
You can talk about your *New York Times*
And *Dallas Morning News*
But the Yellow Rag of Texas
Never runs an ad on booze!

In 1957 Mims took the paper into the University's 75th anniversary, and celebrated it with the largest paper ever published by *The Texan*— 100 pages.

"The administration made an excellent year-long push to get students and student organizations to define goals and identify needs for the 25 years ahead," Mims said. "*The Texan* took the leading role in reporting regularly on this important thumb-sucking process. The birthday year ended with a three-day bash in the spring, including issues forums involving students, faculty and prominent graduate and politicians. While the goal-defining process was a good idea and produced good guidelines for the future, *The Texan* complained that the administration might have written some of the reports ahead of time, rather cynically circumventing consensus process for their own needs."

Carl Howard rounded out the 1950s, and was the decade's only appointed editor. "I probably have the greatest longevity as *Texan* editor," Howard said. "I filled out the last two months of the term of Robb Burlage, editor 1958–59, because he got too many parking tickets and went on probation. Then, by fluke, the editor elected for 1959–60 (George Runge) was forced to resign after it was revealed he hadn't legally been a full-time student when voted in." So the TSP Board appointed Howard to a full term for 1959–60.

Again, under Howard, the administration did not try to directly shape editorial content, but "President Wilson and Dean Ransom invited me pointedly to a luncheon discussion one time when I got their goat."

The story was another *Texan* push for dorm integration.

"When we learned that some of [minority] housing was run down and roach-ridden, we got a photographer down there and wrote a fairly sensational expose. This was indeed embarrassing to the administration, and resulted in further integration of facilities."

During Howard's term, a prankster borrowed *Texan* stationery and forged Howard's name on a letter to Arkansas Gov. Orville Faubus, whose "moss-backed views *The Texan* attacked regularly," Howard said. The forgery invited Faubus to speak at a major dinner on campus, and the governor's office wrote back, accepting.

"I politely straightened it out," Howard said. "And eventually they sent a copy of the forged letter, which was a curiosity I saved for a long time."

The Texan survived the 1950s, largely on the passion of young editors who were willing to face the Tower's wrath to preserve the paper's independence for future staffers.

CHAPTER 7

A Decade of Change: 1960-1970

The 1960s student body and *Daily Texan* were unlike anything before them. No wonder spunky Jo Eickmann took the helm.

"All the *Texan* offices were blue with smoke and bad language," Eickmann said. "A bulletin board outside my door enshrined the smartass remarks of the day. And on a series of bulletin boards in the outer office, Professor Olin Hinkle executed his daily commentary on what we missed, what we got right, and how we displayed it."

Eickmann, though she was the sixth female editor, still dealt with a University that required UT females to sign out of their dorms and could punish them for "unsatisfactory housekeeping" or put them on probation for breaking the 11:00 P.M. curfew. "Women wore skirts, dresses with flats or black (never brown) penny loafers and white socks. We may have been able to strip varnish with our vocabularies, but we dressed like belles," Eickmann said.

In her first editorial, Eickmann vowed to "disturb the public peace in various directions," promised the regular publication of Charles Schultz' *Peanuts,* and to fight any "gentleman's agreement" banning African-American students from participating in SWC Intercollegiate Athletics.[1]

The price of a *Summer Texan* subscription was up to $1.25, and it continued to be published as a tabloid only on Tuesdays and Fridays. The student directory, published within *The Texan,* was used as a ploy to get subscribers.[2]

Eickmann's term marked *The Texan*'s 60th anniversary. The paper celebrated by reprinting its first page, from October 8, 1900. On a national level, Texas Democrats were in high cotton, and Eickmann's staff covered Kennedy's Democratic Convention triumph. Internationally, Korea had fallen wayside to a new Red Crisis: Cuba.

"Castro went too far," Eickmann wrote in July of 1960. "In retaliation for a refusal by company officials to refine oil from the Soviet Union, he seized the $26 million Texaco refinery and snapped the straw that broke the back of United States' sympathies. This proves where Cuba's sympathies do not lie."[3]

The Texan's editorial control was again

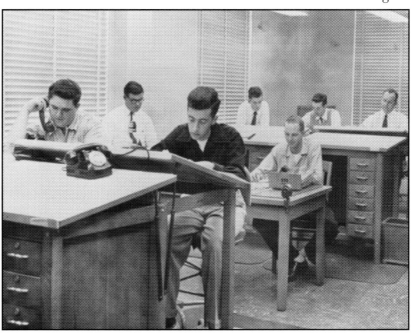

Paste-up room in the 1960s.

assaulted, this time by the TSP and 1960 Student Government president Cameron Hightower.

"There are grave *Texan* errors which especially affect student government," Hightower said. In response, editorial director Lee suggested Hightower and two other students form a watchdog committee to continue to bring *The Texan*'s shortcomings before the board.

Hightower also complained that "it is almost impossible for student government to get any news in *The Texan*." An editorial concerning his platform statements was overly slanted, Hightower said.[4]

It may have been wiser for Hightower to keep a low profile. *The Texan* later uncovered allegations of misappropriations of funds and insufficient hours at work, and Hightower resigned.

Remarkably, the Texas Senate struck the requirement of students having to sign the loyalty oath before getting scholarships, but reiterated that there would be criminal penalties for being in a communist group while on scholarship.[5]

McCarthyism still thrived. Future editor David McNeely reported that the "patriotic" John Birch Society was recruiting students to tape record lectures given by "commie" professors. The society was supposed to "tabulate subversion at the university," and it sent information on three professors to the U.S. House Un-American Activities Committee. *The Texan*, the YMCA, and the Unitarian Church also made the society's suspects list.[6]

"The McCarthy era died hard in Texas," Eickmann said. "Operation Abolition, a movie made by McCarthyites about the 'communist conspiracy,' to abolish the House UnAmerican Activities Committee, was shown to the Law school with considerable enthusiasm. *The Texan* pointed out the inaccuracies in the film and editorialized against the idea to perpetuate the idea that 'some pigs were more equal than others.' TSP was terrified by the response—a number of letters from alleged adults plaintively inquiring whether all students at UT were communists. It was my happy duty to write reasonable refrains to each letter."

THE FIGHT FOR INTEGRATION CONTINUES

The most compelling issue for Eickmann, as it would be for many editors of the '60s, was racial integration. Both on campus and off, segregated

Once Again

This is the editorial from which we cannot bar emotion.

It will have to be a personal matter. For this time, not just those abstract, rather general feelings of justice or even pity are involved.

Empathy IS.

This situation was not the type to make headlines. Even small ones.

It was the type to demand editorial consideration.

The facts are these:

Gwen Jordan returned a favor Saturday n i g h t. She agreed to sing for at least part of the evening with the Chuck Jones band, playing at the annual all-dorm dance at Kinsolving.

Miss Jordan is a Negro student.

After she had sung a few numbers, the band stopped for an intermission. During this intermission, Chuck Jones was approached by Miss Jane Greer, manager of the women's residence halls. Since the dormitories were operated on a segregated policy, and since Miss Jordan was a Negro, Miss Greer said, she would have to check with higher authorities to see whether Miss Jordan's singing in Kinsolving was permissible.

While she was checking, Jones told Miss Jordan that it would probably be better for her to leave.

★　　★

Miss Greer's check with "higher authorities" revealed that the situation was, indeed, proper within the bounds of University policy.

By then, however, Miss Jordan had already left, more than a little upset, embarrassed, humiliated.

And we must protest.

● Not this time because another "incident" has made lingering American folk ways and attitudes "look bad."

● Nor because we still disagree for moral, philosophical, and practical reasons with the University's continued policy of segregation in women's dorms.

● But because the situation was almost a natural outgrowth of a system of regulations that d a i l y reminds Negro students here that they are still not quite accepted as "first class."

● And because a fellow student, one we know and admire, was subjected to a needless humiliation for the sake of we know not what.

In 1961, editor Jo Eickmann continued her pursuit of integration by berating UT officials for removing an African-American student, Gwen Jordan, from an all-dorm dance she had volunteered to help with.

housing, facilities and organizations haunted the University. *The Texan* battled segregation from a variety of angles, with the full support of Student Government.

"There are practical reasons as well as the usual moral arguments for our hope that proprietors of those businesses which cater to at least

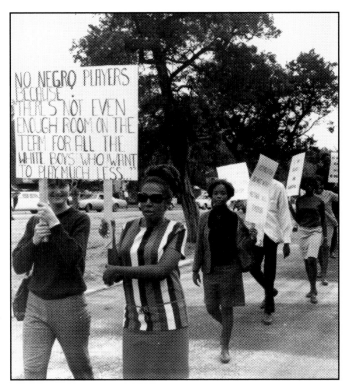

Protesting racist policies at UT.
—Center for American History,
University of Texas at Austin

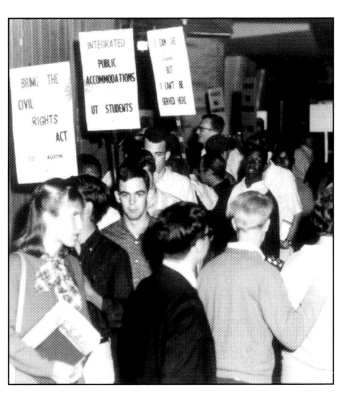

Civil rights pickets.
—Center for American History,
University of Texas at Austin

part of the public realizes the injustice of continued segregation policies," Eickmann wrote.[7]

The year 1960 was one of change for UT integration. As Duren wrote in *Overcoming,* in 1959, "the housing issue mushroomed. *The Daily Texan* investigated black housing and used pictures to illustrate that the dorms were both separate and unequal. A black male student was quoted as saying that on his dormitory application, 'They had scratched through all the white dorms and left the poorest facilities on campus.'

"The student commented that Dorm D was considered integrated, for in addition to housing blacks it housed six Mexican-Americans and one Japanese student. For the women it was a problem of quantity and quality. Whitis House and the Almetris Co-op had so many applications that some women who could not get in gave up going to the University," Duren wrote.[8]

By 1960, after petitions and protests by many African-American students, the University spent an estimated $30,000 to renovate two buildings for extra dorm space. That year was the first year there were actually more rooms than African-American applicants, Duren wrote.[9]

In April of 1961, Eickmann continued her pursuit of integration by berating University officials for removing Gwen Jordan, an African-American student, from an all-dorm dance. Jordan had signed up as a volunteer.

"The situation was almost a natural outgrowth of a system of regulations that daily remind negro students here that they are still not quite accepted as first class," Eickmann wrote.[10]

The Texan joined forces with the student body to fight segregation. In May of 1961, the Student Government presented a proposal for an integrated student body to the Board of Regents, and the UT faculty adopted the following resolution with only a few dissenting votes: "We, the faculty of The University of Texas recommend that the University proceed with racial desegregation of all its facilities and activities in the manner subscribed by the Supreme Court's language, that is, with all deliberate speed."[11]

To support this move, *The Texan* published an integration poll it had taken from 1,000 postcards mailed to students (333 of which were returned). The poll showed 53 percent of students supported equal access to university dorms.

Thirty-three percent said no, 5 percent were un-decided, and 3 percent didn't care.

The Texan also asked whether students sup-ported integrating intercollegiate sports. Seventy-four percent did, 4 percent were undecided, and 3 percent didn't care.

Even its most sensitive question, "Would you live in integrated housing?" got a response of 54 percent yes, 6 percent undecided, 38 percent no and 2 percent don't care.[12]

Off campus, businesses were also reluctant. Two Drag theaters, the Texas and the Varsity, re-fused to admit African-Americans. Students led sit-ins in front of the theaters, often sleeping for days on the Drag's cement sidewalk. Eickmann tried to address both sides of the story, but the theaters would not respond to repeated requests for interviews.

"Until the silence barrier is broken and until the theater's point of view is expressed with words other than 'no comment,' neither can *The Texan* change in the direction of completeness, its cov-erage of the stand-in demonstrations," Eickmann wrote.[13]

Even with burning issues on campus, *The Texan* kept students informed about topics such as the increasingly important space race and ten-sions abroad. The April 12, 1961, *Texan* bannered that there were "unconfirmed reports from unof-ficial sources that Moscow had sent a man into space for 6 days." The following day, *The Texan* confirmed it: "MAN IN SPACE: 'IT'S A HAPPY DAY IN RUSSIA.'" *The Texan* diligently followed the United States and Russia in the space race, and happily boasted on February 21, 1962, "HEY, ONE OF OUR BOYS MADE IT! JOHN GLENN ORBITS."

The Texan's stand on racial integration would ultimately cost it the ability to elect its editor for three years. Coupled with student body and Student Government support, *The Texan* had be-come quite a thorn in the Board of Regents' inte-gration-reluctant side. The administration did not look favorably on a March 1961 meeting where the Student Government voted 15-1 to give full censorship control to *The Texan*'s editors.[14]

The assembly's progressive stride was quickly reined in by the TSP Board. One member re-marked that "I would predict if we send a plan over to the administration for the editor to have more chance to be rash, we will have an ap-pointed editor."[15]

This accurate prediction foreshadowed a very difficult year for 1961–62 editor Hoyt Purvis.

Eickmann ended her term with *The Texan*'s traditional thirty-column editorial. "The blue swivel chair is reupholstered now," Eickmann wrote. "The still-battered Remington has a new keyboard. With blithe disregard for the irreplace-able beauty of objects time worn with well-beloved work, repairmen have changed the face of two editorial parts of *The Texan* Tradition. But for each succeeding blue swivel chair there are still the editors and typewriter. It was good to have been one of the long line of writers and dreamers to have used them."

A STRONG STEP TOWARD SILENCE

For Purvis, the battle started with his elec-tion. His race was so close that the election super-visors had to recount the ballots after announcing he had won by seventeen votes. In the waiting room, cigar still wrapped in cellophane, Purvis fretted. "I'm sorry, I just can't take it yet," he told a reporter covering the race. "I may be the editor with the shortest term of office."[16]

Once in control, however, he took on a lot. "We are not as concerned with following tradi-tions as we are establishing them," he wrote in his introductory editorial. "In recent years, campus readers have become increasingly dissatisfied with *The Texan* news columns. In fact *The Texan* has unintentionally managed to antagonize nearly every potential news source. This makes the aim of accurate and full more difficult than ever. So attempt to understand our position and help us pump in new life."[17]

The Texan reported in June of 1961 that three UT students were among fifteen nationally to train for the first Peace Corps program.

"The exciting innovation elected in last fall's campaign promise by President Kennedy is about to become a reality," Purvis wrote. "For many young Americans the Peace Corps provides the answer to Kennedy's inaugural challenge, 'Ask not what your country can do for you, but what you can do for your country.'"[18]

Despite national progress, the regents re-fused to budge on integration.

"We're not ready yet," was the regents' com-ment in a July 28 front-page story reporting they had rejected a petition to fully integrate the Uni-versity.[19]

"By advocating no substantial change, the university is choosing to regress," Purvis retorted.[20] The regents, to say the least, were not pleased with this constant criticism.

"I think we finally got under the regents' skin," Purvis said. "They had become increasingly irritated by *The Texan*—I think it was because of our civil rights stand. It was also a culmination of frustration against, and inability to control *The Texan*, but it came into prominence during our push for integration."

In October more than 6,000 UT students signed another petition, imploring the regents to reconsider. But the administration didn't even discuss the possibility. To protest, students began sit-ins, the first occurring in Kinsolving Dormitory on October 20.[21]

So it was not a surprise when on Sunday, February 4, 1962, after months of consulting with an "advisory committee" made up of administrators and professional journalists, the regents released the following statement:

"The system of electing a *Texan* editor was established when the University had a few thousand students and *The Texan* averaged four to six pages an issue. *The Texan* now has 17,000 circulation, rivals a professional daily in size and complexity, and demands almost full time work for both editor and managing editor. The appointive process provides better opportunity for selection of an editor on his professional merit."[22]

Purvis used the whole page to fight the decision, with his words and those of his predecessors.

"By making *The Texan* editorship an appointed rather than elected position, the Board of Regents took a strong step toward silencing the major voice of free expression on the campus, and certainly denied students the right to retain a voice in the selection of editors. We doubt seriously that the newspaper men of Texas, who have been given a great deal of credit for bringing about change, have more than a surface understanding of the current operation," Purvis wrote.[23]

Jim Hyatt, *The Texan*'s managing editor, wrote, "We cannot live with an appointed editor if on the TSP Board the appointment procedure stagnates into campus politics and personal grudge battles. Further criticism of *The Texan*, based on inaccuracy and misunderstanding, will be excellent ground for further control of *The Texan*."[24]

Willie Morris also wrote in: "Students should

devote themselves to the idea of a small off-campus paper. Dr. Reddick has argued that the University is larger now than when *The Texan* was set up. Following this logic, so is the U.S. Why don't we appoint our next president? Next, by this same reasoning, why don't we appoint our next sweetheart?"[25]

Realizing an appointed editor was a done deal, Purvis refocused his efforts on empowering the voice of his successor, Sam Kinch.

"It's been claimed that appointing the editor will discourage a potential editor from making outspoken contributions. That condition now exists in the Texas press, some members of which are known for their flaming timidity," Purvis wrote. "We do not at present moment believe that an appointed editor is the end of the world for *The Daily Texan*. We hope, and urge others to add their efforts to insure that appointed editors do not become the beginning of the end of *The Daily Texan*."[26]

Despite the appointment, Purvis felt safe about the future, because of Kinch's and the staff's ability. "I think if anyone had tried to compete against [Kinch] we probably would have bumped them off," Purvis said.

DESEGREGATION AND ASSASSINATION

Kinch used his introductory editorial to emphasize that *The Texan* would not lose its editorial voice under his leadership:

For 61 years now, the position I hold now was an elected one. Out of the few persons each year who were eligible, one was chosen by the student body—the one who put on the best campaign and solicited the most votes.

But things are different now. The editor of *The Daily Texan* is appointed by the student majority TSP Board of Directors. This change, formulated by the board of regents, was met by a storm of protest from those who saw it as somewhat of a subversive plot to decrease student power, or as a move toward making *The Texan* a house organ of the administration or regents.

Mine was among those protests, along with a number of *Texan* staffers because I too was worried about *Texan* editorial freedoms and the significance of student responsibility. I do not think of an appointed editor as any more or less of a free individual than an elected one would be. If at any time during the next year I feel that I am saying what I am told to say, kept from saying what I want to say, or saying what someone else has said, I will end my responsibility as editor of *The Daily Texan.*[27]

The regents' refusal to budge on integration cost them the Peace Corps in 1962, as *The Texan* reported that "A Peace Corps official said Thursday that the University's action on an integration suit filed last year by three negro students was the catalytic agent in the corps' decision not to award $257,000 training contract to the University."[28]

Another reason was the lingering all-white 40 Acres Club, located on the Drag where the current faculty dining center is housed. The establishment's owner, Buck McCullough, said he had a contract to provide for the white faculty, friends, and staff of the University, and that he would not violate that contract.

After much criticism by Kinch, his successor Dave McNeely, and the student body, McCullough reversed himself. He was promptly accused of breach of contract by a UT English professor, so McCullough returned to a segregated facility. The faculty then officially cut ties with the club.

"Dave McNeely and I must have proven that *The Texan* can be a pain in the ass no matter how the editor is chosen," Kinch said.

As in Willie Morris' days, the sportswriters were still up to no good. "We had a sports reporter who became a bit too close to the jocks and was caught, accidentally, scalping student-athlete football tickets for above market prices. Profits were shared with the football players," Kinch said. "Not only did the reporter get fired, we put the story on the front page. And when my fall managing editor resigned abruptly, allegedly taking about half the staff with him, we put that on the front page too."

Kinch steered *The Texan* away from campus issues temporarily, for good reason. In October the Cuban missile crisis escalated, as the Department of Defense threatened to sink any ships bound for Cuba and reported that reconnaissance airplanes had photographed two launchers, with missiles nearby, on the island.

But Kinch didn't let the issue go without a jab at Student Government.

"With crises facing the world and campus, *The Texan* is obligated to report the important things," he wrote. "When the students assembly shows us that it can act in a rational manner on items removed from its own self-interest, it will regain a major place in *The Texan*'s pages."[29]

Friday, January 11, marked a change in *The Texan*'s masthead, as it removed the University seal from behind "*The Daily Texan*," and changed "The First College Daily in the South" to its current title, "Student Newspaper of the University of Texas."

The 1963–64 editor, Dave McNeely, continued the fight for integration, and, as the '60s zeitgeist demanded, questioned everything.

"There are issues that have no black or white answer," McNeely wrote. "For instance, there is integration. How much integration is too much? How fast should integration proceed? Or is it proceeding too slowly? Where does one draw the line on birth control? Or drinking? Can a 19-year-old hold his booze as well as a 22-year-old? Should a 20-year-old help select the President? Will girls corrupt A&M? How many women does it take to ruin that fine institution up on the Brazos? One or one thousand? Or merely the thought of women going there?"[30]

The Texan sent managing editor Richard Cole to cover the desegregation of the University of Alabama in June of 1963, and used the historic occasion to again berate the administration for stalling.

Finally, after years of student and *Texan* protest, the last walls to total university integration fell during McNeely's term. In October of 1963, the regents gave in to integrating all UT activities, including sports—but held out on housing. Finally, after one last Kinsolving sit-in during late April, the regents decreed on May 17, 1964, that the whole University was to be integrated.

Even the 40 Acres Club relented in 1964, and opened its guest privileges to African-Americans. It was a long-awaited victory.

Two changes which directly impacted *The Texan* took place in McNeely's year: The end of cigarette ads in *The Texan*, which the paper reported would "cost $7,000 a year in advertising,"[31] and the announcement that the University planned to build a journalism school, which would have advertising, print, speech, radio and television departments.[32]

Besides integration sit-ins, the University was a rather quiet place in 1963. Student unrest, McNeely said, more often took the form of panty raids, and even they seemed to lack the gusto of years past.

"The panty raid was dreary with one compared to the one in '61, where 2,500 men chanting 'we want panties!' congregated at Kinsolving, and panties flew from women's arms like milk from cows," McNeely wrote.[33]

That lack of enthusiasm may have been partly *The Texan*'s fault.

"I always felt *Texan* staffers were responsible for instigating those raids," Purvis said. "Because they always managed to be right on the scene."

It was a great year for sports editor Bill Little. The Horns were ranked number one, after giving Oklahoma a terrific beating. To top it off, the mischievous Aggies abducted Bevo. But leave it to the Aggies—when the original kidnappers went to return the steer, they discovered it had wandered off, and had to join the search for him or face criminal charges. Little happily reported the next day that Bevo was discovered safe and sound, just looking for a home.

But it was President Kennedy's fateful Texas visit that would mark this year for McNeely and the whole *Texan* staff.

The paper did several preview stories, including a front-page boast, "3:15 Landing for Kennedy, Royal, Ransom will pass Longhorn football to JFK." *The Texan* also took the opportunity

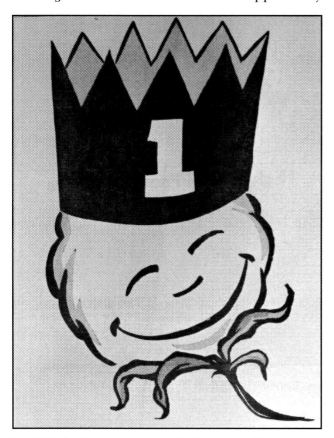

In 1963 the Longhorns were in high cotton, with a number-one ranking and a trip to the Cotton Bowl.

to highlight how politically shaky Texas was—including divisions in the Democratic Party.

Despite the shock, *The Texan* reacted immediately to Kennedy's assassination.

"Within an hour we had four reporters and a photographer on a chartered plane to Dallas. Charmayne Marsh led our coverage up there, and was comparing notes with reporters from *The New York Times* and others," McNeely said. "*The Texan* did not normally publish on Saturdays, but we had a special edition that Saturday. The front page from it is a plaque on my wall from my time as *Texan* editor."

Of the occasion, McNeely wrote: "The pall of death hangs over America. . . . The nation will go on, life will go on. Our new president is eminently capable of leading our country. We will continue our lives. But we will never forget the grief shared throughout the world yesterday when a great man was murdered."[34]

The Texan's coverage of the tragedy was outstanding. It detailed Gov. John Connally's recovery, and brought to everyone's attention that the new president's daughter, Lynda Bird Johnson, was a sophomore at the University. *The Texan* would continue to report on the first daughter's progress, including how Secret Service quarters had to be built into the Zeta house for her.

The Texan also followed Lee Harvey Oswald and Jack Ruby extensively, and McNeely progressively argued that "We deplore Jack Ruby's death sentence, as we deplore any instance in which death is the punishment for a crime."[35]

The issue of whether to elect *The Texan* editor came back up, as a student referendum passed by a 2-to-1 margin in March to reinstate the election. However, another year passed before the regents released their hold.[36]

Charmayne Marsh's year marked the fiftieth anniversary of the Journalism School, and the death of Fritz G. Lanham, *The Texan*'s first editor.

For her editorial policy, Marsh turned *The Texan*'s attention to national affairs, and began battling a TSP policy which stopped her from giving political endorsements.

"*The Daily Texan* has not taken a stand in the 1964 presidential election because it is prohibited from doing so," Marsh wrote. "According to the TSP handbook, because *The Texan* is the only newspaper published for all students of this state-supported university, the editorial columns then should neither support or oppose any such candidate for national or state office."[37]

THE DAILY TEXAN

EXTRA   EXTRA

Student Newspaper at The University of Texas

Vol. 63   Price Five Cents   AUSTIN, TEXAS, SATURDAY, NOVEMBER 23, 1963   Four Pages Today

PRESIDENT KENNEDY MURDERED; OSWALD CHARGED WITH KILLING

A Feast Fit for A President
Everything was ready for the $100 a plate dinner.

A Horrible Mockery
Gay Party Awaited Kennedy

Johnson Takes Oath of Office Before Flying to Washington

By BILL LITTLE
Texan Staff Writer

A First Lady and A New President

Prisoner Denies Slaying of JFK

Defector to Russia
A Crack Marksman

Man of Destiny Met Task With Sincerity

By JOYCE BLEEDMAN
Texan Staff Writer

THE FAMILY

SECOND SON

An Editorial

By DAVE McNEELY
Texan Editor

State Will Try JFK's Assassin

The President, the Day Before

Tension of Negro Revolution Shows in the Faces of Selma

By CHARMAYNE MARSH
Texan Editor

SELMA, Ala.—(Spl.)—"Selma is sick. It is just like a person. You know, everybody has a certain tendency to catch diseases, but they have a resistance to them. The outside agitators have brought us hate germs and they are stirring them up."

A chubby, middle-aged lay minister for the Disciples of Christ Church—Artey Crelman—spat out these bitter words Saturday afternoon. He showed the typical anger and disgust of Selma citizens at the trouble besieging the small Alabama town.

SELMA IS A CITY of more than 20,000. Its shady tree-lined streets usually are quiet, but lately they have been filled with

Four Daily Texan staff members are in Selma, Ala., to cover the voting rights march beginning Sunday. News stories and photographs will be sent back by Charmayne Marsh, Texan editor; Kaye Northcott, Texan editor-elect; Greg Lipscomb, president of the Students' Association and photographer for the trip; and Jeff Shero, Texan columnist.

the rioting of Negroes and whites and the steady patroling of state troopers.

The tension of the Negro revolution is showing in Selma and its citizens.

Clerks in stores are hostile to all who ask questions. Waitresses are suspicious and refuse to talk or do more than take customers' orders. They tolerate, but do not welcome the business of outsiders, the whites who might not be on their side.

Police refuse to give directions or to

answer questions. A Confederate flag adorns each side of their crash helmets and long billy clubs dangle from their belts as police stride around the city.

ON THE STREET CORNERS, members of the National Guard, now under federal control, with stony faces stand watch, shotguns on their shoulders.

Persistent questioners are referred to Dallas County Sheriff Jim Clark. One has to call first to get directions to his office. It may then be entered by going down an alley and to the courthouse's side door. Then, "Sheriff Clark is here," a sheriff's posse member says, not allowing anyone upstairs to Clark's office.

THE SECRETARIES and deputies milling around say no more than is necessary.

The lay minister is not afraid to stop someone who looks new on the street and offer to tell the other side.

"There are about 20,000 Negroes in Dallas County," he said, "and about 600 or '20 Negroes participating in this marching. But most of them are from out-of-town. Some are teenagers and children they (the white outsiders, members of the Southern Christian Leadership Conference, ministers) have drug out of school."

"MOST OF THOSE, helping with the march, who claim to be ministers are not."

He is pastor of both the Cambridge and Plantersville Disciples of Christ Churches. Each has a congregation of some 180 persons, he said. "I give old Gideons, you know, the Bibles. Well before all this trouble, we used to give out one to a five-year-old and a twelve-year-

old. But now they won't even let us in," he said. "Ain't that awful?"

"If they're qualified, why they can vote," he snapped.

"If they (the outsiders) had left us alone, it would have been all right."

THE SPEAKER also manufactures golf clubs at his handcraft pattern shop. "Of my 13 employes 11 are Negroes," he said. "I know 'em.

"I pay them according to what they're worth," he said. "Four days a week, ten hours a day. If they've been with me and know the business, I pay them more, but the others get minimum wages of $1.25 an hour.

"I hope you'll help tell folks the real story," he told this reporter as he climbed into his white, 1964 Cadillac.

Daily Texan *staffers were there when civil rights marchers protested in Selma, Alabama.*

"We decided to get around that by endorsing both Johnson and Goldwater," said then sports editor Paul Burka. "We couldn't find anyone to endorse Goldwater, so I wrote it. We told the students to choose who to support, and although that was deemed a violation of TSP policy, no one enforced it."

Burka contributed much to *The Texan*'s editorial voice that spring, writing on everything from Vietnam to UT football.

"I wrote an editorial against the University's use of red shirts," Burka said. "The day it came out, I had a speeding ticket to appeal. The Justice of the Peace asked me, 'Did you write this?' I said 'yes,' and without argument he said, 'Guilty!'"

Although the University was officially integrated, *The Texan* did not let up on its push for civil rights. When marchers protested in Selma, Alabama, in March of 1965, editor-elect Kaye Northcott, Marsh, *Texan* columnist Jeff Shero, and Greg Lipscomb, "Student's Association president and photographer for the trip," were there.[38]

"The tension of the negro revolution is showing in Selma and its citizens," Marsh reported. "Clerks in stores are hostile to all who ask questions. Waitresses are suspicious and refuse to talk

or do more than take customer's orders. They tolerate, but do not welcome, the business of outsiders, the whites who might not be on their side."[39]

VIETNAM COVERAGE BUILDS

As Kaye Northcott took office, the campus was plunging into a ferocious decade of Vietnam protests. "The draft, like the Eyes of Texas, is inescapable," Northcott wrote. "The once safe college student or married man can no longer rest easy, according to recent announcements from the selective service."[40]

Stories detailing bombing raids and downings of U.S. planes became frighteningly familiar on *The Texan*'s front page.

Inside, however, open-minded *Texan* viewpoints began to aggravate some students.

"*The Texan* is accused of being a communist sympathizer . . . and in other terms anti-American," Northcott wrote. "Throughout the developments in the controversy on U.S. policy in Vietnam, on both campus and world levels, *The Daily Texan* has maintained the right of spokesmen of any and all views to be heard. Unfortunately, many persons have interpreted this stand as whole-hearted support for the so-called radical liberal groups who oppose the president's stand on U.S. involvement."[41]

The Texan did not let up on its criticism of Vietnam all year under Northcott. They diligently reported when Sen. John Tower told Sigma Delta Chi that "we are no longer losing the war, but we are not winning it." Northcott continued with viewpoints about rising draft quotas, and *The Texan* reported what day and month was to start off each year's draft on the front page. Burka also actively protested through the editorial page, with columns such as "WHAT YOU DON'T KNOW, CAN HURT YOU."[42]

"Like the country, the student body (and

even the *Texan* staff) was split on the wisdom of the war," said then sports reporter Sam Keach. "After all, for many of us the next step after the University would likely be Vietnam. Fortunately, I never had to go, but a number of my fellow *Texan* staffers were drafted and served. Some died in Vietnam."

Northcott kept criticizing the war, despite pressure from the administration to stop.

"Finally, the staff's 'enormous' pay checks failed to show up," Keach recalled:

> Repeated calls to check on them brought various lame excuses about where they were. We suspected it was not so subtle pressure on us to change the editorial policy. The irony of this was it didn't bother Kaye, the person they were after.
>
> Finally, being the brave soul I was at 21 years old, I called to Frank Erwin's law office in downtown Austin to make an appointment to see him. The other staffers just laughed at me. They didn't put much stock in it, they thought I'd never get to see him. Erwin's secretary escorted me into his office and after a brief wait, as I sat down in a huge overstuffed chair, the terror of what I was about to do hit me.
>
> All he said was, "Young man, how can I help you?"
>
> I remember the horrible hollow feeling in the pit of my stomach. A chill went down my spine. I suddenly knew exactly how the Christians felt when the Romans threw them down to the Lions, or so it seemed.
>
> I explained to him that the poor working staff at *The Texan* had nothing to do with the editorial page and that all of us needed our pay checks to eat. Several of us (including me) were married and had kids.
>
> Without comment, Erwin wheeled his big leather chair around and picked up the telephone. Hell, I had no idea who he was calling or what he was doing. He dialed a number and as a person on the other end answered, he said, "Norman, [Hackerman, vice chancellor for academic affairs at the time] this is Frank. I understand these poor students who work at *The Daily Texan* can't seem to get their paychecks. Will you check into it? You know they need money so they can eat."
>
> "Anything else you need Sam?" he asked. I thanked him and quietly retreated in disbelief of what had happened. I remember stopping on the lawn of the Capitol for 15 minutes or so to collect myself. As I walked into *The Texan* offices, I was greeted by a group of students who said, "Sam, you're not going to believe this. Our checks just

showed up. We're sure glad you didn't go talk to Frank Erwin." The rest, as they say, is history.

On campus, African-American students made noticeable progress in integration during Northcott's term. In fall of 1965, Violantha Hicks became the first African-American to make the "Ten Most Beautiful" list. Farrah Fawcett was also elected that year.

On campus, the University was debating whether to tear down Memorial Stadium in order to build a new, bigger one at Balcones Research Center.

"Theo Bellmont was dead set on not tearing down Memorial Stadium," Keach said. "In the end, the stadium stayed put, and Bellmont Hall was erected with the west upper deck."

TRAGEDY AT THE TOWER

It is one man and one fateful day for which the 1966–67 *Texan*'s staff is remembered: Charles Whitman, August 1, 1966.

"We were sitting around earlier that morning thinking we need something exciting like a murder," said 1966–67 editor John Economidy, in a thirty-year commemorative issue. "We thought, we need someone to jump off the Tower."

About two hours later, Economidy said, the call came. A man was shooting a rifle from the Tower's observation deck.

"All the photographers were hiding behind the venetian blinds," Economidy said. "They wouldn't go out there. I said, 'Get off your butts and get a Pulitzer Prize.'" Economidy then ventured out himself.

"Whitman dropped one of the kids 50 yards from me," Economidy said. "Shit, I'll never forget that."

The event put *The Texan*'s reporting into the national spotlight, and brought the national press into *The Texan*'s newsroom.

"As the first shots rang out at about 11:35 A.M., curious students and faculty peered from windows and doors. Others ran outside. Those in the open, realizing what was happening, ran for cover," reported issue news editor George Kuempel. "Within minutes, at least a dozen dead and wounded lay on the campus."[43]

"Everybody remotely involved with *The Texan* came in that day and, as I remember, we were all

Smoke rises from Charles Whitman's gun during the 1966 Tower massacre.
—Center for American History, University of Texas at Austin

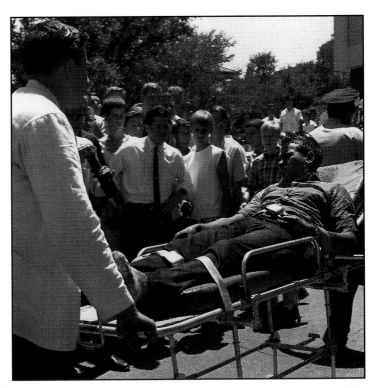

A student wounded by sniper Charles Whitman is taken to an ambulance.
—Center for American History, University of Texas at Austin

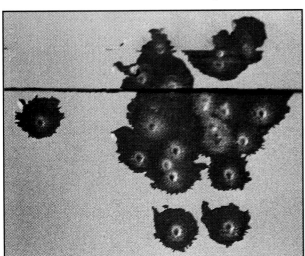

Above: *Whitman's bullets riddled surrounding buildings; some on the Tower still remain.*
—Center for American History, University of Texas at Austin

Right: *From the Tower, Charles Whitman shot and killed people as far away as Sheftall's Jewelry on the Drag.*
—Center for American History, University of Texas at Austin

Whitman's bloody body is removed from the Tower.

—Center for American History,
University of Texas at Austin

really business-like about it," said 1966 reporter James Webb in the 1996 commemorative issue.

"The reaction was very professional," said 1966 *Texan* reporter Marilyn Kuehler in the commemorative. "*The Texan* reporters who were scattered all over campus all just clicked into reporter mode. We were all trying to get into the journalism building."[44]

The Texan's coverage, an extra, was amazing. The paper became a national resource not just for sources, but for equipment. "The national press just descended on us and took over our newsroom. We helped them out and at the same time tried to do our stories too," Kuehler said.[45]

Whitman's shots left the campus numb, terrified. *The Texan* played a major role in the campus' healing, by reminding students of the bigger picture, and showing that life went on.

LET THE PROTESTS BEGIN

The long-outdated "loyalty oath" was finally dropped completely in 1967. But Texas' conserv-

ative climate thrived, as the state experimented with "Blue Laws," which forbade shoppers from buying non-essential products on Sundays. In addition, that year, reporters won the right to information, as the Freedom of Information Bill became law. On the other hand, on campus, the TSP Board passed a resolution limiting editors from appealing information withheld by the editorial manager.[46]

Mary Moody began her term as editor for 1967–68 with a call to reopen the Tower's observation deck, and on June 30, 1967, in a "fittingly quiet and dignified manner," the security guards "simply removed the sign saying it was closed."[47]

More students were avoiding the draft, as Moody wrote "the enlistment response was termed 'tremendous.' There were 1000 spots open in Texas national guard, many filled with law students . . . some are facing the end of draft exemptions and would like to get through school."[48]

The Forty Acres, by 1968, had grown to 262 acres. In an analysis predicting the future growth of the University based on 1968 construction rates, reporter Ed Ford wrote in August 1968, "It is reasonable to assume the new main building will be a four-tower structure of 50 stories. Linking this structure to campus buildings out near Airport Blvd. will be a monorail capable of 80 mph. . . . The University will, in 1990, be ready for a new memorial stadium. . . . Everyone today visualizes an "Astrodome" but by 1990 that will be an old idea. The 1990 stadium will be roofed, with a heli-port on the roof to bring spectators in. . . . The class of 1996 will have a six-year program. . . . If all this seems inhuman to you, reflect a moment on your life to date. Your grandfather grew up with the cranked telephone, his son with a dial phone and crude vending machines. Your child will come into a world more push-buttoned than ever."[49]

On campus, longhairs and sit-ins were growing.

Race relations and anti-Vietnam protests heated. The Chuck Wagon—commons area and dining hall—was the stage. Washington was the devil, the Tower was its advocate. To hell with the draft, hippies, and rednecks. Salute Black Power, and hail the Longhorns. *The Texan*'s liberal roots urged passionate reporters and editorial writers into a frenzied pace of query. *The Texan*'s pages frequently carried anti-Vietnam advertisements calling for students to protest the war, and daily accounts of U.S. retaliatory strikes or the latest Capitol Hill claims were covered.

Even food-quality protests attracted mace.

In October of 1968, editor Merry Clark supported a boycott of the Chuck Wagon and Commons, until the Texas Union Board acted on proposed improvements for the appearance and quality of the eateries' fare. Conspiracy theories that the Tower's hand was in the food to purposefully discourage students from congregating there simmered.

The Texan ran a survey for students to respond to, rating the Chuck Wagon, and demanding improvements.

And as the times required: I have smoked pot in the Chuck Wagon 1.) Frequently 2.) Infrequently 3.) Never.[50]

The Chuck Wagon protests turned violent a year later when the Union Board voted to exclude non-students. Approximately 150 students took over the establishment, screaming, "Hell no, we won't go!" and battled seventy Austin police officers who maced their way in.[51]

In October 1968, editor Merry Clark urged a boycott of the Chuck Wagon and Commons until the Texas Union Board acted on proposed improvements. This student survey asked whether students had smoked pot in the Chuck Wagon frequently, infrequently, or never.

For three hours the crowd had stood steadfast in its demands that the Chuck Wagon be open to everyone—student and non-student. But in the face of police action, many headed for the exits. During that last frantic five minutes [of negotiations] a number of women wove through the crowd passing out wet paper towels to protect against possible tear gas attacks. "Don't rub your eyes, take off your shirts and wrap them about your heads," a voice droned on the bullhorn.

While the crowd pressed toward the two glass doors of the Chuck Wagon, A contingent of twenty-five olive-helmeted Department of Public Safety officers pushed into the north entrance. An equal number of security officers filed in the East Door.

Dishes crashed to the floor as tables were overturned by fleeing demonstrators. *"Sieg Heil, Sieg Heil,"* the crowd screamed with hands raised

An Afternoon of Discussion Ends

When Riot-Equipped Police Move In

A University Tire Gets the Knife

And a Fresh Fight Breaks Out

THE DAILY TEXAN

Student Newspaper at The University of Texas at Austin

Vol. 69   Price Ten Cents   AUSTIN, TEXAS, TUESDAY, NOVEMBER 11, 1969   Twelve Pages Today   No. 67

Chuck Wagon Violence Follows Union Decision

By LYNNE FIOCKE
City Editor

More than 35 law enforcement officers swarmed into the Chuck Wagon Monday, beginning a 90-minute spree of violence in and around the Student Union Building.

Riot-equipped State police and chemical Mace to disperse large crowds in the Union during Saturday night persons, including five students, were arrested.

One woman was injured in a confrontation outside the north door of the Chuck Wagon and later treated at the Student Health Center. There were no other injuries.

Police were called in to enforce a decision by the Union board to close the Chuck Wagon at 4:15 p.m. and arrest anyone who did not have proper identification.

THE ORDER to close the Chuck Wagon came after protesters held a two-hour meeting on the restaurant to denounce a Union Board of Directors' decision, announced Friday, to exclude non-students from the Chuck Wagon.

Protesters held a noon rally in front of the Union and at 1:30 p.m. marched on the Chuck Wagon. Students who were checking identification at the doors of the Chuck Wagon had been warned by management to offer no resistance. Approximately 60 protesters entered the facility with a bullhorn and remained until police arrived at 4:15 p.m.

Union Board President Steve Van told the crowd at 2:30 p.m. that the Chuck Wagon would be closed at 4:15 and persons without proper identification would be arrested. He urged protesters to move to the Main Ballroom of the Union for further discussion.

"Hell no, we won't go," they retorted. After the announcement, Van and student government representatives left for the Main Ballroom to discuss the situation.

FOR 25 minutes spirited discussion on whether to leave or stay filled the room. Speakers competed for the bullhorn while trying to sway protesters.

About 150 persons were in the room at

4:15 p.m. when Assistant University Security Chief W. L. Payne told the crowd that "the doors will be closed. Anyone in here at 4:15 will be arrested, the time officials can't be an excuse. Everyone who remains will be arrested."

Most persons stayed for such as several students and non-students urged the crowd to leave.

At 4:15 p.m., more than 50 Department of Public Safety patrolmen and Austin police were outside the Union. At that time approximately 35 policemen moved into the Chuck Wagon with riot helmets, Mace and nightsticks.

Mace Used on Protesters

By KAREN ELLIOTT
Managing Editor

Curious students packed the halls surrounding the Chuck Wagon Monday afternoon. Time was running out for a roomful of protesters inside.

Hundreds squatted against walls, sprawled on the floor and sat around tables as they nervously cast glances at the growing number of campus security guards and the clock on the wall.

"TIME is drawing close. You have only five minutes," W. L. Payne, assistant chief of campus traffic and security, announced. Anyone in here when the doors are locked at 4:15 will be arrested, regardless of whether he is a student or not.

For three hours the crowd had stood steadfast in its demands that the Chuck Wagon could be open, to everyone — students and non-students. But the force of police action, measured on the walls, a bullhorn passed quickly from one leader to another.

SOME URGED the crowd to go upstairs and meet with the Union Board of Directors. Others urged that the protesters keep sound and maintain their demand for unlimited use of Chuck Wagon facilities.

During the last frantic five minutes, a number of scenes eased through the crowd passing out new paper towels to protect against possible tear gas attacks.

"Don't rub your eyes, take off your shirts and wrap them about your hands," a voice droned over the bullhorn.

"Will that really work?" one woman reporter asked. Most of the persons gathered behind the Chuck Wagon ice cream counter as the deadline drew near.

WHILE THE CROWD pressed toward the two glass doors of the Chuck Wagon, a contingent of 35 olive-helmeted Department of Public Safety officers pushed in-

BY THE time they entered, only a small group of students remained. The officers formed a semicircle in front of the group and began to force them back.

Ernie Haywood, Students' Association vice-president, and several students asked for a few more minutes to persuade students to leave.

The officers continued to push the students back through the east door. The students surged back into the Chuck Wagon and officers pushed at them and forced the group out the door.

Haywood was grabbed by highway patrolmen and thrown on a table. Officers

were about to put handcuffs on him when several reporters told them Haywood is the Students' Association Vice-President. He was released.

THE PUSHING battle between students and officers finally broke the east door.

At the north door in the Chuck Wagon another pushing battle developed. When the crowd refused to disperse, an officer sprayed Mace. Students fled away covering their eyes.

Outside, students gathered around the trucks serving as paddy wagons. Police formed a circle around the trucks.

(See VIOLENCE, Page 3.)

8 Arrested At Protest

Eight persons — five of them University students — were arrested Monday and charged with disorderly conduct. Four also were charged with aggravated assault on a police officer.

The charges resulted from arrests near the Chuck Wagon and Union Building during a late afternoon demonstration.

Nonstudents Paul G. Spencer, 24, of 2206 Guadalupe St. and Albert A. Camino, 17, 404 W. 33rd St., were charged before Justice of the Peace Bob Kuhn with aggravated assault on a police officer. At the time of his arrest, Spencer was free on bond on charges of assault on a police officer and disturbing the peace filed Saturday.

Kuhn set bond for $500 for Spencer.

Spencer was charged Saturday after he was arrested for refusing to leave the Chuck Wagon when vice-president for student affairs, Dr. Bryce Jordan, asked him repeatedly to leave.

Charged before Corporation Court Judge Ronald Earle with aggravated assault on a police officer were University students James C. Sparks, 19, of 1607-A Nueces St. and Gregory Scott Miller, 19, of 2323 San Antonio St. Earle set bond of $500 on each.

Charged before Kuhn with disorderly conduct were University students William Bryan Tummings, 22, of 1401 Winsted Lane, and Michael Huntly Koch, 20, of 1902 University Ave.

Charged before Earle with disorderly conduct were student William Paul Meacham, 20, of 2307 Longview St., Sparks and Miller. Also charged were John Willis McGee, 20, of 709 W. 14th St., Spencer and Camino.

Police officials said late Monday that Meacham, Spencer, Camino and McGee remained in City Jail. Sparks and Miller were released on bond.

Travis County Jail officials said Tummings and Koch had also been released on bond.

Weather:
• Partly Cloudy
• High: Low 80's
• Low: Low 60's

Union Board Statement

When the board assumed responsibility in June for the Chuck Wagon, it began to study what responses could be made to the problems of overcrowding, drug abuse, and use by juveniles. On July 16, the board stated that use of Union facilities was intended for students, faculty, staff and their guests. Guests were defined at that time as follows:

An invited guest shall be an individual who is invited by:

(1) A Union member for a specific purpose under the jurisdiction of the Union;

(2) By the University for conferences, special functions, tours, or official visits; or

(3) By an approved student organization to sponsor Union programs.

To qualify as a guest of a member, the individual must be accompanied by the member while using the building. The use of the Union by a guest shall be limited to the specific occasion for which he is invited, and is not to be interpreted to include regular and repeated use of the facilities. Guests are subject to the same rules and regulations governing the use of the Texas Union as are members of the Union.

From that time until last Thursday, Nov. 6, we have continued to work on the problem. On that day, two plainclothesmen were assaulted in an attempt to take into custody an 11-year-old girl. On Friday, Nov. 7, Dist. Atty. Bob Smith indicated he intended to request a grand jury investigation of activities in the Chuck Wagon. A subsequent conversation with Mr. Smith indicated considerable factual data supporting charges of drug abuse in the Chuck Wagon and its use as a sanctuary for juvenile runaways.

On Friday evening, the board met to

consider these events and with a desire to see if the board, composed of six students and three faculty, could not pre-empt outside action and resolve this problem on its own. At that time, the board decided to limit the Chuck Wagon's use to students, faculty, staff and their families for a two-week period. This would remove control of the problem to the board and give the board sufficient time to develop a long range solution.

On Saturday, one non-student's refusal to leave this ruling resulted in a disruption sufficient to force the board to close the facilities for the day.

Monday, the board re-opened the facility. There were no problems until early afternoon when a group of individuals forced the entranceway. The resulting confrontation forced the closing of the Chuck Wagon for the second time.

In light of yesterday's events, the board takes the following position: (1) It is important to note that in regard to these events and this decision, no pressure was placed on the board by the University administration in any form.)

1. Funds is responsibility for yesterday's actions due to a necessity inside the circumstances to adequately communicate with the society personnel.

2. Requests that, due to honest misunderstanding of varying statements, charges against the University students arrested in the Chuck Wagon and in the Union be dropped.

3. Close the Chuck Wagon for necessary repairs and pending the results of the student referendum on Friday, Nov. 15.

4. The Texas Union will assume financial responsibility for those Union employees affected by this temporary closing.

NINETY PERCENT of the people in Austin feel we have been pushed too long. When juvenile officers can't come in the Chuck Wagon and pick up an 11-year-old girl without pulling guns for protection, something needs to be done," Smith said.

Smith referred to the mobbing of two Austin city detectives who removed an 11-year-old runaway girl from the Chuck Wagon Thursday afternoon.

Police and protesters engaged in a tug-of-war over one woman, whom officers were attempting to load into the truck. During the battle, she escaped but several of her rescuers were arrested.

A battle crushed into the truck, and officers, taunted by profane jeering, unstrapped their billy clubs and charged into the crowd.

One long-haired protester was swung to the ground by his hair. Cringing against the truck he pleaded, "Don't arrest me I'm on probation."

OFFICERS carried him into the walking truck, where he was pushed to the rear and handcuffed to the seat itself.

The first truck, whose three had been slashed, pulled slowly into the street, crowded on either side by demonstrators and curious onlookers. It went north on Guadalupe.

As the second truck followed minutes later, the crowd began to dissipate. Many followed as it turned east on 24th street. Before it cleared St. Peter's Gate, another protester was arrested after a struggle near the historic Battle Oaks.

The Chuck Wagon looked like a battlefield, strewn with broken glass, overturned tables, scattered dishes and spilled liquids.

WALKING THROUGH the debris was Capt. K. B. Hallmark, a 22-year veteran with the DPS.

His men sat quietly in chairs while Chuck Wagon employes cleared glass and other litter. Dist. Atty. Smith leaned against the wall and puffed a cigar as workmen nailed boards across Chuck Wagon entrances.

"This is the worst incident I have been involved in," Hallmark said. "My son goes to school here and I hate it any time we have to deal with students".

Referendum Due Friday

A campus referendum on the controversial non-student use of the Chuck Wagon has been set for Friday.

Lynn Malone, chairman of the Student Assembly Election Commission, said Monday that because of the antiwar moratorium there would be many students who were from campus Friday.

Absentee balloting will take place from 1 to 4 p.m. Wednesday and from noon to 1:30 p.m. and 1 to 4 p.m. Thursday in the Alpha Phi Omega office in Union Building, 307.

"We anticipate won't have the printed ballots ready and the absentee voters will have to write-in, Malone said.

Poll workers should report and follow their assignments that were originally scheduled for next Wednesday, Malone said. Any questions or conflicts may be relayed through the APO office prior to Thursday.

The referendum was called after the last clash erupted Monday in the restaurant when non-students marched into the Chuck Wagon and refused to leave.

A planned referendum on whether Frank C. Erwin Jr. should continue as chairman of the Board of Regents has been postponed indefinitely.

The Senate referendum had been scheduled for Wednesday. It has been postponed to allow more time for the campus to read.

in a Nazi Salute. "Sooey Pig, Oink Oink!" some shouted.

As DPS officials struggled to lock the doors, the crowd began to surge in, throwing ball point pens and kicking at officers. A stream of mace drove them back against the wall and into the Union Courtyard. But as patrolmen secured the door, a rock crashed through, splintering glass to the floor and into one officer's eyes.

Ultimately, eight students were arrested and one injured in the ensuing violence. It was a hint of things to come.[52]

ON THE MOON AND UP THE TREES

Mark Morrison, editor for 1969, had to grow up fast. Man landed on the moon (for which occasion class was canceled). Erwin cut down Waller Creek trees. U.S. soldiers killed U.S. college students. The Longhorns won another national championship. And student control of *The Texan* was again under attack.

It was one of the most demanding years for *The Texan* staff and resources. Students were in the difficult position of avoiding the draft, but knowing another young man would have to take their place.

"When a man 'wins' his fight against the draft," wrote *Texan* columnist Maurice Bourne, "the loser is not the army, government, bureaucracy, establishment etc. The loser is another young man who was not quite so clever at discovering loopholes and was drafted as an alternate."[53]

Although Nixon gave students some hope by setting a 1970 deadline to pull 100,000 troops from Vietnam, reality set in when in December of 1969, lottery numbers came back up. All young men under nineteen born on September 14 were the first called to duty.

The Texan's attackers were not the administration this time, but the Student Government. Five members of the nine-member board voted to limit *Texan* advertising to student housing, and to put that advertising in the hands of the newly created Student Government's Fair Housing Committee. It would have been a fatal blow.

This time, it was Erwin who came to *The Texan*'s aid, in August of 1969, by voicing his disagreement with who had made the decision, not necessarily the decision itself. "I think it is a mistake for officers of the student's association to be on the TSP board, and I have consistently voted to restrict that control," Erwin said.[54]

The Forty Acres and the nation held their breath for Neil Armstrong, and the University canceled classes Monday, July 21, in anticipation of his famous walk.

"Somehow the words 'fantastic,' 'tremendous' and 'great' were inadequate to describe the feeling of the historic moment—but they had to suffice," Morrison wrote.[55]

The year continued its intoxicating mixture of glory and principle when enraged students threw themselves in front of bulldozers. They were trying to stop Frank Erwin from yanking the Waller Creek trees so that he could expand the football stadium.

Erwin, neither inspired nor amused, ordered

The year 1969 continued its intoxicating mixture of glory and principle when enraged students threw themselves in front of bulldozers. They were trying to stop Frank Erwin from yanking up Waller Creek trees so that the football stadium could be expanded. "Arrest all the people you have to," Erwin ordered the police.

When 250,000 Americans gathered in protest of the
Vietnam War in 1969 at the Washington Monument,
Texan *writers John Watkins, Lynn Flocke, and
Carolyn Hinckley were there.*

the police to arrest the students and the workmen to continue. So students took to the trees. Associate news editor Patsy Guenzel and reporter Ruth Doyle covered the spectacle.

"You can't build the stadium addition without the trees coming down," Erwin said. "We spent 18 months studying how to keep the damage to a minimum. If you move the stadium west, you have to move the street west, and the trees have to go.

"Arrest all the people you have to," Erwin continued. "Once these trees are down, there won't be anything to protest."

But "while state city and campus police prepared to remove the demonstrators, they climbed higher in the trees," Guenzel reported.[56]

The trees—and students—lost, but already deeply rooted anger against the administration grew.

"Now all the trees are torn down," Morrison wrote. "A small patch of trees resulted in twenty-seven arrests and embarrassing publicity for The University—because Frank Erwin had to run the show his way. His way was fantastically inept. . . . The days of the University being accurately referred to as Frank Erwin's University must come to an end. It is time for power to be given to the Institution's administrators, faculty members and students, where it belongs."[57]

More campus upheaval followed. All over the country, students and professors had begun protesting U.S. involvement in Cambodia and Laos with teach-ins, class boycotts, and speeches. On October 15, 1969, the nation organized a moratorium on teaching to protest the war. Instead, UT students attended outdoor rallies, and about 12,000 of them marched on the State Capitol.

Former *Texan* editor Ronnie Dugger, then editor at-large of *The Texas Observer*, addressed the crowd: "We are a people of love and peace. We come together today in mourning, in shame and in resolve that the United States shall withdraw from Vietnam. On Monday, President Nixon said, 'There is nothing new we can learn from these demonstrations.' President Johnson thought that too, and he is no longer president."[58]

The Students' Association president then brought 4,500 students to their feet saying, "Our presence here today is a statement to this nation, this state and this university that we have the right and duty to integrally question the course of this nation. The war is not a question of what will hap-

pen to our prestige if we pull out. What is at rock bottom can't go lower."

One month later, 250,000 Americans gathered in protest at the Washington Monument. *Texan* writers John Watkins, Lynne Flocke, and Carolyn Hinckley were there.

"The massive throng, covering a route along Pennsylvania and Constitution avenues, lined with Washington police maintained an almost eerie silence throughout the March," Watkins and Hinckley reported. "Protesters became quite vocal when the march passed the Department of Justice building, a scene of violence later in the afternoon and a protest against the 'Chicago Seven' conspiracy trial."[59]

Then came Kent State, May 4, 1970.

The Texan put the National Guardsmen student massacre on the front page and opened its pages to the swelling student upheaval.

Despite pleas from the students and faculty to close the school in honor of the deaths, the administration refused.

"This is a declaration of war," Morrison wrote in a bannered viewpoint spreading over half the editorial page.[60]

To smart the wound, the Austin City Council refused to give a parade permit to protesting students, and Gov. Preston Smith threatened to call out the National Guard if students defied the decision.

That night, hundreds of students rallied in the Main Mall. Morrison wrote that "many students feared violence, but were prepared to take dangerous action in the wake of Thursday's developments.

"Marchers, if they are to prevent violence, must exercise extreme caution," Morrison warned. "All indications are that troops will be more than prepared to deal with any kind of disruption. Not one thing will be gained if death mars Friday's March. It's up to those who march to assure tranquility; regents and city councilmen seem to have taken every step to assure violence."[61]

The Texan dedicated its entire front page to the next day's chaos. *Texan* associate news editor Cliff Avery wrote:

Then there they were. About 20 police, helmeted and with clubs, an imposing threat a block ahead. The leaders of the march mobilized and made a flanking movement, circling around the police, running hard. Up Lavaca. Again, the

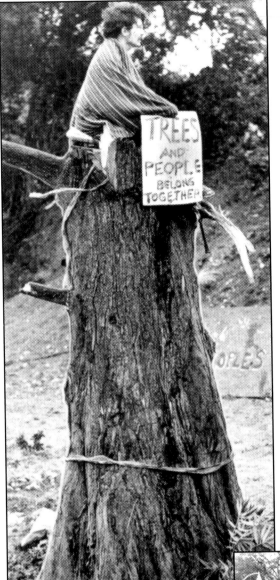

police. Another run around the block. Finally a go-for-broke assault and across 15th street en masse to the Capitol grounds . . . success . . . for a moment.

Confusion. The leaders tried to force the crowd to go around the Capitol, but some still went inside. Office workers and high school ROTC tourists lined the second floor balcony. "Lackey!" one cried.

Then singing a song of peace they drifted to the curb and sat at the feet of the gas masks. A scuffle. Tear gas. Eyes were no longer clear. In the bright afternoon sun, the blue uniforms moved up the green of the lawn, sometimes engulfed by the billowing grey gas they sent up in front of them, and battling the canisters that were unceremoniously tossed back.

Forcing students back to campus, police kept watch with gas and bayonets, until finally the two opposing forces turned their separate ways toward home. For the students this meant another mini confrontation, over the flag at the ROTC building. They lowered it to half mast but campus police re-raised it and stood guard. Then the protesters, weary with the sting of tear gas and spring heat, went for a playful romp in the East Mall fountain. Many swam, many watched and many simply sat and with somewhat glazed expressions mulled over the day's events in their minds.[62]

Above: *Student attempting to save trees from destruction.*
—Center for American History,
University of Texas at Austin

Right: *A fight for the trees which were up for sacrifice near Memorial Stadium.*
—Center for American History,
University of Texas at Austin

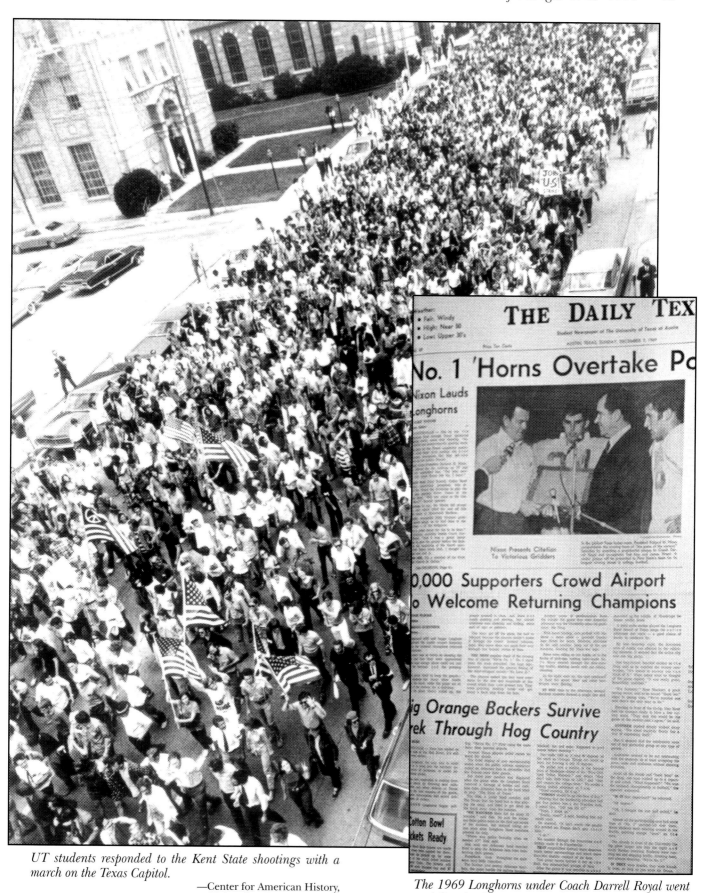

UT students responded to the Kent State shootings with a march on the Texas Capitol.

—Center for American History,
University of Texas at Austin

The 1969 Longhorns under Coach Darrell Royal went undefeated to become National Champions.

THE DAILY TEXAN

Student Newspaper at The University of Texas at Austin

Please Recycle This Newspaper   Austin, Texas, Monday, March 18, 1974   Ten Cents   Sixteen Pages

'We do not fund anything that
we don't control.'

—University System Regent Frank C. Erwin,
March 16, 1972

(See Story, Page 2.)

CHAPTER 8

The Power of the Press Emerges: 1970–1980

The Texan was evolving as technology developed. The paper expanded to three issues in the summer, published Tuesdays, Thursdays, and Fridays.

To explain their daily responsibilities to the student body, the *Texan* printed a full-page story in November of 1970 titled, "*THE DAILY TEXAN*, NO SMALL OPERATION."

"Before *Texans* are deposited at dormitory and apartment doors, at about the same time the milkmen are making their deliveries, many cups of coffee are consumed, wastebaskets filled with crumpled and rejected story leads, and many frustrated attempts made to get a tight-lipped administrator to make a statement. . . . According to TSP Business Manager Loyd Edmonds, the paid news staff will receive salaries amounting to more than $29,000 this year. Pay ranges from $40 a month for copy editors working one night a week to $285 a month for the editor."[1]

Some things never change. As it does now, *The Texan* used about forty tons of paper each month.

Frank Erwin, perhaps best remembered for his orange-and-white Cadillac, was 1970-71 editor Andy Yemma's nemesis, and vice-versa.

Yemma started his term defending students from one of Erwin's many attempts to limit students' speech. Erwin decided the University was through with sponsoring "subversive" speech, and, in response to a series of anti-war gatherings by the Young Socialists Alliance in the Texas Union, Erwin announced that the University would limit the number of non-students to three who attended on-campus meetings. The meet-

ings, which were organized with help from the Students' Association, Erwin criticized as "labeled as classes in Socialism, when in fact they were classes in Communism." Further, Erwin threatened to remove Students' Association funding if they continued the sponsorship.[2]

"I wanted to put the Students' Association on fair notice," Erwin said, "that if they continue to spend this money on these wild-eyed schemes they have in the past, one year from now I will be serious about my amendment."[3]

Yemma wrote in response, "The above rule, . . . ranks (In order) 1.) unconstitutional 2.) discriminatory 3.) ambiguous 4.) absurd. In a day when the so-called silent majority is supposedly crying for strict interpretation of the Constitution, it is sad paradox to see such blatant violation of First Amendment guarantees of free speech and assembly . . . the real intent is clear—to make sure University facilities are not used to express ideas contrary to those the Regents approve."[4]

A student committee was formed specifically to protest the rule, and *The Texan* carried guest columns from members of the Socialists Alliance and others attacking the decision.

The situation intensified as *The Texan* reported that an "alleged wire-tapping device" had been discovered in the Union Ballroom. *Texan* reporter Cliff Avery wrote, "The alleged eavesdropping device is a wire that runs from an input jack of the room's public address system to a telephone circuit box in a storeroom at the end of the room."[5]

It took the regents a few days to see the likely constitutional challenge of their actions—but they

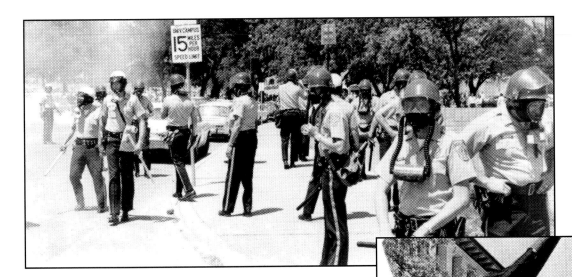

UT Police in riot gear.
—Center for American History,
University of Texas at Austin

Demonstration in the wake of Kent State.
—Center for American History,
University of Texas at Austin

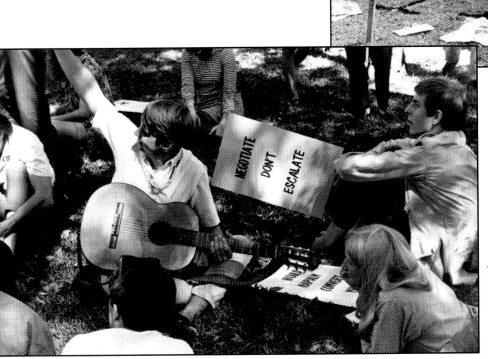

Texan *associate news editor
Cliff Avery said, "It's hard
for people to remember that
young men could actually be
conscripted into the Armed
Forces against their will."*
—Center for American History,
University of Texas at Austin

only gave an inch. At a special meeting, they voted to repeal the rule for meetings on University grounds, saying "it would be unfair to require an organization to be responsible for an audience outdoors where passersby could walk up to the edge and listen," Erwin said.[6] On the other hand, Erwin and the board then looked into ways of enforcing the three-student attendance in University buildings, including canceling memberships of organizations which violated the rule.

Yemma examined Erwin's boardroom tactics. "For awhile it was questionable whether the remainder of the regents had been simultaneously struck dumb by Erwin's flawless logic or were so confident with his arguments that they found it unnecessary to vocally support the omnipotent chairman," Yemma wrote. "As for the unsuspecting opponents of the Regents' rule, it was a clear case of diminishing returns. The quick-witted Erwin sank each speaker's arguments with the intensity of a fiery flotilla. But the classic example of Erwin's keen mind came in reply to a possible test suit against the rule by the Young Socialists Alliance.

"'I'd just as soon as be sued by a Marxist as anybody I know,' he chortled with a boyish grin. Maybe it's such charm that persuades the rest of the board to love him so."[7]

THE EXODUS

Erwin's actions led to a huge faculty bloodletting, referred to as a "general reorganization in the University System."[8] By July, not only had Harry Ransom resigned as chancellor, but so had John McKetta, executive vice-chancellor for academic affairs; Gardner Lindzey, vice-president for academic affairs and professor of psychology; William Livingston, vice-chancellor for academic programs and professor of government; professor of philosophy William Arrowsmith; and Norman Hackerman, former UT president and professor of chemistry.

"It took UT years, if not decades, to recover from the academic damage inflicted by Erwin and his lackeys," Yemma said. "We tried to promote Page Keeton, dean of the law school and a progressive free-thinker, for the UT-Austin presidency, but our endorsement of him might have cost him the position in retrospect (if he ever had a fair chance). We raised a big enough stink that

Erwin got the Regents to stop us from sending free copies of *The Texan* to state legislators, but we raised funds privately to keep *The Texan*s going."

The exodus resulted from the proposed reorganization of the College of Arts and Sciences. UT faculty had one vision for the department, and Erwin had another.

The reorganization, known as "The Watt Committee report," Yemma wrote, was met with "a great deal of hostility from the majority of the faculty in A&S."[9] The report plotted the division of Arts and Sciences into 1.) Faculty of Letters, 2.) Faculty of Social Sciences, 3.) Faculty of Earth and Life Sciences, 4.) Faculty of Physical Sciences.[10] The report stated that the division was necessary to facilitate effective administration and promote the broad liberal arts character of the degree programs of the college—i.e., greater administrative control over the academic content of those departments. Arts and Sciences Dean John Silber led active criticism of Erwin's plan, a decision which eventually cost him his position.

In addition to such challenges, on July 9 Yemma reported that Charles LeMaistre was to be the University's next chancellor. "When the Board of Regents announces its slate of appointments in the 're-organized' university system administration Friday," Yemma wrote, "it will become apparent that Chairman Erwin is quite sure the day of the professional administrator is upon us. . . . There's no question that some of the changes are for the better . . . but the overall impact of this organization all too closely resembles what the chairman had in mind in calling for a new kind of administrator. Placing a non-academic in such a powerful and influential post as the new deputy chancellor for administration will hold an unpardonable offense against the basic concepts of academic freedom. And academic freedom is what this university is supposed to be about, ISN'T IT?"[11]

Dave Helfert, a *Texan* columnist, wryly suggested a solution to several problems facing the University administration: "Regents Chair Frank C. Erwin should simply assume all the powers in the system in name as well as in fact. He should dispense with the bothersome myriad levels of bureaucracy which clog and impede his every attempt to improve the University as he sees fit. A campaign of dissolving such figure head offices as chancellor, president and all those deans would streamline the system, making it easier to enlarge

The "reorganization" of the College of Arts and Sciences sparked intense coverage in The Texan, *especially when Dean John Silber (above) was asked to resign.*

stadiums, repulse marxists and do other things that help the students."[12]

Finally, Erwin had had enough of Silber and the faculty's criticisms. So, through UT ad-interim president Bryce Jordan, he fired Silber.

"John, you are very intelligent, articulate and hardworking. Because of these qualities you make some people in higher education nervous. That is why you must resign or be removed," Erwin said.[13]

The Texan responded with a front-page above-the-masthead editorial denouncing the move. *The Texan* implored the regents to reconsider:

"Now, with one of the last independent voices removed from the scene, Erwin holds an even stiffer reign of terror over the administrators of this university . . . there is one issue, however, on which Erwin cannot be disputed—that John Silber is the most intelligent, articulate hard working man in the campus. *The Texan* therefore appeals to the better judgement of the eight remaining board members to repudiate the efforts of a political hack to destroy a great university as a center for liberal arts education."[14]

Silber countered by saying he had no intention to resign, and urged his fellow faculty not to give in either. *The Texan* responded by starting a petition not only to reinstate Silber, but to reject LeMaistre's proposal to separate the Arts and Sciences College.

One of the more humorous responses to Silber's firing came in the form of a biting parody of the situation written by Yemma and titled "STALLION'S FALL FROM TOWER UNEXPLAINED":

> Reactions were mixed Wednesday, as the news spread across campus that a 900-pound black stallion had fallen from the observation deck of the University Main Building. The nearly tragic event occurred mid-morning, luckily most students were in class.
>
> Asked about what the horse was doing above the 300 foot tower, interim president Bryce Jordan replied, "you'll have to ask Mr. Erwin about that."
>
> Contacted late Wednesday night by *The Texan* staff in the 40 acres club, Erwin refused to comment.
>
> "I've been misquoted by *The Texan* so many times recently, if you want a quote out of me you can write down your question and give it to Mike Quinn, and he'll get an answer out of me. Quinn however, is out of town for two weeks on vacation."
>
> LeMaistre, when asked for comment,

responded, "I'd rather you get that information from President Jordan or the veterinarian performing the autopsy."

> The veterinarian, who wished to remain anonymous, told *The Texan* he could not comment unless he had the permission of the Board of Regents.

> The report included a "Bulletin" reporting that: "Contacted at his stonewall ranch early Thursday morning, former President Lyndon Johnson confirmed that the horse which fell from the Tower Wednesday morning fit the description of a stallion missing from his ranch.

> "'I don't know what Frank knows about this,' Johnson said. 'But if it turns out to be my horse, he has some explaining to do!!'"[15]

The Arts and Sciences spectacle ended with the college divided into three separate sections, with a provost instead of a dean. Silber eventually left UT for Boston University.

THE BAUER HOUSE CONTROVERSY

Even though the regents loosened their hold of student meetings in September of 1970, they couldn't resist tampering with Texas' Open Meetings Laws.

Over an unposted, informal telephone vote in November, the regents decided to keep the Chuck Wagon closed to non-students, despite a student referendum to open it back up. *The Texan* learned of their vote, and front-page articles incited loud student protest.[16]

"The board's secret telephone meeting may have been illegal," Yemma wrote. "It was irresponsible to take this action without the benefit of a hearing on the issue."[17]

The regents squirmed, justifying their telephone conversation as "not really a vote" since the issue had been decided previously. However, they were unnerved enough to hold an emergency meeting to decide if they should vote on whether they could waive the law which forces them to post written notice of emergency meetings five days beforehand and re-vote on the Chuck Wagon. Predictably, they affirmed their earlier "non-vote."[18] The meeting was held during half-time of the UT-TCU football game in Fort Worth's Daniel Meyer Coliseum.

"The decision is akin to the proverbial burglar going back to ring the doorbell after he's

caught robbing the house," Yemma wrote in a response titled "MORE EFFLUVIA FOR CESSPOOL."[19]

The Texan was about to endure a major restructuring, as its fifty-year charter would expire in 1971. It was a dangerous time, since Erwin wanted nothing more than to kick the paper off campus. LeMaistre was to lead a board of newspaper editors and publishers, who were already suggesting that *The Texan* become more of a journalism lab, or that UT fund a second paper to compete directly with *The Texan*. Knowing Erwin's guiding hand was behind all the subtle improvement suggestions, *The Texan* opposed any major changes.

The Texan increased its peril in February by publishing one of the biggest scoops in its history —what came to be known as "The Bauer House Controversy."

Reporters Ron Martin and Jorjanna Price, in a *Texan* copyrighted story titled "NO BIDS TAKEN ON MANSION," revealed suspected overexpenditures on the Bauer House, a mansion which was to be "remodeled" for Chancellor LeMaistre. Remodeling turned into demolishing and rebuilding the house—complete with guest house and a bath house. *The Texan* broke that the residence, said to cost $225,000, may have exceeded $1 million in refurbishment costs, without taking competitive sealed bids for the work as state law required.[20]

"Repeated efforts by *The Texan* to obtain exact figures have been refused by university officials," Price and Martin wrote.[21] So *The Texan* led a campaign to find out where this additional money came from, and published an above-the-fold accounting of the known house's costs the next day.

The Texan's in-depth investigation literally met a brick wall. When an independent appraisal team tried to estimate the house's value, they were not allowed inside the structure. Undaunted, Martin and Price continued to pound away, and found that while the administration claimed no state tax dollars were spent, $163,000 was appropriated in March 1969 from the Permanent University Fund Board by the regents.[22]

The University's spokesmen felt no need to comply with the Freedom of Information Act, either. Yemma's requests were answered by the director of planning buildings and facilities, E. D. Walker, in the following disclaimer: "Generally university records are public documents, but our normal policy isn't just to open them to anyone who requests them, for obvious reason. We couldn't open them to anyone who comes in off the street and says he want to see them," Walker said.[23]

And there may have been no paperwork, as the contractor, under oath, testified that the contract was oral, and that after spending beyond the

$163,000 allocated by the board, he just continued to work because he "had an account number, and just drew on that account."[24]

Even if *The Texan* couldn't get the records, the paper's persistence piqued legislators' interest. An ethics investigation, to which the contractor and Erwin had to testify, followed.

Erwin balked at the investigation. After all, he reasoned, since no "appropriated funds" were being used in the construction, no approval by the governor or legislature was necessary. The legislature balked back, saying Erwin hadn't exactly asked to tear down the state property, either.[25]

"We mortified Erwin politically when we revealed that the UT System Administration had incurred huge cost overruns, maybe $1 million by our estimates, to demolish and reconstruct the Bauer House," Yemma said. "There was a state Senate investigation and Erwin claimed an anonymous donor gave them $600,000 for the project so that no state funds had to be used. Erwin also claimed that *Texan* reporters were hounding wealthy alumni in the middle of the night trying to find out who the donor was. We were aggressive, but not that aggressive; we assumed such a search would be fruitless," Yemma said.

Not quite fruitless, as the Senate's investigation led to the $163,000 being returned to the fund. The $600,000 "donation" was also returned, and interest earned on the Permanent University Fund eventually covered the cost.

"The issue died down, but it was quite a scandal and we won some awards for the coverage," Yemma said.

For one future *Texan* staff member, the work of Martin, Price, and Yemma made quite an impact. "I was a teaching assistant in the journalism school when *The Texan* broke the story," said future editorial manager Ron Gibson. "Although I did not have much contact with *The Texan* at the time, I was tremendously impressed by the information they uncovered."

Finally, on March 12, 1971, Frank Erwin formally stepped down as chairman of the regents, even though he did not leave the board. The day began with a regents' meeting in the Tower and ended with a formal dinner at Municipal Auditorium. More than 2,000 students protested and heckled both events. Not only were four hecklers arrested, but police discovered a homemade bomb outside the entrance.[26]

"REGENTIAL CHALLENGE" CONTINUES

Although Erwin had stepped down, *Texan* staff members knew he would still control the rechartering. They expected retaliation.

Lori Rodriguez faced Erwin's vengeance, which surfaced in the form of LeMaistre's request that *The Texan* not receive its $2-per-student subsidy in December of 1971, reporter Steve Winch wrote.[27]

"There were no reasons given, and there was the knowledge that such a refusal will prevent *The Texan* from the all-out aggressive reporting that leads to Bauer-house type disclosures," Rodriguez wrote.[28]

Although *The Texan* editorialized on the threat, no analysis appeared on its pages. However, future editor Mike Godwin outlined what took place in a 1987 *UTmost* article titled "*THE DAILY TEXAN* DOES NOT BELONG TO YOU (BUT IT USED TO.)"

The charter, established in 1922, which incorporated TSP into the University, but also provided for its autonomy, had two major flaws, Godwin wrote. The first was a limitation of the charter to fifty years, which according to then student body president Bob Binder was necessary because of a 1920 non-profit corporation law. The second, Godwin wrote, was a clause providing that in the event of a dissolution of the corporation, all assets would revert to the Board of Regents.

As general manager Loyd Edmonds explained in Godwin's article, the charter "was a time bomb" ticking away at TSP. Godwin wrote that LeMaistre called for a rechartering which "proposed to shift control of TSP from students representing the whole student body to students selected from the journalism school."

The plan would also make the editor appointed rather than elected.

"Ostensibly, the plan was motivated by the Regents' legitimate concern about 'professionalism' at *The Texan* and its ongoing relationship with the journalism school," Godwin wrote. "But Erwin, a hopeless extrovert, was incapable of keeping his real intentions secret. One evening in April 1971, over drinks at the 40 Acres Club, Erwin revealed to then TSP Board member Tim Donahue that he was going to '[——] the *Texan*.'"[29]

The TSP Board, knowing their charter expired July 6, 1971, voted to amend it and add a seven-month extension to give themselves more time. Yet the regents sued TSP on July 9, 1971, to recover their assets. Six days later, Godwin reported, TSP responded with a counter suit.

"It took a great deal of courage for the current TSP board to meet this Regential challenge head-on," Rodriguez wrote. "It took courage and dedication for this student newspaper to remain editorially free and unrestrained."[30]

The Texan was defended by legislators and the national press, and the changes were depicted as Erwin's attempt to silence a free-enterprise. *The New York Times* ran an in-depth story on May 21, 1971, detailing the fiasco, and hundreds of faculty signed a resolution to protect the paper.

Finally, with work from UT President Steven Spurr and Edmonds, the "Declaration of Trust" which made the TSP an independent entity, but whose assets belong to the regents, was created. The charter set up a board of six student representatives and five faculty representatives, and continued the tradition of electing the *Texan* editor.

Rodriguez' term ended with two more student protests. The first occurred when 3,000 students marched on the State Capitol to protest Nixon's continuing bombing of Vietnam. Rodriguez urged students to unify, oust Nixon, and end the war—but through voting, not violence. "We can stop Nixon and the war, if not now, then at the polls this fall," Rodriguez wrote. Second, *The Texan* and student body were alarmed to discover that the University had hired a long-haired undercover drug enforcement agent as a Jester RA. *The Texan* decried the move, which led to twenty-two student arrests, and wondered, "If you can't trust your RA/ Who can you trust?"[31]

But the years of activism tired the campus. More and more, letters to the editor requested that *The Texan* stop sensationalizing protests and focus on more important issues like getting an education and a job. It was a philosophical turn which had crept up on the campus for years, and which would become more obvious as the decade continued.

ON PACE WITH NEW TECHNOLOGY

Under 1972-73 editor David Powell, and 73-74 editor Michael Eakin, *The Texan* underwent major changes. In August of 1973, the University celebrated the grand opening of the Jesse H. Jones Communications complex, to house the recently expanded communications school as well as *The Texan, Cactus,* and *Ranger. The Texan* paid $205,000 in return for guaranteed space in the complex. The financial stability which allowed *The Texan* to make the move was largely due to Loyd Edmonds' contributions. Under his leadership, from 1956 to 1982, *The Texan*'s budget increased from $235,000 to $2,384,000.[32]

A close friend and co-worker of Edmonds, Dolores Ebert, would write upon his retirement, "In budget-making I have learned to think $2,000,000 without blinking."[33] Reporter Carol Thurston wrote that the complex had a research auditorium, equipped with audience-response instruments, which would "record respondent's electric current charges" to measure if something was keeping the respondent's attention or not.

The complex cost $9 million, and had $2.5 million in new equipment. One such piece was *The Texan*'s new press. "The new press means a change from letter press to offset printing, a thirty-two-page newspaper to replace the current sixteen-page limit, improved quality of reproduction and more versatility in use of color," Edmonds said.

The Texan commemorated the last run of the old press by "turning the rules" around a front-page article August 21, 1973, marking its demise.

"With this issue, the paper abandons the hot type, letterpress methods which it has used since the paper's birth in 1900," *Texan* reporter Steve Renfrow wrote. "The sturdy old Duplex tubular, with 16-page capacity and a capability of running 18,500 issues per hour, will give way to a Goss Urbanite Offset press with a thirty-two-page capacity and a speed of 45,000 issues per hour. The old pressroom on Little Campus, where temperatures often reach 105 to 110 degrees will be replaced by an air-conditioned pressroom in the basement of the TSP Building."[34]

Additional changes to *The Texan* included expanding summer publication to four days a week, and eliminating the use of *The Summer Texan.* From then on, *The Daily Texan* name would be used year round.

KEEPING UP THE PRESSURE

Despite the new trust agreement, Erwin wasn't through meddling with *The Texan.* Yet the ranks of *Texan* defenders had swollen significantly, so Erwin had a tougher time of it.

First, in April of 1973, an administrative quest to prevent *The Texan* from endorsing city council candidates was struck down by a district judge. In response, Rep. Joe Allen sponsored a bill providing "that no language in any appropriations act shall be construed to prohibit or restrict the utilization of facilities of an institution of higher learning in connection with the publication of any newspaper, magazine or other periodical," reported *Texan* staffer Jeanne Janes.

Allen said, "We are concerned with whether or not this rider was developed to restrict the freedom of the press by the elimination of the editorial viewpoint. This the legislature can not do," Janes reported.[35]

Then, in January of 1974, UT President Steven Spurr began calling for the elected editor to be appointed from the journalism school. He did so, as was done so many times before, in the interest of increasing the "professionalism" on *The Texan*'s staff.[36] Editor Eakin argued, instead, that "Spurr's recommendations were absurd. If *The Texan* is to be a free newspaper, it must have an elected editor, not one which is appointed by a board that is 1/2 appointed by the president."[37]

Erwin's final major attack, as Eakin put it, to "eliminate the opposition" on *The Texan* also came in January of 1974 when Erwin urged the regents to make optional the $1.65 fee students paid for *The Texan*. He suggested the regents follow an attorney general's ruling that only students who take a full-time course load—then a whopping eighteen hours—should have to pay fees.[38]

Unsurprisingly, *The Texan* was headlong into another state investigation when the proposal surfaced. "Though we cannot say in certainty, the new coldness may in part reflect the extensive research attempts initiated by *The Texan* two weeks ago," Eakin wrote. "On January 4, 1974, *The Texan* utilized the new open meetings legislation to request previous unitemized information on the University's voluminous oil and gas leases."[39]

The Texan kept the pressure on Erwin. Eventually, he was forced to testify in front of the "Constitutional Convention Committee on Education" for University Fund expenditures such as three expensive paper shredders for the chancellor's office and comptroller's office, and numerous expensive plane rides for LeMaistre.

Before lashing back, Erwin paid an unexpected visit to *The Texan*'s offices. "Erwin's visit was quite an uncommon occurrence," wrote assistant to the editor Ken McHam. "Some work stopped as staffers turned to watch him look around. A uniformed campus cop accompanied him, opening every locked, unwindowed door with a master key. Erwin was just looking around.

"Or perhaps he perceived it as a bold excursion into the enemy camp—a coup in the way of Indian warriors. We want to dispel any notion that *The Daily Texan* is the enemy of Frank Erwin; Erwin is an intelligent, distinguished, shrewd and powerful man that could have been a hero in some other context. Within the context of rapidly changing social roles, he has cast himself in a villain's role by opposing those changes without understanding them."[40]

Finally, on Friday, March 15, 1974, *The Texan* and Student Government were dealt Erwin's hardest blow, when the Board of Regents voted to axe funding for both.

The Texan staff was in Waco at the time, receiving their fourth Southwest Journalism Conference sweepstakes award. "It was a to-the-barricades weekend," said managing editor John Yemma. "Conspiracy theories abounded. We phoned Walter Cronkite. We concocted a dramatic *Texan* front page that was blank except for the nameplate and the stirring, perhaps apocryphal words of Frank Erwin: 'We do not fund anything we don't control.'"[41]

"What I remember is that our desire to so protest was not abridged by Loyd Edmonds, or Bob Hilburn, or the TSP Board, and, of equal importance, when I took the mess of Waco Hotel bills and dumped them on Edmonds' desk he graciously overlooked who stayed with whom, and what was consumed," Yemma said.[42]

South Mall protest.
—Center for American History,
University of Texas at Austin

The Texan's protest was bolstered this time by Texas Sen. Lloyd Doggett, and Reps. Ronnie Earle, Sarah Weddington, Wilson Foreman, and Larry Bales' demands for Erwin to reconsider.[43]

Erwin backed down a little, but retorted that the whole exercise wouldn't be necessary "if you can find a way to keep *The Texan* from making administrators' jobs so difficult."[44]

"The very day we were fighting for the permanent fund," Erwin said, "with all those close votes and tie votes, *The Texan* had an editorial opposing its retention. That didn't help much."

The legislators growled that "if the University didn't find money for these entities, the legislature would look at them with a 'jaundiced eye' at the University's appropriations bill."[45]

The protest culminated in a 3,000-student South Mall rally demanding the board alter their view. Eakin began circulating a campus petition, for which he wished to get 30,000 signatures, and hinted at a campus strike if the regents did not reconsider.[46]

For *The Texan*, two UT students composed a poem describing the predicament:

"BEWARE THE IDES OF MARCH"

To the editor:

"Friends, students, countrymen lend us your ears,
We come to bury *the Texan*, not to praise it
The evil that men do lives after them,
The good is often interred with their bones
So let it be with *the Texan*. The Noble Erwin
Hath told you *the Texan* was ambitious
If it were so, it was a grievous fault
And grievously hath *the Texan* answered it.
Here under leave of Erwin and the rest—
for Erwin is an honorable man
So are they all honorable men
Come we to speak at *the Texan*'s funeral
It was our friend, faithful and just to us:
But Erwin said it was ambitious;
And Erwin is an honorable man
What the poor hath cried; *the Texan* hath wept;
Ambition should be made of sterner stuff."[47]

On April 29, 1974, *Texan* reporter Virginia Timmons reported that during preregistration, students would have two fee cards —one for *The Cactus*, locker, shower and parking permits, which worked on a negative check-off system, and one for the Student Government, *The Texan*, "cultural entertainment," and men's athletics with a positive check-off system. Edmonds said if 15,000 of the 30,000 students expected to register did not check-off *The Texan*, it would not make its present operating budget of $50,000, and changes would be made.

"The paper will be placed out as usual and will operate on the honor system," Edmonds said. "However, if funds are not met, *The Texan* will have to dip into its reserve monies made from previous earnings. Also, some cutbacks will have to be made . . . as in reducing the number of pages in circulation. We hope to get more faculty and staff to subscribe."[48]

Whether or not the positive check-off system was designed to confuse students, it certainly did, and *The Texan* ran numerous ads and stories urging students "Don't check off the *Texan*" in order to support the newspaper.

Finally, after preregistration ended, the regents countered by lowering the full academic load from eighteen hours to twelve hours. Their timing, some suspected, was just an attempt to show the Student Government and *The Texan* who controlled funding, and occurred just as Eakin and Yemma were writing their thirty columns.

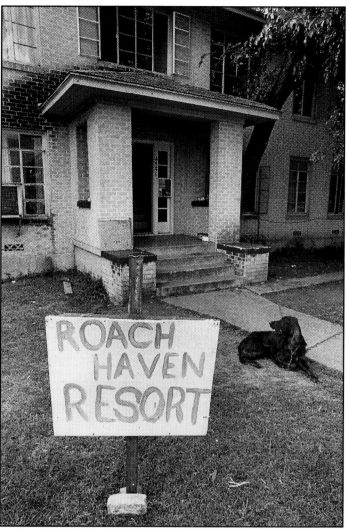

The Drag in 1977.

Apartments near campus weren't always pristine. Even the dog won't live in this 1977 "Roach Haven."

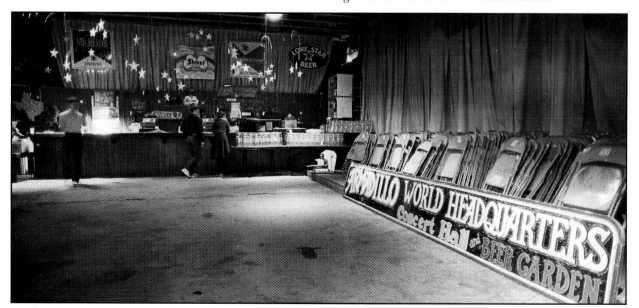

Students grieved over the 1978 closing of Armadillo World Headquarters, a place where longhairs and rednecks could share a beer and music peacefully.

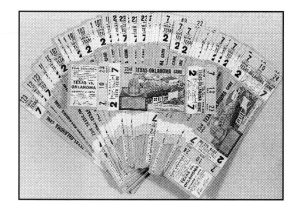

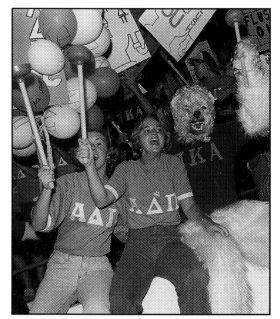

Top left: *A ticket to the big OU game in 1978, as it does today, meant a ticket to a big, drunk weekend.*

Middle left: *UT/OU pep rally, 1977.*

Below left: *Greek student life, 1978.*

Top right: The Texan *followed Heisman Trophy winner Earl Campbell closely in his final year with the Longhorns, 1977, and afterward as he became the number-one draft pick for the Houston Oilers.*

Middle right: *The men of Jester, 1979.*

Bottom right: *The UT Band cuts loose at a 1979 disco party.*

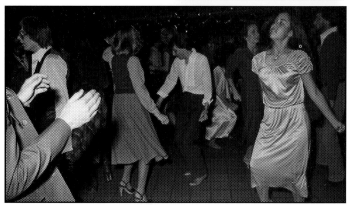

Eakin noted, "It is my hope that *The Daily Texan* will continue to grow and thrive; increasingly, however, I feel the time of repressions may be on the way. If repression, either subtle or otherwise, is to be the case I fear for the continued life of this university, a fragile place already plunging into the depths of mediocrity."[49]

STREAKING, POT, AND "DATING"

Despite the turmoil, nationally with Nixon and at home with Erwin, the University was an amazing place to be in the 1970s. "There was always smoke in the air, either tear gas or pot," 1971–72 editor Rodriguez said.

On campus, and especially around Littlefield Fountain and the South Mall, a streaking craze had infected the student body. To serve students' interests, *The Texan* published the National Safety Council's tips on the hobby, including "Wear sneakers and wear reflectorized tape—this is especially important for night streaking. The council suggests streakers make 'bumper numbers' or 'tail lights' from tape and imaginatively adorn the anatomy with tape on the front, back and sides."

When 600 students gathered on 21st Street between Moore-Hill and Jester for a mass-streaking, *The Texan* was, of course, there, although no one can confirm whether reporters James Dunlap, Paul Bender, and Paul Watler were covering or uncovering the event.

"The initial atmosphere was similar to a drunken pep rally," they wrote. "Periodically, the cries of 'streak!' would rise and the crowd would run from one end of the street to the other in an attempt to see the person brave enough to risk arrest. To shouts of "Eat More Pork," an officer in a patrol car in the midst of the students attempted to turn his car around, but students began rocking the car. At this point, police ran toward the car and began dispersing the crowd with mace and clubs."[50]

'Streakers' Make Dash On Campus

Phone booth stuffing, goldfish swallowing, flagpole sitting, panty raiding ... and now, streaking.

"I want to report the first streak of the year," said an unidentified caller to the Texan office.

A "streak" is a dash across campus or other public place in the nude.

He reported he and six other males ran around the east wing of Jester Center in the nude Monday night. The Texan later received several calls from Jester residents who saw a group of naked men running around the dorm.

An Associated Press story from Gainesville, Fla. reported that a University of Florida college student arrested for streaking said an anonymous donor would give $200 to a drug treatment center if students can complete 12 successive streaks on the campus there.

However, threat of police action wouldn't keep the staff from baring it all.

Pot wasn't uncommon in *The Texan* newsroom during those years.

"Absolutely," 1975–76 editor Scott Tagliarino said of his staff's use. "If you could find it. Mostly at *Texan* staff parties. But one night several staffers—not me—got stoned and decided it would be a great editorial statement if they 'streaked' naked across campus. No big deal; just a lot of laughs."

Texan editors were not above the trend, however, as Tagliarino observed that "Mary Walsh, who followed me as editor, had the distinction of being photographed in the nude on the front page of *The Texan* for an article on the attraction of Hippy Hollow during the summer."

When *Texan* staffers were clothed, the typical attire, Tagliarino said, was "Levi cut-offs, Jesus sandals, and T-Shirts. The best looking editor in this attire was Buck Harvey, who preceded me. Buck set the standard for sexy, editor attire, and unfortunately I followed him in what was a poor male replacement."

The 1970s *Texan* staff, much as they do now, spent a great deal of time and money in The Hole in the Wall. And has been the trend since nearly its birth, the unique relationships struck in *The Texan* newsroom were often continued after deadline.

"Inner-office dating was an occupational hazard," Tagliarino said, "particularly after a long week and a long night at the weekly *Texan* party on Friday night. I'm not sure we would call it dating today, but you always ended up with someone on Saturday morning."

"My first managing editor [Melissa Segrest] and I tried once to draw a chart with lines connecting all the various people who had dated," Beth Frerking said. "It looked like a spider web. We finally gave up and never finished it, partly because we couldn't decide whether one night stands counted as dating."

Texan reporter Karen Tumulty said, "I was in a sorority, a

The old Duplex tubular press, with sixteen-page capacity and capability of running 18,500 issues per hour, gave way to a Goss Urbanite offset press with a capacity of thirty-two pages and speed of 45,000 issues per hour in 1974.

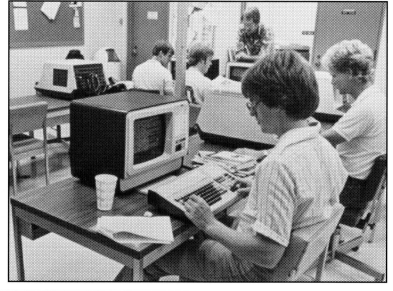

VDTs were used to edit, delete, save or send copy from the 1970s to the early 1990s.

Old Press Runs Last Issue

very strict one where getting caught with a joint meant getting kicked out, and sometimes it felt as though I were living on two different planets that were only about seven blocks apart. But as time went on, I really began to feel that I was learning far more at *The Texan* than anywhere else, and *The Texan* began taking up a larger and larger share of my social life. I just loved hanging out there," Tumulty said. "Graduation was nothing short of devastating. I still have several pages of photos from the –30– party in my photo album at home."

THE CUTTING EDGE

The Texan underwent another major change technologically in 1974, when it graduated to the interim between computerization and typesetting. Then, in 1977–78, the paper ventured into total computerization and switched wire services. As Tumulty described, "There was something of a flap when we had to drop AP and start taking UPI exclusively; the *American-Statesman*, it turns out, had protested the student rate we were getting from the AP. It was the clearest evidence that we had really arrived, and were genuinely giving them a competitive headache. I still think *The Texan* practiced some of the best journalism in Texas."

"Computers were brand new to our group," said 1978–79 editor Gary Fendler. "The ability to compose a story on a VDT/CRT, save it, and then pass it to a copy or section editor electronically was cutting edge. Actually, in our time it was bleeding edge. Why? Because while you may have time today to grab a cigarette, more often than not the computers 'ate' our copy on the transfer or, more commonly, when we pushed 'save.' So, after an hour or two writing a pulitzer prize-winning story, we would push 'send' and poof, off into cyberspace went the copy—lost forever without a trace. The computer jocks would come out from their work space, sit at the offending terminal, have you recite precisely the steps you took just prior to the story's disappearance, and after a few seconds authoritatively declare the story was gone. Then they would just as quickly exit. The only thing remaining was to recompose the story, and seldom in as quality a form as the first version."

The production headaches occurred in part because *The Texan*'s move to VDTs was cutting edge. "Ironically enough, almost every job I had

after that meant a step backward: *The San Antonio Light*, where I went after graduation, was using scanners, and the *Los Angeles Times*, when I started there in 1981, was still using manual typewriters," Tumulty said.

Perhaps the most famous *Texan* staffer to emerge from the 1970s was Berke Breathed. His

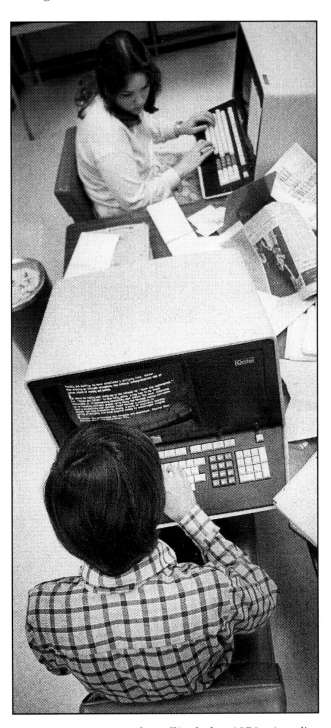

Computers were new to the staff in the late 1970s. According to 1978-79 editor Gary Fendler, more often than not, the computers ate copy when the "save" button was pushed.

daily strip, "Academia Waltz," would light up *The Texan*'s editorial page from 1977 to 1979, with its witty eye on University life. Breathed brought up real University issues, such as problems with integrating Greek life, student drinking, sex, or other more pedagogical endeavors through a distinguished style that he would later employ in the Pulitzer Prize-winning strip "Bloom County." Breathed even challenged *The Texan*'s policy against publishing obscene language.

"Breathed helped stir the pot with a couple of cartoons spiced with naughty words," Fendler said. "At first TSP blocked their publication so we ran blank space in the pages. Ultimately, TSP backed away, but at the time, even though I argued strongly for the right to publish Berke unedited, I always felt the issue was less than noble. I mean, really, here we are round adults arguing for the right to use curse words in a newspaper. Right principle, somewhat empty issue. A pyrrhic victory of sorts."

Each victory, however, helped *The Texan* become more independent, and less likely to fall underneath the whims of an administrator like Erwin ever again.

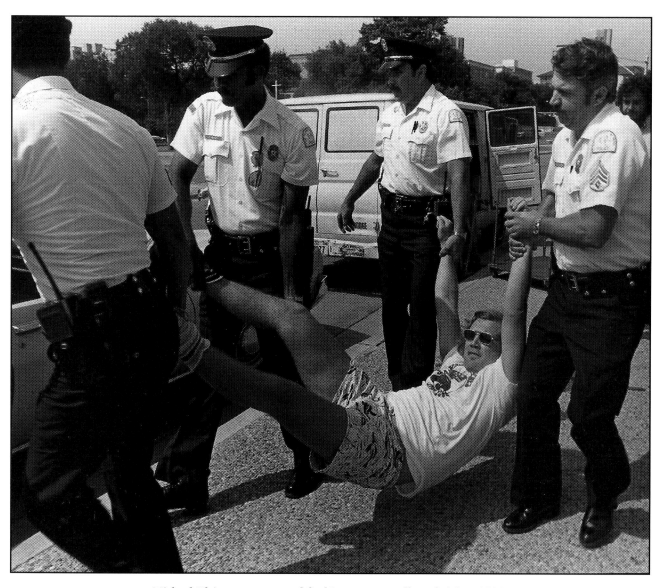

Michael Kleiman was arrested for his attempt to sell sandwiches, 1979.

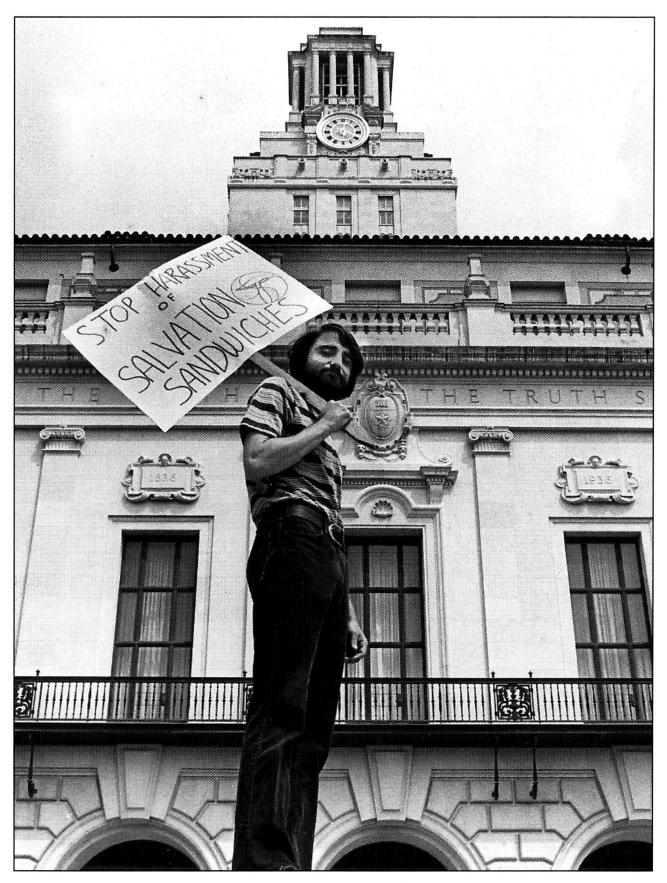

Even sandwiches caused a stir in the '70s.

CHAPTER 9

Some Things Never Change: 1980-1990

What would become the most memorable event for 1980–81 editor Mark McKinnon really started with 1979 editor Beth Frerking.

That year, Shah Mohammed Reza Pahlavi fled Iran and religious leader Ayatollah Khomeini eliminated most of Iran's elite. Then, on November 4, Iranian militants seized the U.S. Embassy, taking sixty-two American hostages. The Iranians demanded the U.S. send the Shah, who was receiving cancer treatment in New York, home for punishment.

Protests started in Houston. *The Texan*, through a UPI article, reported that angry Houstonians were demanding Iranian students go home.[1] On campus, opinion was mixed. "We will simply kill one million Iranians utilizing nuclear weapons," one engineering student wrote in the "Firing Line." He opined, "That seems a fair exchange—one American dead equals one million dead Iranians. Should the Iranian students in the United States protest, we will simply round them up and throw them off the end of a New York City pier and allow them the privilege of swimming home."[2]

Several fraternities seized the opportunity to combine activism with beer. The members of Pi Kappa Alpha "demonstrated"—on their front lawn with a keg—in favor of deporting Iranians and the Shah.[3] Heated West Mall protests ensued; some shouting matches lasted more than nine hours. *The Texan* ran several un-bylined accounts of the rallies, in which many of the Iranian students interviewed refused to give their names. Some students covered their faces in photo-graphs, fearing their families in Iran would be retaliated against.

As the hostage situation worsened, Sen. Barry Goldwater, among others, called for the deportation of protesters. The Justice Department reminded Americans that "aliens can not be deported simply for protesting." On campus, too, feelings intensified.[4] Editor Frerking implored students to remain rational. "Americans have every right to protest the takeover, within the limits of peaceful protest," she wrote. "But rabid reactions, especially those which might result in violence toward Iranian students here could seriously endanger the hostages' lives. And that must be avoided above all."[5]

But it seemed neither the student body nor the government was listening. Many American students supported President Jimmy Carter's November 10 decision to "check the immigration status" of Iranian students. *Texan* reporter Jenny Abdo wrote that "a crowd, comprised of mostly American students, roared that U.S. tax dollars should not be going to educate Iranian students. Saeed Zabihi, one of the few Iranian students at the rally, was escorted away by University police, who said 'We want to make sure he doesn't get hurt.'"[6]

Immigration authorities prowled, scrutinizing each Iranian student's status. By November 28, 1979, the visas of 190 of the approximate 220 UT Iranian students were investigated. Thirty-five were found not to meet immigration requirements.

"The University of Texas has absolutely no obligation to accommodate the INS while it inter-

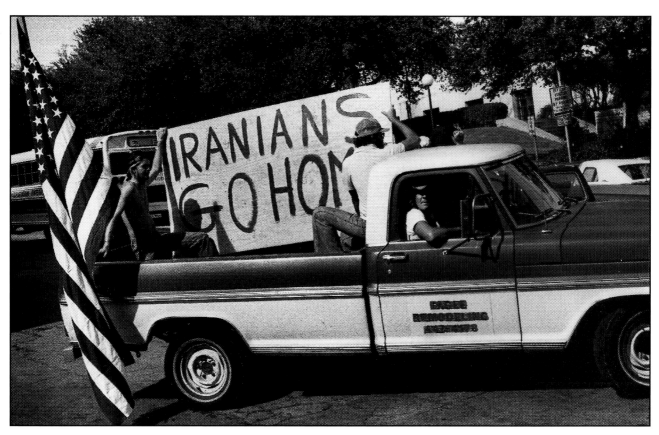

Above: *The student body was sharply divided on how to treat Iranian students during the hostage crisis in 1979. Many demanded their protection, and others, such as this truckload, wanted them out.*

Below: *Iranian students protest pressure and scrutiny put upon their INS status during the Iran hostage crisis.*

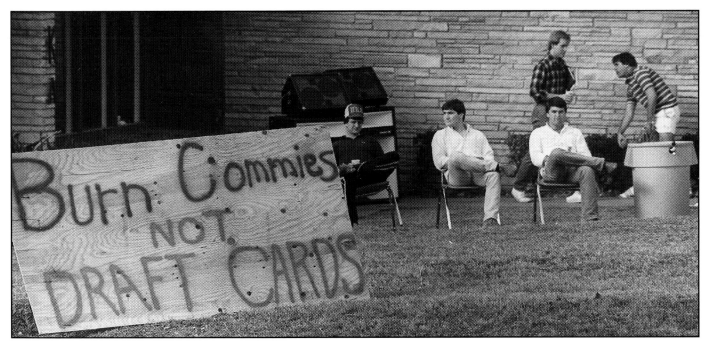

Members of Pi Kappa Alpha combine beer and activism on their front lawn while demanding that UT send Iranian students home.

views Iranian students here," Frerking wrote. "Let the INS do its dirty work elsewhere."[7]

The issue was brought closer to home when Carter moved the Shah from New York to Lackland Air Force Base in San Antonio. Tempers and tension rose.

On January 31, 1980, according to a *Texan* report by Patricia Yznaga and Ron Saint Pierre, when a former Iranian UN ambassador was introduced to speak on campus, Iranian and American students began chanting "Death to the Shah." Dean of Students James Hurst threatened expulsion, and the UTPD arrested twenty-four Iranian students for "disruptive activities." No Americans were arrested.[8]

"The students showed up at the address and demonstrated in a very understated and modest way," McKinnon said. "They sort of stayed in the back and had some signs . . . it was nothing terribly disruptive. Nevertheless, because of the climate at the time, the campus police completely overreacted, arrested them, and then the county prosecuted them. It was clearly a political witch-hunt."

But to prosecute the students, the police needed more evidence. So the Tower requested the *Texan*'s photographs of the event—both published and unpublished—which were mostly taken by *Texan* staffer Jan Sonnenmair.

The administration was not pleased by *The Texan*'s response.

"We told the administration to stuff it when they asked for our photographs/negatives of the anti-Shah of Iran rally held on campus," Frerking said. Fortunately for Frerking, she did not have to face the Tower's wrath. The subpoena for the negatives didn't arrive until after her term—it fell into McKinnon's lap.

"We chose not to turn [the negatives] over for reasons of the First Amendment privilege," McKinnon said. "We had a lot of support from other papers like the *Statesman*, and we got Jim George as our attorney, who is one of the best First Amendment attorneys in the country."

According to *Texan* staffer Scott Lind, McKinnon and George tried to avoid turning over the negatives or being held in contempt of court by arguing the photos showed only protesting American students, not the arrested Iranians. McKinnon went to court.

"McKinnon took the stand to answer whether the negative sought by the subpoena depict the alleged disruption in the ballroom," Lind reported. "Testifying, [he said] he called photographer Jan Sonnenmair, who took some of the photos. McKinnon said he asked her what the contents of the negatives were. She answered 'people.' McKinnon asked her to 'be more specific.' She said, 'Mark, go to sleep,' and hung up."[9]

The judge of the County Court of Law No. 3 was not amused. And on Tuesday, September 2, he threw McKinnon in jail. The ordeal attracted worldwide media attention.

"A lot of money and a lot of resources were spent by the county for a ridiculous prosecution," McKinnon said. "There was a lot of attention on the issue, because it had consequences not just for *The Texan* but for all the media in Texas. It was getting stories from around the world . . . it was weird because my wife left on an airplane for a trip the day I went to jail, and when I was found in contempt, there was every expectation that I was going to be remanded to the county facility until I turned over the photographs. So when they initially fingerprinted me and the door closed behind me, two things were going on: It was pretty exciting to be the object of so much attention—it felt good to stand up for a principled fight, but all that said, I also thought, 'six months from now in the county jail, this may not be all that much fun.' But thanks to Jim George, I was sprung the next day, and ultimately the charges were dropped."[10]

His stand reaffirmed *The Texan*'s independence, from both the Tower and the courts.

WARFARE WITH THE GREEKS

Although McKinnon said the subpoena "was definitely the most controversial thing to happen on campus," he managed also to get "into some heavy, heavy, heavy warfare with the fraternities," as some Greeks just couldn't outgrow old, racist views.

In the 1981 Greek Week parade, Zeta Psi's entry featured a man dressed in Mexican peasant costume pulling a car labeled "border patrol," and Phi Delta Theta's float included a car carrying an "intoxicated" black man, *Texan* staffer Carmen Hill reported.

And some campus sororities refused to sign the 1981 *Cactus Yearbook* policy that all organizations covered in its pages must not discriminate.

They only wanted "to preserve their heritage and membership," the sororities declared, and decided to form an independent yearbook.

"During the Greek Week parade," McKinnon said, "one fraternity member sent us a letter that was extremely racist . . . it was clear that he had had no idea it would be printed. We printed it, and it created such an uproar that he denied having written it. I was hung in effigy by the fraternity

outside their window, and we had to have a handwriting analysis done to prove he'd written it."

The letter, "An open letter from a Greek to all non-Greeks," said: "We find you detestful because you are drug-oriented, anti-nuke, anti-establishment, anti-money and smelly" and "this is the last time your kind can viciously stab at our kind and get away with it, because in ten years you will all be working for us."[11]

Unfortunately for McKinnon, the handwriting analysis confirmed that the letter was forged. "McKinnon expressed regret . . . he said it was never his intent to harm [the student] but rather to show the attitudes expressed in the letter exist among Greeks and non Greeks," *Texan* staffer Ann Broe reported.

The misunderstanding resulted in *The Texan*'s current policy of requiring "Firing Line" contributors to identify themselves. McKinnon advised future editorial boards not to accept any Firing Lines unless the writer was identified in person.

IN-HOUSE EDITORIAL CONTROL

On Wednesday, January 14, Berke Breathed returned to *The Texan*, this time as a syndicated cartoonist from *The Washington Post*. His strip, "Bloom County," was carried on *The Texan*'s editorial page.

Finally, after 444 days in captivity, the fifty-two remaining U.S. hostages in Iran were freed. *The Texan* ran a double truck to mark the occasion, and covered several local angles to bring the story home. Reporter Catherine Chriss found that "Throughout the drizzling cold rain Monday, University students and faculty went about the typical rigmarole of the first day of classes. . . . No one seemed really ecstatic or jubilant about the signing of the release that will eventually lead to the release of the 52 hostages. . . . It was like no one could believe it was true this time."[12]

As always, the University's culture was changing. The country had entered the Reagan Years, and Texas had entered the "Dallas" years. Coke's long-running relationship with the University continued, as the company decided to test on the Forty Acres brand-new machines that would accept $1 bills.

And the entire country, on April 10, 1981, watched breathlessly as space shuttle *Columbia* launched America into a new era of technology.

"The 9.6 billion shuttle project is the key to the nation's future in space," *The Texan* reported. As the shuttle orbited the earth, future editor Lisa Beyer completed a three-part series on the spacecraft, detailing its inner workings and problems to the student body. When *Columbia* landed at Edwards Air Force base in California on April 14, 1981, more than 350,000 people gathered to welcome the astronauts home.[13]

That year, Don Puffer, a former editorialist, was elected editor. Even without Student Government elections to bring students to the polls, Puffer won 1,949 votes.

But Puffer's term has the dubious distinction of being the first and only year in which *The Texan*'s editor and managing editor resigned under pressure from the staff. The point of contention was editorial control—not outside the *Texan*'s staff, but within.

A letter supported by many on the news staff "contained seven complaints involving the alleged infringement by other staff members of *The Texan* news department functions," staffer David Elliot reported.

"Specifically, the letter accused Puffer of allowing news copy to undergo alteration after it had been read by the news editor. Puffer was also accused of altering news play for graphic purposes and creating an editorial imbalance affecting news play," he reported.[14]

The mutineers, led by former news editor Jenny Abdo, claimed "these complaints have been brought to the attention of the editor and managing editor several times. No measures to correct the problem have been taken in the 46 issues this semester. We believe we can no longer work under conditions involving unethical practices and unprofessional behavior."[15]

Puffer lashed back, accusing Abdo and the others of a political power play. He refused to resign, and accused them of threatening the paper's quality with their action.

Eleven staff members, all of whom worked in *The Texan*'s news department, submitted a letter calling for Puffer's resignation to the executive committee of the Texas Student Publications Board."[16]

The letter expressed the group's intention to quit if the committee did not ask for Puffer's resignation. The committee refused, saying such action would exceed its legal authority. So the eleven, along with an uncounted number of other staffers, walked out on November 3.

By the week's end, Puffer and managing editor Paula Angerstein resigned. Reactions were mixed. Loyd Edmonds said he "begged Puffer to stay on," as did Bob Hilburn. TSP Board president Betsy McCole said it was probably better for *The Texan* that Puffer resign. Some staffers quit over the coup, and some expressed relief that *The Texan* could finally get back to the business of putting out a high-quality publication.

"Both sides of this dispute have been pretty vicious to each other," said TSP Board member

Several members of The Texan *staff crammed into a November 1981 meeting of the Texas Student Publications Board to demand the resignation of editor Donald Puffer.*

Warren Burkett. "A lot of people stayed because they liked *The Texan*, a lot of people left because they liked *The Texan*."[17]

Thus, the paper found itself with another unprecedented challenge: selecting a new managing editor and editor to finish out the year.

The afternoon after Puffer and Angerstein left, the TSP Board appointed John Schwartz, then editor of *UTmost*, as *Texan* editor. Brian Dunbar, a former managing editor, would help out until permanent selections could be made.

Schwartz, in his first editorial, urged students not to abandon *The Texan* because of the internal conflict. "The last few days have seen major changes at *The Daily Texan*," Schwartz wrote. "For the first time in some 30 years, the editor has resigned—forced out by his own staff. We're still a little shell-shocked down here, and trying to put things back together. *The Daily Texan* is a pluralistic environment, where everyone has his own ideas about what the paper needs. Most people feel they haven't heard all the details of the recent conflict. The staff still hasn't sorted them all out, were you to ask five staffers down here what really happened, you'd get at least six answers. There was little evil involved, but a lot of insanity. Accusations flew on both sides, making *The Daily Texan* look like a dirty place. But a long hard look at the details reveals no evil schemes, no sabotage. Instead we see a fight that might have been averted, but ran out of control. It should never have happened, but after a certain point, there was no going back. It's over now. *The Texan*'s on the mend, and its time to look ahead. We feel that after recuperating, we'll feel better than ever. But that will be for you to judge. Watch this paper, and don't cancel your subscription."[18]

Tuesday, November 10, the full TSP Board approved Schwartz to complete Puffer's term, which he did.

A TIME OF PLENTY

The '80s staff was as punkish as the music. Maureen Paskin, 1982 summer managing editor, painted the *Texan* offices blue and mauvish pink, then covered her own office in aluminum foil. The big, green dirty "Scott Lind" sofa—so named because he either seemed to live, or really did live, on that sofa—couched 1982–83 editor Lisa Beyer and others. And the entertainment depart-

ment, Beyer said, "was referred to by Bob Hilburn [editorial manager] as 'the opium den.' It was all darkness and funky posters and lots of smoke."

When entertainment writers weren't holed up in the den, they were at Raul's, the crossroads for an exploding '80s new wave/punk scene.

"We were all so [———] crazed," said entertainment writer Louis Black. "There was lots of drugs, lots of sleeping around, lots of writing . . . everything else was secondary."

Film students, writers, and musicians were producing work at a dizzying pace. Creative minds drifted on and off *The Texan's* pages long after leaving the University to write about them, but there just wasn't enough space.

Quietly, in the *Texan's* entertainment office, the *Austin Chronicle* was born.

"The first meetings came out of there," said publisher Nick Barbaro. "For entertainment writers, there was no place to go from the *Texan*—I hadn't been taking classes for a year, and I was still writing."

Five out of six of the *Chronicle's* original writers came from the *Texan*. The first issue of the *Chronicle* came out in September 1981.

The early 1980s were a time of great wealth for *The Texan*. Lots of advertising dollars meant lots of pages. The influx of copy and the retirement of Bob Hilburn brought Ron Gibson to the *Texan* basement. "The '80s can be divided into two segments: the time of great plenty, and the time of very little," Gibson said. "There was a huge boom in the early '80s as *Texan* classifieds went way up. We were averaging 24 total pages a day."

"Our philosophy in the '80s was different too," Gibson said. "There was a saying . . . if you want to know what's going on in Austin, read *The Texan*. If you want to know what's going on at UT, read the *Statesman*."

In 1980 the *Texan* had technological growing pains. There was "a significant unsatisfied demand on campus for the text processing services of a UNIX-based computing system," according to TSP minutes. Finally, the *Texan*, in a joint agreement with the College of Communication, got $14,500 to buy additional storage hardware.

The Texan's computer system, as in the rest of the University, was a series of "dumb terminals," VDTs that were connected to a central computer.

"Writers would input the copy into the computer through the VDT, there they could edit the copy, delete words or send to storage," the TSP minutes explained. The backshop could then print out a tape of the words. The upgrade gave the paper cutting edge technology, such as the "hand" function, which allowed writers to pick up and move blocks of text at a time.

When there were insufficient terminals in the newsroom for *Texan* reporters, they would often work from the journalism department's "newslab" in the TSP building, Beyer said.

"The newsroom and the newslab were connected by one of those pneumonic tubes, so we could shoot hard copies of stories and phone messages and whatnot from one place to the other. It made a fabulous *thunk*," she said.

POLITICS AND THE TRADITION OF RACISM

During this time, the Student Government was trying desperately to revive itself.

"I remember John Schwartz commenting that the people who were spearheading the effort to revive it would quit if they could only get laid," Beyer said. "As I recall, there was a referendum about the proposal, but in any event [the Student Government] was revivified. Then came the campaign. The folks who'd lost in their effort to stop student government created a campaign for 'Hank the Hallucination,' a character in a far-out *Texan* cartoon strip, Eyebeam, drawn by Sam Hurt. I thought this was pretty hilarious. But the Hankists took it very seriously and were extremely furious with me when I refused to endorse Hank,

preferring instead Paul Begala, who has since become President Clinton's adviser. In the event, in the first round of balloting, Hank, as a write-in candidate, beat out all the other candidates."

In the end though, Begala won.

Racially, the *Texan*, although liberal at heart, was seen as an insensitive publication. But it got its first African-American editor in 1983 when then managing editor Roger Campbell was elected.

"I'm damn proud to be the first black editor," Campbell said in election coverage by reporter Richard Stubbe. "Especially here at the University of Texas."[19]

Once editor, Campbell pushed the University's racial climate into the forefront, just as the University was preparing to celebrate its centennial. "As the University approaches the pomp and circumstance of its centennial celebration," Campbell wrote, "there are signs that racism is still as much a tradition as UT football."

Campbell pointed to the case of an African-American UT cheerleader who wasn't reappointed to the squad, and a male UT cheerleader's rationale of the decision. "'Blacks usually don't have the gymnastic skill that whites do,'" Campbell reported the male cheerleader saying. "'The orientals and Mexicans are being totally ignored in this issue, and I think it's because they didn't complain and because the team is mostly black.'

"For an institution that to this day is still attempting—or so we are told—to meet the same desegregation orders it faced when it first allowed blacks to enter, this incident is a most regrettable one," Campbell wrote.[20]

During Campbell's year, the U.S. House of Representatives voted 338-90 to set aside the third Monday in March as Martin Luther King Jr. Day.

"Finally, more than 15 years after his tragic assassination, Martin Luther King Jr. may be rightfully honored," Campbell wrote.

Campbell wrote viewpoints less frequently than

Bevo and the Silver Spurs, 1980.

previous editors, preferring to directly control news policy. This met with mixed opinion, according to 1989 editor Mike Godwin. "*The Texan* staff found that Campbell seemed to be peremptory in his decision-making. Campbell, in turn, felt the staff was stubbornly unprofessional in its resistance to his efforts to run the paper," Godwin said.

During his term, Campbell challenged the merit of electing the editor. Members of the TSP Board and Campbell felt *The Texan* would be more professional if the editor were appointed. After a battle involving the Student Government and many former *Texan* staffers, the elected editor was retained.

Racial hatred rose on campus again during 1985–86 editor Russell Scott's term, when two white students attacked former Black Student's Alliance president Randy Bowman with a pipe and bottle. Bowman, who was a vocal advocate for integrating fraternities, suffered a concussion and nerve damage.

The timing of the crime limited *Texan* news coverage—it made the last issue of the spring semester. But Scott didn't let the attackers escape scrutiny.

"It frightens me to think there are practitioners of such corrupt and dead ideals among us . . . the attackers no doubt felt solace in the fact that their crime went relatively unnoticed—those of us staying on will not forget," Scott wrote in the first editorial of his term.

A TIME OF TENSION

On the business side, *The Texan* was trying to crawl out of a crippling drop in advertising, brought on by the real estate crash.

"For other papers, after a nose-dive in advertising it leveled off," Gibson said. "Not for *The Texan*, though. Only since Kathy Lawrence arrived in 1994 has the linage gone back up."

But even with a thinner paper, *The Texan* responded to national crises with the same passion.

"You can do amazing things when the juice starts to flow," Gibson said. "So many college papers, when you see the resources they have, relatively few of them would be able to do the things we've done over the years. It's real news we deal with, and we deal with it well."

During the *Challenger* crash January 1986, "our guy was on the road to Houston within minutes and we had a local reaction as well," Gibson said.

Reporter Brian Edwards joined national journalists in the breaking story from Johnson Space Center. *The Texan* combined his reactions from NASA with UT reaction from reporter Martha Ashe. Ashe interviewed UT professor Karl Heinze, who'd ridden the *Challenger* in 1985. *The Texan* ran a special section the day of the crash, and when President Reagan and 10,000 family members, dignitaries, and press gathered at Johnson Space Center to mourn, the *Texan* was there. Photographers Kelly Pace and Robert Cohen shot the event, and Edwards returned to report.

AIDS fear also gripped the nation, and the *Texan* took the issue head-on.

"Debra Muller and Sean Price gave more in-depth coverage of AIDS than had been seen at the University," Gibson said. "AIDS was still fairly new. Their articles put to rest the myths about transmission. We saw the opportunity to package it as a tabloid, [and] ran of a few extra thousand and made them available to UT students as a service to the nursing school, to the Department of State, we sent it to U.S. senators and congressmen. It eventually won the national award for editorial leadership from the *Los Angeles Times*."

Apartheid in South Africa also gripped the campus, and UT students demanded the system divest Permanent University Fund money from companies dealing with that country.

At an "unauthorized" rally April 14, 1986, forty-two UT students were arrested after refusing to surrender a shanty they'd constructed on the West Mall. The University cited a number of reasons for the arrests, including a University rule that allowed rallies only between noon and 1:00 P.M. The arrests incited an even bigger protest the following Friday, when 182 students were taken by UTPD.

"The rally began at noon, when about 20 people who were arrested recently . . . stood on a concrete planter on the West Mall, wearing gags and holding their hands behind their backs," Ashe and Lisa Gaumnitz reported. "From 12:30 to 1:00 P.M. the demonstrators held a banner that read 'Apartheid Kills—Divest Now.'"

The protesters wouldn't budge, and "at 1:15

THE DAILY TEXAN

The student newspaper of The University of Texas at Austin.   Wednesday, January 29, 1986.   25¢

Vol. 85, No. 82

Shuttle explosion kills seven

NASA officials refuse speculation on cause of tragedy

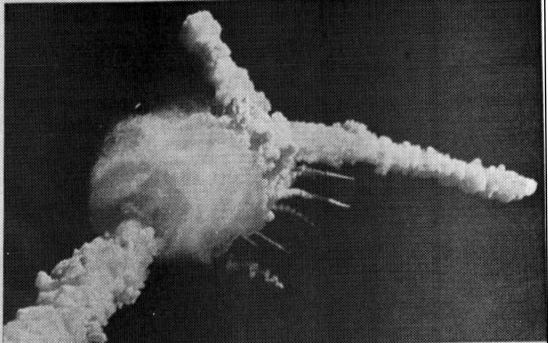

Space shuttle mission 51-L explodes shortly after liftoff from Cape Canaveral, Fla. One of the two solid-fuel boosters took an erratic course over the Atlantic after the explosion Tuesday.

More on the shuttle tragedy

- **Challenger crew** — The men and the women who died in the fiery blast above the Florida coast represented a cross section of America. Page 2.
- **Future for NASA** — If we supposed to be a banner year for the space agency. Now NASA's ambitious plans lie in shambles. Page 2.
- **Teacher remembered** — Christa McAuliffe was supposed to be the first teacher in space. She became the first civilian to die on a space flight. Page 2.
- **Project delays** — Some UT space projects may be delayed by the shuttle explosion. Page 10.
- **UT students react** — Students on campus joined the rest of the nation in watching the horrifying images from the Kennedy Space Center. Page 10.
- **Austin finalist reflects** — Austin high school teacher Steve Warren was among the finalists for the Teacher in Space program. Page 10.

isaster touches many at UT

Reagan mourns loss of U.S. astronaut crew

The January 1986 explosion of space shuttle Challenger stunned students. Minutes after the tragedy, a Texan reporter and photographers were on the road to the Johnson Space Center.

P.M., at least 25 UTPD and 22 helmeted APD began arresting students in groups of 10."

Russell Scott ended his year as editor in style —he got arrested.

The staff decided to have a "terrorist" costume theme at the annual TSP banquet due to the numerous hijackings, embassy bombings, and U.S. air strikes against Libya. Scott wore a sheik's robe, with an alarm clock and road flares taped to his chest. But not every patron was amused. Scott wrote in a later viewpoint:

> As a yellow creek of butter melted down the sides of my baked potato, four of Travis County's finest, in big-brimmed headpieces, sprung from the rabbit hole.
>
> As flares and red tape were ripped from my chest in the doorway of the Texas Tumbleweed, I felt like that kid, Billy in *Midnight Express.*
>
> "We've had a complaint that someone had a bomb," they said.
>
> "They're road flares," I said.
>
> "You're under arrest," they said.
>
> The feast was about as threatening as a six-year-old's birthday party with brats throwing ice cream. In my costume, I was one of several dozen 'terrorizing' *Texan*oids dressed in camouflage and battling it out with squirt guns.
>
> When I was led outside, leaving my orphaned potato, the TSP celebrants ran outside, thinking the cops were an addition to the endless procession of the evening's jests. Right quick the

UT Dean of Students, TSP general manager *Texan* managing editor and staffers were threatened with arrest if they didn't back off—things were eiree and serious.

Scott was taken to jail and quickly sprung with a $1,000 bond. The APD promised not to press charges—if he didn't file a complaint.

Demands for divestiture did not go away. Finally, on the morning of October 20, 1986, sixteen students marched into UT President William Cunningham's office and took it over.

"The sit-in lasted well under an hour," wrote *UTmost* contributor Scott McLemee.[21] "Police entered by smashing through windows, since the doors of the office were locked with Kryptonite locks and blocked with desks."

Student reaction was divided about this show of passion. Cunningham was not swayed at all. Editor David Nather criticized the demonstration.

"How embarrassing. . . . Take over the main building? Now there's a fresh approach," he wrote.[22]

On the other hand, "If [*The Texan*] didn't make a big deal out of events you think are 'old' and 'boring,'" wrote one "Firing Line" contributor, "by running them on the front page, your protesters might do more interesting things."

Although some considered him too stubborn, Cunningham was admired by Nather's editorial board. "Does Cunningham oppose divestment?

On the morning of October 20, 1986, sixteen students marched into UT President William Cunningham's office and took it over to protest UT Permanent Fund investment in South Africa. The sit-in lasted less than an hour.

In the current budgetary crisis, 'yes'," wrote columnist John Anderson. "Cunningham doesn't apologize for the positions, he, as University president, must take. He states his views, and if you don't like them, that's okay. Go ahead, disagree with him, but respect his views. There's something to be said for his candidness."

Cunningham's stubbornness frustrated the 1980s' last editor, Karen Adams, far more. Tuition was skyrocketing, legislative support was dwindling, and student services were suffering because of it. But Cunningham remained silent.

In an open letter to Cunningham, dated January 19, 1990, Adams wrote: "Let's face facts. Since the fall semester began, your approval rating has taken a beating, and your credibility with students is at an all-new low. Anyone can see why."

Adams and other student leaders pressured Cunningham to address class availability issues; they went unanswered. Adams ran six columns of blank space that had been reserved for the president's response to a specific editorial on class availability issues.

"This really hacked Dr. Cunningham off," Adams said. "I don't think [he] was ready for a bunch of uppity kids hitting him hard in the public relations department."

The friction didn't help the *Texan* reporters, Gibson said. "Adams was furious at Cunningham. *The Texan* wanted information the University didn't want to release . . . they were going to file an FOI, but Cunningham warned Karen that if she did, he'd release the information to the *Statesman* first."

Another time, "Cunningham also was addressing students at Batts during Mike Casey's time as managing editor," Gibson said. "A *Texan* reporter was there, and Cunningham picked him out of the audience and said, 'I don't want you to cover this. You can stay, but you can't record it.' Mike had to inform Cunningham's office that the reporter had every right to be there, because the meeting had been advertised to students."

Another Greek Week racial outburst rounded out Adams' term.

"A car used by Delta Tau Delta was painted with racial slurs . . . and the Phi Delta Thetas distributed a T-shirt bearing the caricature of a black man similar to the 'Sambo' caricatures of the last century," wrote *Texan* staffer Michael Margolis.[23]

Adams dedicated her entire page to criticizing the fraternities, "because to be silent in light of the cases is to applaud those who committed the acts."

Texan columnist Scott Stanford wrote of the event, "The racial slurs that appeared on a car by Delta Tau Delta during the Round Up parade could hardly have been a surprise given that Round Up is a traditionally racist activity that takes place at a traditionally racist University in a traditionally racist state."[25]

Students united against the Greeks' ignorance. Phi Delta Theta and Delta Tau Delta were indefinitely suspended, and *Texan* staffer Brandon Powell led a march down the Drag to protest the racism. The tumult that ensued led to the termination of the Greek Week parade, and to numerous cultural sensitivity programs for UT Greeks.

A Greek Week racial outburst was spawned in 1990 when Delta Tau Delta's parade car appeared with racial slurs painted on it, and Phi Delta Theta distributed a T-shirt bearing the caricature of a black man similar to the "Sambo" character.

CHAPTER 10

RULINGS, POLICIES, AND NEW PERSPECTIVES: 1990–1999

January 15, 1991, after months of U.S. demands that Iraqi despot Saddam Hussein release his clamp on Kuwait, American forces mobilized Operation Desert Storm. Students wondered what the mobilization would mean—would there be a draft?

Aaron DaMommio reported that "as the crowd argued, the original protesters chanted, hell no, we won't go! We won't die for Texaco!"[1]

The deadline for Iraqi withdrawal passed without action, and on January 17, 1991, *The Texan* bannered the headline: "WAR ERUPTS IN GULF." The entire *Texan* staff participated in covering various angles of Operation Desert Storm. Reporter Dane Schiller wrote that the Secret Service was ready if necessary. Reporters DaMommio, Dave Loy, and Heather Wayment went to the Capitol rotunda where hundreds of anti-war protesters marched and held a candle-light vigil.

Kevin McHargue, 1991–92 editor, got four extra pages to create a special section. "The War in the Persian Gulf" detailed everything from President Bush's address following the initial assault to extensive AP graphics detailing what equipment was being used and where the U.S. warplanes were striking.

The "Firing Line" reflected a heavy anti-war sentiment among the student body. "We're reminded daily of the 58,000 of our young men who were slaughtered in vain in Vietnam," wrote one contributor. "Now we sit on our hands and watch as our

politicians offer hundreds of thousands more . . . wouldn't our forefathers be proud?"[2]

"Images" editor Greg Weiner urged students to ignore a "no peace, no class" movement on campus, which was pushing students to boycott class until the war ended. "This is a time of crisis," Weiner wrote, "but nothing indicates that sacrificing educational opportunity will solve it."[3]

The Texan localized its coverage by reporting on the plights of about 100 UT students who were

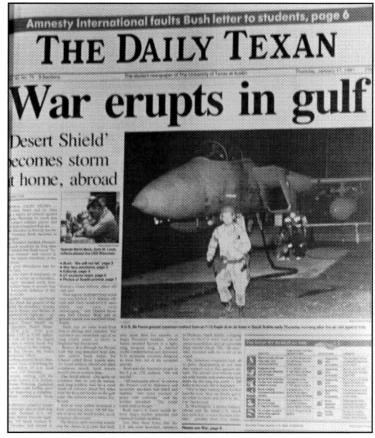

to ship off, and wouldn't recover their tuition. "As people give blood and fly flags and light candles, lawmakers should do what they can to help," McHargue wrote. "If the only thing Texas can give its soldiers are refunds and course credits, at least give them that" (which the legislature eventually did).[4]

FINANCES AND POLICY

After a threadbare late '80s and a 1991 recession, *The Texan* was in serious financial trouble: it was $250,000 in the hole. At that time, the student services fee *The Texan* received allowed it to be offered to each student for less than a dollar a year.

To help *The Texan* out, student leaders proposed using some of the proceeds being set aside to build a new student services complex across from the health center, to help *The Texan* to crawl out of its deficit. McHargue politely denied the offer, saying the $250,000 gift would taint its credibility.

"We can not afford to gamble even with the appearance of impropriety," McHargue wrote. "Although student leaders made the offer in good faith and with good intentions, the best response from TSP would be, 'thank you, but no thank you.'"

In the year's Student Government and editor elections, until the evening before the vote, the TSP Board had maintained it would appoint the editor because none of the interested candidates met all the qualifications. At the last minute, the board reversed itself. But the election was still delayed, because UT President Cunningham wouldn't approve the board's revised requirements. Cunningham's refusal might have been motivated by a bias against one of the candidates.[5]

Then TSP Board member Kate Jeffrey said "that during a discussion with Cunnningham at a media party last semester, he did not think Greg Weiner, government senior and current applicant, was a fair reporter," *Texan* staffer Dianne Smith wrote.[6] Finally, after negotiating to allow the revised qualifications for only one year, Matthew Connally was elected editor on April 11.

The University was feeling the continued effects of a legislature hell-bent on weaning UT off state funds, as from 1991 to 1993 it pushed a budget slicing UT's funding by $50 million. A trend of steadily increasing tuition was about to barrel upwards to help make up the difference. "The shift in priorities from academic to economic has compromised quality and overloaded education's resources without a significant payoff," McHargue wrote. "The state has asked Texas universities to become engines of economic development while at the same time cutting their resources."[7]

On campus, years of dealing with AIDS turned into a push to have condom machines installed in all campus restrooms, but Cunningham wouldn't hear of it.

"I don't want to turn this University into a sleazy motel," Cunningham said.[8]

State Democrats disagreed.

"We have to get beyond the shyness in discussion of sexual matters," said Rep. Ron Wilson, D-Houston, in an article by Angela Shah. "AIDS doesn't discriminate."

AD CONTROVERSY

Matthew Connally's term was marked by a challenge to *The Texan*'s advertising policy that would continue years after he left, as *The Texan* struggled to avoid printing a now infamous revisionist ad: "The Holocaust Controversy, A Case for Open Debate," by Bradley Smith.

The ad denied the Holocaust's reality and alleged that "no executions in gas chambers existed in any camp in Europe which was under

Holocaust ad provokes theft, draws criticism

German control. There was no German policy . . . to deliberately kill the internees."

Among the many problems surrounding the ad was that payment for its publication had already been accepted. A second was an outdated TSP Handbook, which had no firm policy on whether the paper had to accept the ad.

Managing editor Michael Casey filed an appeal on behalf of the staff, urging the board not to print the ad, but the staff had mixed opinions on the matter. Future editor Rebecca Stewart argued that "we wouldn't run an anti-black ad on MLK Day. We wouldn't run an anti-Christ ad on Christmas. Why should we run this? If they plan to run it during the first week of December, it's going to be during Hanukkah."

Connally supported publishing the ad, with accompanying editorials attacking the revisionist's premise. "Let the readers decide if it is true or not," he said.[9]

At a November 26 meeting, the TSP Board voted to overturn a review committee decision to run the ad, but failed to get enough votes to carry the motion. Finally, on December 15, TSP board member John Murphy switched his vote, and the board rejected the ad—but only until it could be re-evaluated under clearer advertising guidelines. The issue would quiet down, but only for a few months.

Totally unrelated to the Holocaust ad, Connally's religious beliefs almost cost him his staff. It started in the fall, as Connally's religious stands leaked out in his viewpoints. For example, his November 20, 1991, article praised the Inter-Varsity Christian Fellowship's activities.

"Today, don't be surprised if all the soaps between 11 A.M. and 1 P.M. get interrupted with a newsflash," Connally wrote, "that today an extraordinary scene is taking place at the University of Texas. There is an intelligent, respectful discussion going on at the free speech area. . . . Those who are open minded enough to get over the initial blanket generalization that anyone who brings up the claims of Christ in public is ipso facto a mindless bozo will stop and listen. . . . There's no doubt about it, Christians have telescopic vision, an almost completely intolerable quality in American today. They believe in truth."

Then on the Friday before Easter, Connally devoted the entire editorial page to celebrating Christ. The staff was enraged.

"Connally was a devout Christian, and decided in the springtime to devote the entire editorial page to how great Jesus is," Gibson said. "It was, to say the least, not a great use of the page, and many members of the community, especially members of the Jewish community were seriously offended. It took managing editor Mindy Brown talking to the staff to keep them from walking out."

The year 1992 also marked the first annual Hope Week for the University, sponsored by Alpha Phi Alpha. Many sorority and fraternity members gathered during what would typically have been Greek Week to reflect on the 1991 Sambo incident, and to promote racial harmony.

Connally ended his year criticizing the board's latest decision—to accept the revisionist ad.

"A college newspaper must be an open forum for ideas, in editorials and advertisements. Those wishing to have an open forum do not decide what issues are expressed. They allow the ideas to speak for themselves. But they are also responsible for determining whether an issue lies in the sphere of legitimate controversy."

The board changed its mind once again on April 30, when it dropped the ad on legal advice, *Texan* staffer Teri Bailey reported. The issue would resurface under 1992–93 editor Geoff Henley.

THE HOPWOOD CASE

"This could be a year of tremendous change for the University," Henley wrote in an August column welcoming students back to campus. "Debates over issues such as multicultural education and affirmative action in UT hiring and admissions politics could significantly affect the university as academics battle over the relationship of politics and education."[10]

He was right. On September 29, 1992, Stephanie Haynes and Cheryl Hopwood, who were denied admission into the UT Law School, filed a reverse discrimination suit against the University. Haynes would eventually drop her name from the case, and the litigation which would end affirmative action in Texas higher education became known as "The Hopwood Case," or simply "Hopwood."

Reporter Teri Bailey followed the case throughout the fall and then in spring 1993.

Court rules against affirmative action at UT law school

Officials fear end to policies

TSP aims for more involvement of minorities in its publications

Jenny Lin
Daily Texan Staff

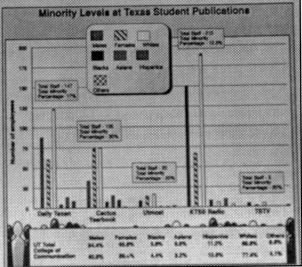

THE DAILY TEXAN

Protest demand met

'It's healing time'

Rev. Jackson calls for unity in UT speech

THE DAILY TEXAN

RACIAL BATTLEGROUND

THE DAILY TEXAN

The student newspaper of The University of Texas at Austin   Tuesday, July 2, 1996   25¢

Hopwood ruling stands

Supreme Court will not hear appeal in affirmative action case

UT students denounce, praise latest decision

"The UT Law School is definitely discriminatory," said Lino Graglia, a UT law professor, in an article by Bailey. "They admit Blacks and Hispanics that would never have been given a second thought if they were white." *The Texan*'s coverage found statistics revealing that resident African-American and Hispanic students were admitted with lower GPA and LSAT standards than non-minority applicants. Henley supported the case.

"With luck, the equal protection clause will also find Townes Hall," Henley wrote.[11]

The lawsuit opened up a Pandora's box of opinions and racial chasms on campus, and throughout the year *The Texan* provided a forum to air the hundreds of opinions on affirmative action.

PRESIDENTIAL NEWS

In August of 1992, darkhorse presidential candidate Gov. Bill Clinton and running mate Sen. Al Gore came to campus. Henley was unimpressed. He took the opportunity to slam one of Clinton's main campaign stands—universal health care.

"Seeing droves of robust young Americans so willing to abandon responsibility and embrace Gov. Bill Clinton's coercive health payment plan should leave the sane bereft," Henley wrote.[12]

It was no secret that Henley, like Connally before him, held conservative views. "It's refreshing to see that *The Daily Texan* has a right wing, union-bashing young Republican for editor this semester," one "Firing Line" contributor remarked.[13]

The University also selected a president to replace Cunningham, who became system chancellor. The same day the *Texan* lauded President Clinton's democratic election, Henley predicted UT Law School Dean Mark Yudof had been preselected, and criticized the regents for trying to fool students that the selection was actually a democratic process.

"If we are to have a governing body that acts independently of the wishes of those it governs, then let us at least be honest about it," Henley wrote. "Students already know we have no real say in such matters; we should at least be allowed the dignity of an honest evaluation of our input."[14]

Unfortunately, Henley's tip-off was completely wrong, and the regents surprised everyone by naming an outsider, University of Illinois President Robert Berdahl.

"Henley and then student body president Howard Nirken got the short list for names of the new university president," Ron Gibson said. "A source let Geoff know it was a done deal, that Yudof was it. However, we got it totally wrong. It was one big scoop, one big scoop of something else."

"One big scoop of something else" may have better described *The Other Texan*, a flash-in-the-pan creation printed in the fall of 1992 and funded by the Council of Graduate Students. *The Other Texan* violated copyright when it lifted a *Texan* ad, showing Dean of Students Sharon Justice holding a superimposed *Other Texan* instead of *The Cactus*, as she did in the actual ad. And above the ad, *The Other Texan* had her say, "Since I began reading TOT, I quit my job and dedicated my life to exposing the lies of the UT administration."[15]

NEWS ON CAMPUS AND BEYOND

Besides Hopwood and a new president, *The Texan* focused on Title IX, legislation which set out to even funding and support for women's athletics. Reporter Steve Scheibal followed the story closely from the spring, and carried the beat into the summer.

Even with a fill of hard news on campus, staffers went beyond the Forty Acres for the news.

Texan photographer Ted S. Warren doubled as a "really aggressive reporter," Gibson said, and would often shoot the stories he wrote. When a pipeline in Brenham, Texas, exploded, Warren shot the story from a helicopter and then wrote a feature on newlyweds who lost their home to the ensuing blaze. Reporters hit the road and uncovered life in South Texas' *colonias* in an award-winning package named "Faces from the Border."

On the state level, future 1993–94 editor Rebecca Stewart followed the 73rd legislative session as it drowned in concealed weapons bills and a Texas Supreme Court ruling finding their previous school funding unconstitutional. *The Texan*'s pages carried the latest chapter of many versions of what would be remembered as "The Robin Hood Plan."

Then the Holocaust ad resurfaced. The board voted in January to reject the ad, but reversed itself a month later. The ad was printed in February.

"No one doubts the veracity of the Holocaust," Henley wrote in an accompanying editorial. "Regrettably, the venue [Smith and co-author David Cole] chose for their thesis wasn't a thesis by William Ariel Durant or other famous historians, but an advertisement in today's *Daily Texan*. The ad, which I rejected to run on initial review and in the first appellate stage, will challenge our readers and anger many others."[16]

It did anger others. *The Texan* received a bomb threat, and 3,000 of the papers were stolen for publishing the advertisement.

"Richard Lytle, TSP general manager, said he hired UT police officers to patrol the newspaper's offices as 'a precautionary measure' due to fears expressed by staff members of a delayed response to the ad," reported *Texan* staffers Mike Brick and Jeff Mead. And Chabad, a University Jewish organization, discussed boycotting *The Texan*.[17]

Even UT President Berdahl took exception to the decision, and submitted a guest column February 22. "I am very disappointed by the decision to run an advertisement that seeks to foster doubts about the Holocaust," Berdahl wrote. "The appearance of the advertisement is an unfortunate occasion for *The Daily Texan* and the University. I am confident, however, that the campus community will use this occasion as an opportunity to renew its opposition to religious prejudice, racism and bigotry in all their forms, and to reaffirm and strengthen its dedication to the humane principles that underlie our democratic society."

That spring, reporters James Wilkerson and Mike Brick competed with national press in covering the fiery end of the Branch Davidian cult in Waco.

The reporters phoned in stories from Waco and lived in their car for days. *Texan* photographer Alicia Wagner caught the complex burning to the ground and graphic artist Korey Coleman recreated the standoff's final moments.

"Brick's and Wilkerson's coverage of Waco was excellent . . . I just thought they were never coming back," Gibson said.

PRODUCTION ADVANCES

The summer of 1993, *The Texan* switched from the clunky yellow and brown PDP 11/70 terminals by Digital to Macintosh classics. The changeover presented a fun challenge for systems analyst Michelle Carlson.

"We had all been working off one mainframe, and all the reporters typed their stories in on dumb terminals," Carlson said. "We piecemealed the installation, and it was exciting. I had gotten bored because there was nothing more to learn from the old system. I felt marketable again.

"We all worked as a team to get the system running in time for the first paper," Carlson said. "The first two nights of publication, I stayed here until the paper went to bed, because we all wanted to make sure we could really put out a *Texan* on Macintoshes."

The switch significantly changed the paper's production and quality. "Before the Macintoshes, students would plan the paper on dummy sheets, and it would eventually have to all be pasted up," said composing room supervisor Sue Jones. "The old computers had codes for different column widths, fonts and point sizes. But it was done in only one column, a galley strip. After the students were done, the story would be sent to a typesetter, or 'photon.' This was just strictly type. Then paperfilm was developed with a developer fix, then the production staff took the galleys of type and pasted them up according to what was dummied on the grid sheets."

Editor Mary Hopkins' term (1994–95) was marked by the first time *The Texan* switched to a full-color press—the front page and section heads were printed in color almost every day. Although initial attempts show the paper out of registration, it was not long before production manager Mike Kirkham and night manager Richard Finnell got the paper up to speed. The second development was *The Web Texan*, begun by Carlson and On-Line director Jim Barger. *The Texan* was the first college newspaper on the Internet, and by 1996 was receiving 17,000 hits a day.

DECISIVE ACTIONS

Newswise, the *Texan* coughed up Freeport McMoRan, leaded fountains, and asbestos removal on the front pages of 1995.

Reporters relentlessly hammered Cunningham and the University for its dealings with Jim Bob Moffett, chairman of the much maligned development company Freeport McMoRan. When

not trying to tear up Barton Creek for apartment complexes, the company made the front page for questionable treatment of workers at a mining site in Irian Jaya, or for questionable influence over the Forty Acres through massive donations to the University. Cunningham himself was making a hefty fee for sitting on the company's board of directors, and the *Texan's* trumpeting of the suggested impropriety did not amuse.

"At the close of a long and ugly semester, seven of us were sitting in the newsroom early in the evening, debating whether to retire to our respective abodes to study or to spend the evening at Hole in the Wall, toasting yet another semester of academic underachievement," said then managing editor Kevin Williamson.

"It was no surprise that [Cunningham] had finally resigned; it really was no surprise that he had chosen that day. . . . The University prefers to conduct any controversial business during holiday breaks or finals week in order to avoid unwanted attention from faculty and students—particularly those chain-smoking, touched-with-the-pallor-of-death, academically marginal students who call *The Daily Texan's* subterranean digs home."

But that didn't stop the staff, which published a *Texan Extra* with a skeleton crew. Williamson continued:

> We decided to bring out a special edition, a dinky—one broadsheet page with news on the front and the editorial page on the back—as a special end-of-semester present to the Chancellor. . . . Our special edition adhered to all of *The Daily Texan's* reliably high standards for reporting and comment. Rob Rogers made sure that the tone was restrained and professional, as it always was. But that dinky was not really a work of reporting—it was a raised middle finger, one last "[——] you" from us to the administration before going on to fail our finals.
>
> It all seemed terribly important at the time, and that sense that one's work is of significance will drive students to spend upward of 60 hours a week in the *Texan* basement. We loved the University, but only hate—and perversely gleeful hate at that—can motivate seven students to spend all night before finals producing a two-page paper and driving it to New Braunfels to be printed (TSP would not call in a press crew to print such a thing). Only pissed-off students will march around campus hand-delivering dinkies, posting them on kiosks and sliding them under doors. And I know that the always sober, always

decent Rob Rogers had something unprintable in his heart when he pitched that paper onto Cunningham's lawn at 5 A.M. He had, after all, written a check out of his personal funds to cover the cost of printing. (Rob was the only person at *The Texan* I can imagine having had enough funds at the end of a semester to underwrite such an endeavor.) I bombed my finals, but I got a nifty plaque from TSP.

The paper entered its 96th year with a history-making ruling from the 5th U.S. Circuit Court of Appeals. On March 19, 1996, the court found in favor of Cheryl Hopwood, ruling that the Law School's affirmative action policies were unconstitutional. The ruling affected all federally funded institutions in Texas, Louisiana, and Mississippi.

UT scrambled to decipher whether the ruling forced an end to all racially based scholarships and programs. To be safe, it halted most programs in order to avoid additional lawsuits. Angry student groups rallied on the West Mall, demanding that all race-based programs cease, as other angry student groups pushed the University to show some backbone and protect the already dismal number of minorities on campus. The University's reputation with minorities already suffered from a racist past—how could it keep attracting a diverse student body to the school now? Attorneys for the University looked to the U.S. Supreme Court for guidance, and were met with deafening silence July 1, 1996, when the justices decided not to hear Hopwood.

Because the University had halted its affirmative action programs, the Supreme Court decided to wait to rule nationally on the issue until it found "a program genuinely in controversy." The result: Texas, Mississippi, and Louisiana had to end affirmative action; the rest of the nation did not.

"It is absolutely devastating and bizarre that three of the states with the worst histories on race relations are told that they and they alone cannot take race into account to achieve the goals of either diversity or desegregation. It's a blow to the University," UT System legal counsel Samuel Issacharoff said in an interview that day with *The Texan.*

The Court's ruling fired up the staff of *The Texan.* The paper responded with a special section headed by *Texan* reporters Amy Strahan and Mike Carr, editor Tara Copp, and managing editor Rob

Russell. The section provided a timeline of the affirmative action battle, a full page of editorial response, and reactions reaching all the way to the White House.

"Obviously, the opinions by Justices Ginsburg and Souter recognize the importance of the issue, and don't rule our future considerations of the issue. But . . . there is going to be some level of uncertainty as they sort out the case law," said White House spokesman Mike McCurry.

AN EXPLOSIVE REMARK

Hopwood as a case was over, but affirmative action would emotionally strangle UT to the end of the century. It dominated "Firing Lines," student body elections, and in fall 1997 would bring the campus to near riot. The cause: UT law professor Lino Graglia's remarks at a news conference announcing the formation of a new UT student group opposed to affirmative action. Graglia said that Hispanic and African-American cultures do not look upon failure with disgrace and that "blacks and Mexican-Americans are not academically competitive with whites in selective institutions," *Texan* staffer Lisa Falkenberg reported.

Graglia's comments engulfed and deeply divided the campus. While many faculty, politicians, and students roared for his head, others cheered the professor for speaking his mind. National media grabbed hold of the racial tension and put the Forty Acres on the front page. Within days, Rev. Jesse Jackson swooped onto the South Mall to denounce Graglia; CNN, the AP, and numerous other national media eagerly awaited what looked to be an explosive rally. It was explosive, but fortunately only in the rhetorical sense.

"Heated words engulfed 5,000 students Tuesday as the Rev. Jesse Jackson condemned institutional racism in higher education and called for student unity amid controversial comments by UT Law Professor Lino Graglia," *Texan* reporter Zack McClain wrote.

" 'You're making a choice today to go forward by hope and inclusion and not backwards by fear and exclusion,' Jackson told the students who packed the South Mall.

" 'The school must know that he represents a national disgrace. . . . The school must act to regain its credibility and its integrity,' Jackson said."

UT Student Government President Marlen Whitley demanded that UT administrators ensure diversity on campus. "If we can't have affirmative action, then we need immediate action," Whitley said. "We are about valuing difference, about studying difference, about celebrating difference, about appreciating difference—until difference doesn't make a difference."

The Texan's editorial response was uncharacteristically conservative.

"Jesse Jackson overreacted when he said Graglia's remarks illustrate the 'struggle for America's definition of itself,' said the Viewpoint. "Though he once said that citizens should not be judged by their skin color, now he finds it to be their defining characteristic. Somehow equating opposition to Graglia with the heroic stands of Rosa Parks, Martin Luther King and Medger Evers, Jackson inflated both his ego and the importance of Graglia's statements."

ON TO 2000

The Texan's editorial response was not surprising, as it had taken a more conservative stand under editor Colby Black. But the very vocal, liberal passion engulfing campus did not make their board a very popular one. Staff resentment over the board's conservative stands that fall, and particularly over two cartoons and an editorial singling out high-profile affirmative action supporter and graduate student leader of Students for Academic Opportunity Oscar DeLa Torre, led to a vote of no confidence against the editor and a small student protest of *The Texan*.

"The anti-*Texan* protest was so ridiculous it would have been funny—if I wasn't working there," said *Texan* staffer Amy Strahan. "SAO formed a circle to march, the YCT's camped on the steps with signs. Reporters stopped working to come out and gawk. Students on their way to class could catch a glimpse of a race protest countered by a protest of that protest and the protestees eating lunch on the side. Somebody annoyed by the chanting began blaring heavy metal out of their dorm room to complete the weirdness. God, I love UT.

"Sholnn Freeman [then managing editor] used to call the fall of 1997 'the battle for the soul of the *Texan*.' Not quite. It was a bunch of punk reporters and would-be politicos trying to hash out how far the editorial page could go in promoting campus debate. They went too far."

The paper got past the protest and no-confidence vote; Black finished his term. With the spring came new elections, new promises, new goals, and new staff under 1998-99 editors Michael Mulcahy and his successor, 1999-2000 editor Rob Addy.

As it had since its inception, *The Texan* graduated an "old guard" of writers and welcomed a new crop of idealistic reporters to four more years of adventure. Born at the beginning of the century, the paper looked forward—to the beginning of a new millennium.

ENDNOTES

Chapter 1

1. *The Texan*, October 8, 1900.

2. Margaret C. Berry, *The University of Texas: A Pictorial Account of its First Century* (Austin: University of Texas Press, 1980), p. 372.

3. Quoted in Ronnie Dugger, *Our Invaded Universities* (New York: Norton, 1974), p. 8.

4. Ibid., p. 10.

5. Ibid., p. 8.

6. *The Ranger* was published by John O. Phillips from 1897 to 1900. *The Calendar* was founded by R. W. Wortham and published from 1898 to 1899. Margaret C. Berry, p. 202.

7. *The Texan*, December 9, 1903.

8. Letter to Escal Duke, March 3, 1941. Quoted in "The Life and Political Career of Fritz G. Lanham." Escal F. Duke, master's thesis, August 1941.

9. *The Texan*, October 8, 1900.

10. Ibid., October 22, 1900.

11. Ibid., April 26, 1911.

12. Ibid., October 8, 1900.

13. *The Ranger*, May 26, 1900.

14. *The Texan*, January 8, 1901.

15. Ibid., October 29, 1900.

16. Duke, p. 24.

17. *The Texan*. January 22, 1901.

18. Duke, p. 106.

19. Ibid., p. 110.

20. Ibid., p. 8

21. Ibid., p. 11.

22. Ibid., p. 82.

23. *The Texan*, June 5, 1901.

24. Ibid., December 9, 1903.

25. Ibid., October 4, 1904.

26. Ibid., September 28, 1907.

27. Ibid., June 8, 1908.

28. Ibid., January 16, 1909.

29. Duke, p. 21.

30. *The Texan*, May 8, 1901.

31. Ibid., September 28, 1904.

32. Ibid., October 23, 1908.

33. Ibid., May 29, 1909.

34. Ibid., April 3, 1909.

35. F. Edward Walker to D. B. Hardeman, November 6, 1934. Paul J. Thompson papers, Center for American History.

36. *The Texan*, February 16, 1910.

37. Ibid., February 26, 1910.

38. D. A. Frank to D. B. Hardeman, December 17, 1934. Paul J. Thompson papers, Center for American History.

39. *The Texan*, February 15, 1911.

40. Ibid., May 3, 1911.

41. Ibid., October 22, 1902.

42. Joe B. Frantz, *The Forty Acres Follies* (Austin: Texas Monthly Press, 1983), pp. 102-104.

43. *The Texan*, January 5, 1910.

44. Ibid., November 2, 1906.

45. Ibid., December 12, 1908.

46. Ibid., March 27, 1901.

47. Ibid., February 12, 1901.

Chapter 2

1. George Wythe to D. B. Hardeman, March 5, 1935. Paul J. Thompson papers, Center for American History.

2. *The Texan*, January 22, 1913.

3. Ibid., February 19, 1913.

4. Ibid., March 19, 1913.

5. Ibid., March 22, 1913.

6. Ibid., March 26, 1913.

7. Ibid., April 19, 1913.

8. Ibid., April 23, 1919.

9. *The Daily Texan*, September 24, 1913.

10. Ibid., November 7, 1915.

11. Ibid., January 16, 1916

12. Ibid., September 24, 1914.

13. Ibid., October 15, 1914.

14. Ibid., November 13, 1914.

15. Ibid., October 15, 1915.

16. Ibid., January 22, 1915.

17. Ibid., February 26, 1915.

18. Besides Landrum, another *Texan* staffer of this time also achieved journalistic prominence. Stanley Walker, who worked at the paper from 1915 to 1918, later became editor of the *New York Herald Tribune*. While Walker discussed his life at the University in a book called *Back To Texas*, he men-

tioned nothing about his work at *The Texan*. See Stanley Walker, *Home to Texas* (New York: Harper, 1956).

19. William Clifford Hogg papers. 1897-1932. Volume III. January 11, 1916-November 24, 1916. Center for American History, The University of Texas at Austin.

20. Will C. Hogg papers. "The University of Texas." Volume IV. February 1, 1917-May 20, 1919.

21. Ibid.

22. Will C. Hogg papers. "Ferguson—University Controversy—Printed material." Box 2J316.

23. Ibid.

24. John A. Lomax papers. Center for American History. Box 3D167.

25. Will C. Hogg papers. "Ferguson—University Controversy Newspaper Clippings— 1917." Box 2J316.

26. *The Daily Texan*, October 12, 1916.

27. Will C. Hogg papers. "The University of Texas." Volume IV. February 1, 1917-May 20, 1919. Letter dated January 2, 1918. Center for American History.

28. *The Daily Texan*, November 8, 1916. Quoted in Lewis Gould, *Progressives and Prohibitionists: Texas Democrats in the Wilson Era* (Austin: University of Texas Press, 1973), p. 197.

29. *The Daily Texan*, December 3, 1916.

30. Will C. Hogg papers. "The University of Texas." Volume IV. February 1, 1917- May 20, 1919.

31. Gould, p. 203.

32. Will C. Hogg papers. "Ferguson's War on the University of Texas. A Chronological Outline." Published by Ex-Students' Association. May 28, 1917.

33. John A. Lomax papers. "Random Recollections of the University 'Bear Fight'" Box 3D168. Folder 3. "University of Texas Career. Gov. James E. Ferguson controversy." Judge Batts' papers contain no mention of the meeting.

34. *The Daily Texan*, February 4, 1917.

35. Ibid., February 6, 1917.

36. Ibid., February 8, 1917.

37. Ibid., April 7, 1917.

38. Ibid., April 12, 1917.

39. Ibid., April 10, 1917.

40. Ibid., April 11, 1917.

41. Ibid., April 25, 1917.

42. Ibid., April 27, 1917.

43. Ibid., May 24, 1917.

44. Ibid., September 26, 1917.

45. Ibid., October 19, 1918.

46. *The New York Times*, February 16, 1999, p. A12, "Scientists Uncover Clues to Flu Epidemic of 1918."

47. *The Daily Texan*, November 11, 1918.

48. Ibid., November 18, 1918.

49. Ibid., November 15, 1918.

50. Ibid., November 19, 1918.

51. Ibid., November 20, 1918.

52. Ibid., November 21, 1918.

53. Ibid.

54. Ibid., January 6, 1919.

55. Ibid., April 21, 1918.

56. Ibid.

57. Ibid., April 20, 1918.

58. Ibid.

59. Ibid.

60. Ibid., April 25, 1918.

61. Ibid., April 30, 1918.

62. Ibid., May 2, 1918.

63. Ibid., May 3, 1918.

64. George Wythe to D. B. Hardeman, March 5, 1935. Paul J. Thompson papers, Center for American History.

Chapter 3

1. *The Daily Texan*, November 3, 1920.

2. Ibid., October 20, 1920.

3. Ibid., November 23, 1920.

4. Ibid., January 6, 1921

5. Ibid., January 7, 1921

6. Ibid., February 1, 1921.

7. Ibid., February 2, 1921.

8. Ibid.

9. Ibid., March 12, 1921.

10. Ibid., May 31, 1921.

11. Mike Godwin, "*The Daily Texan* does not belong to you (But it used to)," *UTmost* magazine, 1987.

12. TSP Board Minutes, September 24, 1928.

13. "Proceedings of the United Board of Publications of the University of Texas." TSP Archives.

14. Ibid.

15. TSP Board minutes, June 30, 1922.

16. Ibid., December 31, 1922.

17. Ibid., November 10, 1924.

18. Ibid., January 21, 1925.

19. Ibid., June 9, 1925.

20. *The Daily Texan*, May 11, 1924.

21. Ibid., November 24, 1921.

22. Ibid., October 12, 1922

23. Ibid., October 26, 1922.

24. Ibid., November 30, 1944.

25. Ibid., April 5, 1924.

26. Margaret C. Berry, "Student Life and Customs, 1883-1933, at the University of Texas," Ph.D. thesis in education. Columbia University, 1965, p. 492.

27. TSP Board minutes, January 10, 1927.

28. *The Daily Texan*, October 18, 1928.

29. TSP Board minutes, September 14, 1927.

30. Lomax to Batts, April 15, 1927. Batts (R. L.) papers, Center for American History.

31. TSP Board minutes, February 4, 1928.

32. Ibid., March 5, 1928.

33. Ibid., March 15, 1928.

34. Ibid., April 4, 1928.

35. Report of Manager of Publications, TSP Board Minutes, April 4, 1928.

36. TSP Board minutes, April 4, 1928.

37. Ibid., April 13, 1928.

38. Ibid., July 17, 1928.

39. Ibid., May 9, 1930.

40. *The Daily Texan*, January 24, 1929.

41. TSP Board minutes, January 23, 1929.

42. Ibid., February 14, 1929.

43. Ibid., May 20, 1929.

44. *The Daily Texan*, December 14, 1921.

Chapter 4

1. *The Daily Texan*, September 21, 1930.

2. Ibid., September 23, 1930.

3. Ibid., October 9, 1930.

4. TSP budget summaries, Paul J. Thompson papers, Center for American History.

5. Ibid.

6. TSP Board minutes, January 14, 1931.

7. Ibid., October 8, 1930.

8. Ibid.

9. Ibid., January 14, 1931.

10. Ibid.

11. Ibid., June 8, 1931.

12. William T. McGill to TSP Board, July 14, 1931. Paul J. Thompson papers, Center for American History.

13. TSP Board minutes, July 31, 1931.

14. *The Daily Texan,* January 11, 1932.

15. Ibid., January 12, 1932.

16. TSP Board minutes, March 23, 1932.

17. Harry Y. Benedict to C. S. Pats, January 1, 1932. Benedict papers, Center for American History.

18. *The Daily Texan,* April 30, 1932.

19. Ibid., May 4, 1932.

20. Ibid., May 25, 1932.

21. Ibid., November 9, 1932.

22. Ibid., March 15, 1933.

23. Ibid., September 29, 1934.

24. Ibid., October 5, 1934. (That editor later visited the White House and had his picture taken with Roosevelt. The photo ran on *The Texan's* front page.)

25. TSP Board minutes, September 21, 1932.

26. *The Daily Texan,* April 26, 1933.

27. Ibid., April 27, 1933.

28. Ibid., April 28, 1933.

29. Ibid., May 2, 1933.

30. Ibid., October 19, 1933.

31. Ibid., January 7, 1934.

32. Ibid., January 10, 1934.

33. Ibid., March 28, 1934.

34. Ibid., September 28, 1934.

35. TSP Board minutes, March 9, 1934.

36. Ibid.

37. Ibid., May 2, 1935.

38. *The Daily Texan,* December 6, 1935.

39. Ibid., May 5, 1935.

40. TSP Board minutes, November 5, 1935.

41. Ibid., November 7, 1935.

42. Ibid., July 28, 1936.

43. *The Daily Texan,* April 26, 1936.

44. Ibid., April 30, 1936.

45. Ibid., May 22, 1936.

46. TSP Board minutes, July 28, 1936.

47. Ibid.

48. Ibid., December 21, 1936.

49. *The Daily Texan,* August 6, 1936.

50. Ibid., January 26, 1937.

51. Ibid., August 16, 1936.

52. TSP Board minutes, October 1, 1936.

53. Ibid., September 28, 1936.

54. Ibid.

55. Ibid.

56. Ibid., October 1, 1936.

57. Ibid., October 16, 1936.

58. *The Daily Texan,* October 7, 1936.

59. Ibid., October 21, 1936.

60. Ibid., October 13, 1936.

61. General Faculty Minutes, October 13, 1936.

62. *The Daily Texan,* October 14, 1936.

63. TSP Board minutes, November 7, 1936.

64. Ibid., November 23, 1936.

65. *The Daily Texan,* January 8, 1937.

66. Ibid., January 26, 1937.

67. Ibid., March 7, 1937.

68. TSP Board minutes, April 28, 1937.

69. Ibid.

70. Mike Godwin, "The Daily Texan Does Not Belong to You (But it used to)," *UTmost,* 1987.

71. Harry Benedict to Malcolm K. Graham, April 29, 1937. Benedict papers, Center for American History.

72. *The Daily Texan,* September 30, 1937.

73. Ibid., October 3, 1937.

74. Ibid., October 5, 1937.

75. Ibid., January 27, 1938.

76. Ibid., January 28, 1938.

77. Ibid., January 30, 1938. This headline does not read quite the way the writer intended.

78. Ibid., February 4, 1938.

79. Ibid., February 6, 1938.

80. Ibid., February 10, 1938.

81. Ibid., March 6, 1938.

Chapter 5

1. TSP Board minutes, April 16, 1941.

2. *The Daily Texan,* November 11, 1941.

3. Ibid., December 7, 1941.

4. Ibid., December 9, 1941.

5. Ibid., December 16, 1941.

6. TSP Board minutes, January 14, 1942.

7. *The Daily Texan,* February 3, 1942.

8. Ibid., August 16, 1942.

9. Ibid., August 9, 1942.

10. Ibid., August 16, 1942.

11. Ibid., February 23, 1943.

12. Ibid., July 18, 1943.

13. Ibid., January 19, 1944.

14. Ibid., May 8, 1945.

15. Ibid., August 9, 1945.

16. Ibid., August 14, 1945.

17. Ibid., August 19, 1945.

18. Ibid., June 7, 1942.

19. Ibid.

20. Ibid., June 11, 1942.

21. Walter E. Nixon to A. M. Aikin, Jr. A. M. Aikin papers, Center for American History.

22. *The Daily Texan,* June 14, 1942.

23. Ibid., July 2, 1942.

24. Ibid., October 3, 1942.

25. Ibid., January 13, 1943.

26. Ibid., January 14, 1943.

27. Ibid., January 15, 1943.

28. Ibid.

29. Ibid.

30. Ibid., January 16, 1943.

31. Ibid., July 22, 1943.

32. Ibid., September 5, 1943.

33. Ibid., September 8, 1943.

34. Ibid., September 15, 1943.

35. Ibid., September 12, 1943.

36. Ibid., December 10, 1943.

37. Ibid., May 10, 1944.

38. Ibid., June 18, 1944.

39. Ruby Black had earlier been editor-in-chief of the summer edition, but Wilke was the first woman to be editor during the normal academic year.

40. *The Daily Texan,* July 6, 1944.

41. Ibid., July 16, 1944.

42. Ibid., July 27, 1944.

43. Ibid., August 3, 1944.

44. Ibid., October 1, 1944.

45. Ibid., October 10, 1944.

46. Ibid., October 12, 1944.

47. Ibid.

48. Ibid., November 17, 1944.

49. Ibid., October 13, 1944.

50. Ibid., October 15, 1944.

51. Ibid., October 17, 1944.

52. Ibid., October 20, 1944.

53. TSP Board minutes, October 19, 1944.

54. *The Daily Texan,* October 22, 1944.

55. Ibid., November 2, 1944.

56. Ibid., November 3, 1944.

57. Ibid., November 5, 1944.

58. Jim Nicar, "Academic Freedom," *Texas Alcalde,* November/December 1994.

59. *The Daily Texan,* November 17, 1944.

60. Ibid., December 10, 1944.

61. Ibid., December 22, 1944.

62. Ibid., January 14, 1945.

63. Ibid., January 23, 1945.

64. Ibid., January 28, 1945.

65. Ibid., February 4, 1945.

66. TSP Board minutes, February 2, 1945.

67. *The Daily Texan,* February 15, 1945.

68. Ibid., June 13, 1945.

69. Ibid.

70. Ibid., July 26, 1945.

71. Ibid., July 29, 1945.

72. Ibid., September 30, 1945.

73. Ibid.

74. Ibid., October 10, 1945.

75. Ibid., May 29, 1946.

76. Ibid., May 24, 1946.

77. Ibid., May 28, 1946.

78. TSP Board minutes, May 27, 1946.

79. Ibid.

80. *The Daily Texan,* May 28, 1946.

81. Ibid., May 31, 1946.

82. Ibid., June 11, 1946.

83. Ibid., June 14, 1946.

84. Ibid., September 15, 1946.

85. T. S. Painter to Dudley Woodward, September 17, 1946, Center for American History.

86. Ibid.

87. Adrian Moore to Dudley Woodward, April 9, 1948. Woodward papers, Center for American History.

88. Dudley Woodward to C. R. Granberry. Woodward papers, Center for American History.

89. Dudley K. Woodward to David Warren, February 20, 1948. Woodward papers, Center for American History.

90. E. E. Kirkpatrick to Dudley K. Woodward, February 23, 1948. Woodward papers, Center for American History.

91. Palmer Bradley to Dudley K. Woodward, March 9, 1948. Woodward papers, Center for American History.

92. Dudley K. Woodward to Palmer Bradley, March 10, 1948. Woodward papers, Center for American History.

93. Palmer Bradley to Dudley K. Woodward, March 11, 1948. Woodward papers, Center for American History.

94. Paul J. Thompson to Harrell E. Lee, December 15, 1948. Thompson papers, Center for American History.

95. Ibid., November 16, 1948.

96. *The Daily Texan,* October 18, 1946.

97. Ibid., November 8, 1946.

98. Dudley K. Woodward to T. S. Painter, January 2, 1948. Woodward papers, Center for American History.

99. *The Daily Texan,* December 8, 1946.

100. T. S. Painter to Dudley K. Woodward, January 9, 1948. Woodward papers, Center for American History.

101. T. S. Painter to regents, ca. December 1947. Woodward papers, Center for American History.

102. *The Daily Texan,* February 20, 1947.

103. Ibid.

104. Ibid., February 12, 1947.

105. Ibid., January 25, 1941.

106. Ibid., March 27, 1941.

107. Ibid., March 28, 1941.

108. Ibid., April 3, 1941.

109. Ibid.

110. Ibid., May 16, 1941.

111. Ibid., February 25, 1943.

112. Ibid., February 26, 1943.

113. Ibid., March 18, 1943.

114. Ibid., March 5, 1943.

115. Ibid., March 18, 1943.

116. Ibid., March 19, 1943.

117. Ibid.

118. Ibid., March 20, 1943.

119. Ibid., January 19, 1947.

120. Ibid., November 16, 1947.

121. Ibid., January 14, 1942.

122. Ibid., February 6, 1943.

123. Ibid., February 9, 1943.

124. Ibid., August 1, 1943.

125. Ibid., May 5, 1944.

126. Ibid., May 9, 1944.

127. TSP Board minutes, March 27, 1945.

128. *The Daily Texan,* March 1, 1946.

129. Ibid.

130. Ibid., March 3, 1946.

131. Ibid., March 19, 1946.

132. Ibid., November 24, 1946.

133. Ibid., December 3, 1946.

134. Ibid., March 9, 1947.

135. Ibid., March 26, 1947.

136. Ibid., May 14, 1947.

137. Ibid., July 10, 1947.

138. Ibid., January 16, 1948.

139. Ibid., July 21, 1948.

140. Ibid., September 28, 1948.

141. Ibid., September 29, 1948.

142. Ibid., October 29, 1948.

143. Ibid., November 25, 1947.

144. Ibid., April 23, 1947.

145. Ibid., November 26, 1946.

146. Ibid., November 28, 1946.

147. Ibid.
148. Ibid.

Chapter 6
1. *North Toward Home* interview with Willie Morris.
2. *The Daily Texan,* June 3, 1949.
3. Ibid.
4. Ibid, May 2, 1951.
5. Ibid., June 5, 1949.
6. Ibid., June 3, 1949.
7. Ibid., June 5, 1949.
8. Ibid.
9. Ibid., June 9, 1949.
10. Ibid., June 12, 1949.
11. Ibid., August 23, 1949.
12. Ibid., June 7, 1950.
13. Ibid.
14. Ibid., June 9, 1950.
15. Ibid., October 4, 1950.
16. Ibid., October 19, 1950.
17. Ibid., January 11, 1951.
18. Ibid., January 14, 1951.
19. Ibid.
20. Ibid., January 11, 1951.
21. Ibid., March 20, 1951.
22. Ibid., May 2, 1951.
23. Ibid.
24. Ibid., June 5, 1951.
25. Ibid.
26. Ibid.
27. Ibid., July 3, 1951.
28. Ibid., June 5, 1952.
29. Ibid., October 7, 1952.
30. Margaret Berry, *Brick by Golden Brick,* p. 78.
31. *The Daily Texan,* June 3, 1953.
32. Ibid., March 30, 1954.
33. Ibid., April 6, 1954.
34. Ibid., September 16, 1954.
35. Ibid., January 11, 1955.
36. Ibid., October 7, 1955.
37. Ibid., June 5, 1955.
38. Ibid., September 28, 1955.
39. Ibid.
40. Ibid.
41. Ibid., November 5, 1955.
42. Ibid., November 11, 1955.
43. Ibid., February 7, 1956.
44. Ibid.
45. Ibid.
46. Ibid.
47. Ibid., February 9, 1956.
48. *North Toward Home* interview with Willie Morris.
49. Ibid.
50. *Overcoming, A History of Black Integration at The University of Texas,* by Almetris Marsh Duren, p. 5.

Chapter 7
1. *The Daily Texan,* June 14, 1960.
2. Ibid.
3. Ibid., July 1, 1960.
4. Ibid., October 20, 1960.
5. Ibid., June 14, 1960.

6. Ibid., May 9, 1961.
7. Ibid., February 7, 1961.
8. *Overcoming,* by Almetris Marsh Duren, p. 5.
9. Ibid.
10. *The Daily Texan,* April 20, 1961.
11. Ibid., May 10, 1961.
12. Ibid., May 11, 1961.
13. Ibid., February 7, 1961.
14. Ibid., March 10, 1961.
15. Ibid., April 19, 1961.
16. Ibid., March 18, 1961.
17. Ibid., June 13, 1961.
18. Ibid., June 23, 1961.
19. Ibid., July 28, 1961.
20. Ibid.
21. Ibid., October 1, 1961.
22. Ibid., February 4, 1962.
23. Ibid.
24. Ibid.
25. Ibid.
26. Ibid., March 11, 1962.
27. Ibid., June 1962.
28. Ibid., June 29, 1962.
29. Ibid., October 23, 1962.
30. Ibid., June 5, 1963.
31. Ibid., June 21, 1963.
32. Ibid., June 25, 1963.
33. Ibid., October 18, 1963.
34. Ibid., November 23, 1963.
35. Ibid., March 15, 1964.
36. Ibid.
37. Ibid., October 28, 1964.
38. Ibid., March 21, 1965.
39. Ibid.
40. Ibid., October 12, 1965.
41. Ibid., October 22, 1965.
42. Ibid., March 9, 1966.
43. Ibid., August 2, 1966.
44. Ibid., commemorative issue, 1996.
45. Ibid.
46. Ibid., November 6, 1966.
47. Ibid., June 30, 1967.
48. Ibid., November 10, 1967.
49. Ibid., August 16, 1968.
50. Ibid., November 12, 1968.
51. Ibid., November 10, 1968.
52. Ibid., November 11, 1968.
53. Ibid.
54. Ibid., August 5, 1969.
55. Ibid., July 22, 1969.
56. Ibid., October 23, 1969.
57. Ibid., October 24, 1969.
58. Ibid., October 16, 1969.
59. Ibid., November 16, 1969.
60. Ibid., May 7, 1970.
61. Ibid.
62. Ibid., May 8, 1970.

Chapter 8
1. *The Daily Texan,* November 15, 1970.
2. Ibid., June 1, 1970.
3. Ibid.

4. Ibid., June 4, 1970.
5. Ibid., June 9, 1970.
6. Ibid., June 13, 1970.
7. Ibid., June 16, 1970.
8. Ibid., July 7, 1970.
9. Ibid.
10. Ibid.
11. Ibid., July 9, 1970.
12. Ibid., July 10, 1970.
13. Ibid., July 28, 1970.
14. Ibid.
15. Ibid., August 13, 1970.
16. Ibid., November 9, 1970.
17. Ibid.
18. Ibid., November 13, 1970.
19. Ibid.
20. Ibid., February 24, 1971.
21. Ibid., February 28, 1971.
22. Ibid.
23. Ibid.
24. Ibid., March 9, 1971.
25. Ibid., March 23, 1971.
26. Ibid., March 14, 1971.
27. Ibid., December 2, 1971.
28. Ibid., December 3, 1971.
29. *UTmost,* September 1987, p. 42.
30. *The Daily Texan,* January 21, 1972.
31. Ibid., January 24, 1972.
32. Ibid., commemorative issue, August 27, 1982.
33. Ibid.
34. Ibid., August 21, 1973.
35. Ibid., April 5, 1973.
36. Ibid., January 18, 1974.
37. Ibid.
38. Ibid.
39. Ibid.
40. Ibid., February 7, 1974.
41. Ibid., commemorative issue, August 27, 1982.
42. Ibid.
43. Ibid., March 19, 1974.
44. Ibid.
45. Ibid.
46. Ibid., March 21, 1974.
47. Ibid.
48. Ibid., April 29, 1974.
49. Ibid., May 6, 1974.
50. Ibid., March 8, 1974.

Chapter 9

1. *The Daily Texan,* November 5, 1979.
2. Ibid., November 8, 1979.
3. Ibid., November 9, 1979.
4. Ibid.
5. Ibid., November 7, 1979.
6. Ibid., November 11, 1979.
7. Ibid., November 28, 1979.
8. Ibid., February 1, 1980.
9. Ibid., September 2, 1980.
10. Ibid.
11. Ibid., April 21, 1981.
12. Ibid., January 21, 1981.
13. Ibid., April 14, 1981.
14. Ibid., November 4, 1981.
15. Ibid.
16. Ibid.
17. Ibid., November 9, 1981.
18. Ibid.
19. Ibid., April 7, 1983.
20. Ibid., August 12, 1983.
21. *UTmost,* November 1987, p. 11.
22. *The Daily Texan,* October 21, 1986.
23. Ibid., April 11, 1989.
24. Ibid.

Chapter 10

1. *The Daily Texan,* January 15, 1991.
2. Ibid., January 17, 1991.
3. Ibid., January 18, 1991.
4. Ibid.
5. Ibid., March 5, 1991.
6. Ibid.
7. Ibid., March 21, 1991.
8. Ibid., November 13, 1991.
9. Ibid., November 9, 1991.
10. Ibid., August 28, 1992.
11. Ibid., October 1, 1992.
12. Ibid., August 28, 1992.
13. Ibid., October 1, 1992.
14. Ibid., November 6, 1992.
15. Ibid., December 2, 1992.
16. Ibid., February 19, 1993.
17. Ibid.

INDEX

E D I T O R S

OF

The Texan

AND

The Daily Texan

EDITORS

Fritz G. Lanham
1900-1901

Ben H. Powell
1901-1902

H. Moreland Whaling
1902-1903

Alexander Duessen
1902-1903

Alexander Weisberg
1903-1904

Alexander Pope
1904-1905

Clinton G. Brown
1904-1905

D. A. Frank
1904-1905

John C. Townes, Jr.
1905-1906

EDITORS

Joel F. Watson
1906-1907

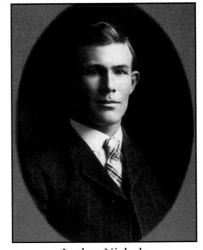

Luther Nichols
1906-1907

Eugene Harris
1907-1908

William A. Philpott
1908-1909

Mark McGee
1909-1910

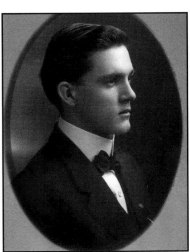

George Hill
1910-1911

Marion Levy
1911-1912

George Wythe
1912-1913

Ralph Feagin
1913-1914

EDITORS

Lynn Landrum
1914-1915

Steuard McGregor
1914-1915

Daniel Williams
1915-1916

Roy Hawk
1916-1917

Silas B. Ragsdale
1917-1918

F. Edward Walker
1918-1919

Milton Ling
1919-1920

Hulon W. Black
1920-1921

Reavis Cox
1921-1922

EDITORS

William Harry Jack
1922-1923

Henry Fulcher
1923-1924

Moulton Cobb
1924-1925

Stewart Harkrider
1925-1926

Granville Price
1926-1927

Sam C. Johnson
1926-1927

Trueman O'Quinn
1927-1928

Jimmie Payne
1928-1929

Wm. Kay Miller
1929-1930

EDITORS

David Hall
1930-1931

Joe T. Cook
1931-1932

Bob Baldridge
1932-1933

Joe Hornaday
1933-1934

D. B. Hardeman
1934-1935

Joe Storm
1935-1936

Ed Hodge
1936-1937

Ed Syers
1937-1938

Pat Daniels
1938-1939

EDITORS

Max Shelton
1939-1940

Boyd Sinclair
1940-1941

Jack B. Howard
1941-1942

Ralph Frede
1942-1943

Robert Allen Owens
1942-1943

Jack Maguire
1943-1944

Weldon Brewer
1943-1944

Helene Wilke
1944-1945

Horace Busby
1945-1946

EDITORS

Faye Loyd
1946-1947

William G. Noble
1946-1947

Cecil R. Hodges
1947-1948

Jo White
1947-1948

Bob Hollingsworth
1948-1949

Ray Greene
1948-1949

William H. Smith
1948-1949

Dick Elam
1949-1950

Charles Trimble
1950-1951

EDITORS

Ronnie Dugger
1950-1951

Russ Kersten
1951-1952

Anne Chambers
1952-1953

Bob Kenny
1953-1954

Shirley Strum
1954-1955

W. W. (Willie) Morris
1955-1956

Nancy McMeans
1956-1957

Robert Elton (Bud) Mims
1957-1958

Robb Kendrick Burlage
1958-1959

EDITORS

Carl Dean Howard
1959-1960

Jo Eickmann
1960-1961

Hoyt Hughes Purvis
1961-1962

Sam Kinch, Jr.
1962-1963

David M. McNeely
1963-1964

Charmayne Marsh
1964-1965

Kaye Northcott
1965-1966

John Economidy
1966-1967

Mary Morphis Moody
1967-1968

EDITORS

Merry Clark
1968-1969

Mark Morrison
1969-1970

Andy Yemma
1970-1971

Lori Rodriguez
1971-1972

David Powell
1972-1973

Michael Eakin
1973-1974

Buck Harvey
1974-1975

Scott Tagliarino
1975-1976

Mary Walsh
1976-1977

EDITORS

Dan Malone
1977-1978

Gary Fendler
1978-1979

Beth Frerking
1979-1980

Mark McKinnon
1980-1981

Don Puffer
1981- Nov. 1981

John Schwartz
1981-1982

Lisa Beyer
1982-1983

Roger Campbell
1983-1984

David Woodruff
1984-1985

EDITORS

Russell Scott
1985-1986

David Nather
1986-1987

Sean Price
1987-1988

Michael Godwin
1988-1989

Karen Adams
1989-1990

Kevin McHargue
1990-1991

Matthew J. Connally
1991-1992

Geoff J. Henley
1992-1993

Rebecca S. Stewart
1993-1994

EDITORS

Mary Hopkins
1994-1995

Robert Rogers
1995-1996

Tara Copp
1996-1997

Colby Black
1997-1998

Michael Mulcahy
1998-1999

Rob Addy
1999-2000